SOCIAL DEVELOPMENT IN THE THIRD WORLD

Jan Drewnowski

Social Development in the Third World

Level of Living Indicators and Social Planning

Edited by J G M Hilhorst
& M Klatter

Published in co-operation with
The Institute of Social Studies at The Hague

CROOM HELM
London • Sydney • Dover, New Hampshire

Croom Helm Ltd, Provident House, Burrell Row,
Beckenham, Kent BR3 1AT

Croom Helm Australia Pty Ltd, First Floor,
139 King Street, Sydney, NSW 2001, Australia

British Library Cataloguing in Publication Data

Social development in the Third World: level
of living indicators and social planning.
1. Social indicators–Developing countries
I. Hilhorst, J.G.M. II. Klatter, M.
300'.72 HN980

ISBN 0-7099-1324-9

Croom Helm, 51 Washington Street, Dover,
New Hampshire 03820, USA

Library of Congress Cataloging in Publication Data
Main entry under title:

Social development in the Third World.

Bibliography: p.
1. Quality of life–Developing countries–Addresses, essays, lectures. 2. Social indicators–Developing countries–Addresses, essays, lectures. 3. Developing countries–Social policy–Addresses, essays, lectures.
I. Hilhorst, J.G.M. II. Klatter, M.
HN980.A85S63 1985 361.6'1'091724 84-23747
ISBN 0-7099-3730-X

Printed and bound in Great Britain
by Billing & Sons Limited, Worcester.

CONTENTS

PREFACE

This volume is dedicated to Jan Drewnowski for whom indicator research has been a principal concern from his time at the United Nations Research Institute for Social Development until his retirement as Professor in Economic and Social Planning at the Institute of Social Studies, The Hague.

The papers presented in this volume are original and were prepared in the course of 1981. The editors are very grateful to the authors for their willingness to contribute to this work. The fact that so much well-considered reasoning has been devoted to a subject that Jan Drewnowski helped to shape in the 1960s is an expression of the esteem in which we all hold him for his work and personality and of our admiration for his originality.

We also wish to express our thanks to Jean Sanders for her careful editing and for seeing the manuscript through all its production phases, and to Netty Born for her meticulous type-setting.

The Editors

1 SOCIAL INDICATORS: A GENERAL INTRODUCTION

J.G.M. Hilhorst

I Since World War II in particular, students of development problems, especially those who are concerned with development policy, have shown a growing interest in quantification, generally sharing the view that societal welfare or changes therein cannot be measured in a single number and that many aspects must be taken into account.

This view is expressed in a 1949 FAO publication which lists seven elements of rural welfare: health; levels of income and consumption; conditions of work; literacy and skills; social adjustment; individual security; and beliefs, customs and standards of behaviour. The members of the working group argue that each of these elements or components of rural welfare can be quantified by a series of indicators, e.g. life expectancy at birth; the incidence of diseases; the amount and distribution of income; aspects of housing; the position of women and children, and so on. In turn, the authors hold that these elements are related to what they called determinants: economic conditions, community facilities and social structures. They also give a long list of indicators for these determinants, some of which are capable of quantification.

This early post-World War II example has been elaborated in order to clarify three things: (a) at that time, there was a clear realization that not all important societal phenomena can be quantified; (b) the authors recognized the need to consider a great many aspects of society (they list 62 indicators of elements); and (c) an understanding of society is an essential ingredient in the construction of indicators. We shall return later to this last point, and for the time being will concentrate on the first two aspects.

The FAO effort was made almost simultaneously with work done in other parts of the UN system such as ECOSOC and ILO. An important step was taken in 1954 with the publication of a report on the definition and measurement of standards and levels of living. At that time, the concern of the agencies was largely with the framing of policies to raise the levels of living in developing countries. The report says that the data are required 'to assess need as well as to record progress in meeting need' (UN 1954: iii). The report is important in that it enters into a series of problems which are still at the centre of discussion on social indicators.

First of all, it reserves the term 'standards of living' for making reference to aspirations or to what ought to be, while the expression 'levels of living' is designed to refer to actual conditions of life in a particular area or country. Thus, a distinction between 'normative' and 'observed' indicators is introduced. The importance of normative indicators is that they serve as a basis for evaluation: in a way, therefore, they constitute 'targets' of policy.

Secondly, the report observes that a choice as to which indicators ought to be included in an 'element' or 'component', and a decision as to which elements to incorporate in an overall indicator of levels of living, constitute value judgements. It will be clear that the exclusion of an indicator or of an element in fact means the giving of zero-weight to that particular aspect. Whether attaching a zero-weight necessarily constitutes the expression of a value judgement, however, remains to be seen.

Thirdly, the report distinguishes between material and non-material aspects of the level of living. This same distinction continues in the literature up to the present day, for instance in work by Liu (1978) and Bayless and Bayless (1982), who separate physical from psychological components. The UN report, meanwhile, goes on to say that 'the concept of levels of living should have reference to the satisfaction of all types of needs and wants' (UN 1954:5). It is important to note that at this point the report introduces not only the distinction between material and non-material, but implicitly also raises the problem of objective or subjective indicators. The report says that the inclusion of indicators of non-material components would make international comparisons more difficult since the latter would refer to values and beliefs inherent in different cultures, but it also recognizes that even interpersonal comparisons can only be made under the assumption that the individuals have common values. This problem has a corollary in the acceptance of the idea that the satisfaction of needs by individuals can be aggregated.

Fourthly, the report enters into the problem of the statistical characteristics of indicators. If a number of indicators are selected to describe aspects of a given component of the level of living, should these indicators be independent or should one prefer those that exhibit interdependence? And also, should indicators be chosen which represent the availability of facilities, or should one prefer indicators that refer to their use? Again, is the number of patients using the services of nurses to be considered as an indicator of the state of health in a country, or should we prefer statistics on the incidence of terminal diseases? The definition of what are indicators of target variables and what are indicators of instrument variables becomes a crucial factor here.

The 1954 report selected eleven components of the level of living: health, including demographic conditions; food and nutrition; education, including literacy and skills; conditions of work; the employment situation; aggregate consumption and savings; transportation; clothing; recreation and entertainment; social security; and human freedoms.

In 1961 a new UN report was published, in which it is noted that of the components accepted in 1954 'some appear to be more directly related to the measurement of levels of living than others.' Thus, for instance: 'It is doubtful whether transportation should be considered a component of the level of living: transportation is primarily a means to the achievement of other goals, and in some circumstances may represent a social cost' (UN 1961: 3-4). The eleven components are therefore reduced to nine: health; food consumption and nutrition; education; employment and conditions of work; housing; social security; clothing; recreation; and human freedoms. Also, the number of indicators is reduced. Subsequently, the first Report on the World Social Situation appeared in 1963 (UN 1963).

II *Indicators of Levels of Living* are thus intended to represent dimensions of welfare (cf. Baster 1972). As such, they are generally drawn up to be used for designing and monitoring policies, and are to be distinguished from *social indicators*. Both differ again from *development indicators*. The latter became of interest when the UN Research Institute for Social Development started a research programme on 'the contents and measurement of development' (UNRISD 1968). In Baster's view development indicators represent 'a direct measurement of an economic or social variable... or, more often, an indirect measure of some non-measurable phenomenon' (Baster 1972:4). The difference between these indicators and the systems in which authors have tried to bring them together, and those of level of living indicators is small but important: development indicators do not contain reference to human freedoms.

The literature on development indicators makes a sharp distinction between social and economic indicators: the former refer to health and demographic states, nutrition, education, housing and communications; the latter include transport and services, agriculture, industry, and trade. Other literature on indicators does not make this sharp distinction, although it seems advisable; it is also accepted in one of the classics of the field: *Social Indicators* edited by Bauer in 1966. Nevertheless, the contributors to that volume helped to create some of the existing confusion. One of them, Gross (1966) warns in his preface against possible misunderstanding of the term. Advocacy of *social* indicators, he says, should not be read as depreciation of *economic* indicators. 'Social', in his view, should be understood as 'societal' or 'pertaining to the social system'. And in this context, social accounting should be understood as referring to 'an ordered set of relevant indicators, without particular reference to how they may have been traditionally labeled' (Gross 1966: xvi).

A fourth concept which is also part of the social indicator research toolbox is denoted by *quality of life* (QOL). As Carley (1981: 34) observes, QOL research refers mainly to research that pays explicit attention to subjective social indicators.

QOL indicators as understood by Liu (1978), for instance, imply the creation of a social index. This requires the selection of variables, their measurement, the standardization of the measurements, and finally, the attachment of weights to the standardized measurements before they are aggregated into an overall index of the quality of life in a given area. There are still considerable problems with this approach, especially in the stages of standardization and weighting (Cf Sinden 1982). The element of subjectiveness comes into the picture in that the indicators include a number that refer to individuals' perception of their well-being.

Thus, the term social indicator in expressions such as 'social indicator research' or 'social indicator movement' in fact refers to something that requires further definition. The literature on this aspect bears witness to the problem: many authors start with a list of definitions made by other authors, subsequently criticize these, and then go on to add to the list. There seems to be some convergence of opinion, however, in the direction that social indicators refer to social phenomena; that is to say, to those social phenomena that are subject of social policy, and that they should be useful for policy monitoring and evaluation. Deviations from this line of convergence are dictated either by the specific interest of the researcher (theory vs policy), or by the way in which data are collected, and/or the degree of their availability.

It seems useful to indicate the definitional boxes in which the contributors to this volume should be placed. Nancy Baster seems to follow the UN line, even if in her introduction she equates indicators of levels of living with those of quality of life. She goes on, however, to say that ways are still being sought to integrate 'social indicators with economic and other aspects of development'. Apthorpe, on the contrary, is closer to the notion put forward by Gross, namely, that social indicators refer to aspects of society. He speaks of development indicators in order to avoid the dichotomy economic:social, which in his view is unwarranted. Ellis, in Chapter 4, enters the relatively new sphere of a composite index on QOL, when he takes subjective aspects of welfare into account. Correa, in Chapter 6 places himself, as does Sovani in Chapter 7, in the framework of the UN concepts, while Koskiaho in Chapter 10 also takes this view.

III Before turning to the issues mentioned in the 1954 UN report, it seems useful to give further consideration to some aspects of thinking on social indicators. Early on, under the impact of statisticians in particular, the idea was launched that social indicators should be put in the framework of a systematic approach that would take account of the problems of consistency, representativeness, and aggregation and disaggregation. Gross proposed such a system and so did Stone (1973). Similarly, OECD developed a system that was agreed upon by its member states (OECD 1973). The approaches taken to the construction of these systems vary widely, and are closely related to the two motivations for social indicator research: understanding and action. In addition, values played a role. Thus, Drewnowski (1974) proposed a system starting from the idea that the economy is instrumental to society and that social variables are more important than economic ones. Although one may agree with this view, it is a value judgement.

Those systems that are designed primarily with a view to facilitating action, organize the indicators either in accordance with the governmental set-up of a country or in relation to social goal areas, as did the 1949 FAO report. OECD also uses the latter approach and so does Drewnowski, while the former approach was taken in Britain (CIPFA 1979) and in the USA by Fitzsimmons and Lavey (1976). The more theoretically-oriented systems are related either to the life-cycle, such as the system of Social and Demographic Statistics developed by the UN (UNSO 1971, 1974) and those by Land and McMillen (Land 1975; Land & McMillen 1980). Correa's approach in Chapter 6 is similar to that of Land. As a footnote to the development of what Gross called a Social Accounting System (SAS), the Social Accounting Matrices (SAMs) (see Chapter 5 by Van Heemst) may be considered as an attempt to relate systems of national accounting (SNAs) to some systems of social accounting: a partial overlap would exist in the supporting tables needed for a SAM and a SNA, and similarly between a SAM and a SAS.

IV The incorporation into a system of indicators of development of those that refer to social phenomena poses rather serious problems of definition and measurement. Correct inclusion would require that the essentials of these phenomena are caught in numbers. If health were to be included, for example, is longevity the essence of health, so that the indicator to take would be 'life expectancy at birth'? Or if education is to be included, would combined primary and secondary enrolment, together with the vocational enrolment ratio, constitute the essentials of education? Although, of course, those who reported on the UNRISD study on the *Contents and Measurement of Socio-Economic Development* (UNRISD 1970) did not argue that these magnitudes represent the essentials of the phenomena 'health' and 'education', they are given as core indicators of socio-economic development, creating, for the furtive (and therefore unwise) reader the impression that they are considered important to indicate what is health or what is education. The point we are trying to make here is that indicators of social phenomena are but poor substitutes for what are qualitatively much richer concepts. It would seem that to create definitions of social phenomena in a meaningful way, while at the same time making their measurement possible, has generally been considered an effort that could not be successful. Thus, although the essence of social stratification would seem to lie in the rules that govern interrelations between individuals and groups belonging to different strata, quantitative discourse on social stratification is largely in terms of how many people belong to each stratum and of their average economic worth in terms of income and wealth.

How, then, is it possible that, although there seem to be good arguments against the quantification of social phenomena, we have been able to witness an increasing stream of numbers on them? Two reasons may be advanced: one might be that even social scientists have been unable to resist the Western scientific paradigm. They, as well as the economists, the geographers and so on, have tended to give their field a strong basis similar to that enjoyed by the natural sciences. A second reason might be found in the demands made by society on the social sciences. Instruments of analysis are developed by scientists and theories are proposed in response to such demands. Thus, it is interesting to note that the theory of monetary and fiscal policy goes back to the Middle Ages when feudal lords and town councils had the right of coinage and learned treatises were written on how to maintain a constant or increasing flow of revenue by manipulating the precious metal content of coins or their official exchange rates. Moreover, while Europe and the United States and, through them, many other parts of the world, were governed by the liberal principles of *laissez faire*, responsibility for social phenomena, which are generally the concern of social indicator research, remained largely with private persons, groups or institutions and *local* government, while monetary policy and trade policies were made by the *national* authorities. Problems of social justice, of employment, of public health, etc., were not to become issues of national government policy until the workers had organized themselves effectively. Only then, and sometimes in support of this movement, did quantitative information on social phenomena start to flow more easily.

It is wellknown that policy making requires the translation of action into budgets, and decisions on policy need the quantification of objectives. Econometrics was born in the 1930s; in the post-war period it developed into an adult subject. But as governments were forced or felt the need to centralize, econometrics was no longer sufficient. As social policy became increasingly a concern of national government, preoccupation with the quantification of social phenomena grew: not only in the West, but also in the East and South.

As this happened, social indicator research in many countries was initiated by economists whose concerns were very largely with quantification of the objectives of government action, identification of the costs involved in meeting targets, and the monitoring of government action in terms of the degree to which these targets were met. This concern largely determined the aspects of the social phenomena that they defined and measured, and the changes therein that they monitored. As a proxy for education, for example, they might take literacy. As a proxy for quality in (formal) primary education, some might measure the percentage of pupils who would pass all grades of the primary school without failing once. For health care, they might use the number of doctors or the number of hospital beds per 10,000 inhabitants. From the point of view of a particular kind of social policy, the measurement of these aspects makes considerable sense. As long as the supply of hospital beds falls very much short of the demand for them, the construction of hospitals and their equipment with beds would seem to be an improvement in curative health care. Others might argue, however, that the discrepancy is indicative of a shortfall in preventive health care and that more should be spent on measures in that direction. The point here is not to go into the intricacies of public health planning, but to indicate at least two issues: (a) relationships may exist between the various indicators that measure aspects of a given social phenomenon; (b) significant disagreement may exist with regard to the importance of a given social indicator in terms of the action which it is supposed to inspire.

V It was established quite early on in social indicator research that there were relationships between individual indicators. The need was felt to use a composite index, especially for purposes of international or interregional comparison, as is done in QOL research, and considerable problems arose in connection with the weights that should be attached to each individual indicator. This problem became more complex when, towards the end of the Viet Nam war, attention was drawn to the importance of the physical environment for the quality of life; not only social and economic indicators, but also references to the environment then had to be included.

The problem of weights appears in at least two forms: first, in terms of the choice of the various aspects of life which can be quantified: the exclusion of some aspects means giving them a zero weight; secondly in terms of the existence of relationships among the various aspects of a given phenomenon and those between the various phenomena themselves which have been selected as relevant for an overall indicator. If such relationships exist, one indicator partly reflects at least one other indicator and their 'communality' might cause the attachment of too heavy a weight.

The problem raised here is not altogether new, as we shall try to show. Taking the problem within the framework of those whose concern is action, the issue is as follows: if today our composite index has a value Z_o based on the weights attached to each of the various indicators and their values, what action should be undertaken to acquire a desirable value Z at some distance in time? The difference $Z\text{-}Z_o$ would be indicative of the action required and of the price tag to be attached to it. This price would, of course, also be a function of the number of years required to attain the target value Z.

To pose the issue in this way, and for the action-oriented QOL researcher this would be the way, implies a return to the problem of measurability of the welfare function, a problem that has played havoc with welfare economics for the last forty years. It goes back, on the one hand, to the problem of whether individual utility functions can be aggregated into a national one and, on the other, to whether a welfare function (in which in principle all components of welfare feature) can be measured at the national level (by, for instance, interviewing the political leadership). Economists are aware that no solution to this problem exists; that is to say, no solution that is satisfactory from a methodological point of view.

But if all this is correct, two types of interrelations between indicators would seem to exist: first, those determined by the nature of the phenomena, aspects of which are turned into indicators (with all the pertinent problems of definition); and second, a relationship that expresses a desired state of interrelationship. In theory, the first type of ('objective') relationship is measurable, although it would have to be separated from the effects of policy action. The second type of ('voluntarist') relationship can, of course, also be measured. But as a utility function this can only be done at the level of the individual (or group, in very specific conditions).

Composite indicators, therefore, pose a problem of objectivity at two levels. The first occurs in the phase of comparative description (for a single country over time or for various countries at a given time): do the weights represent the value system of society or those of the researcher(s), and should they be constant? This problem includes the one concerning measurement of the relationships between phenomena and aspects thereof. The second problem of objectivity is related to the weights used in computing the values of Z as a target magnitude. The problems raised in this section are closely related to the approaches of Drewnowski and Land. Both speak of the necessity to base social planning on quantitative models which express relationships between the quantifiable aspects of social and economic phenomena. Thus, if models contain what Tinbergen (1956) has called 'target variables' and 'instrument variables', and if these models are able to describe what happened in the past, then systems of social indicators serve not only action, but also at least description.

Land (1981), for instance, would seem to agree with Drewnowski (1974) when he argues that changes in the values of the various indicators for a given population require explanation if policy measures are to have a rational basis. Land's models – or systems of equations – are attempts at theorizing change in social indicators. Since these indicators do not necessarily catch the essence of the phenomena (whose aspects they describe in numerical form), neither do they necessarily further a better understanding. They do provide for consistency in policy design, however, especially if embedded (as Land argues) in population statistics.

What remains, of course, is the problem of determining the values of the target variables, that is to say, the standards and norms of the 1954 UN report.

VI Some difficulties of objectivity in social indicator research have been increased considerably by the advent of sociologists upon the scene, particularly as regards the introduction of what were referred to explicitly as *subjective* indicators, measuring as they do the perception by individuals of their well-being. It is perhaps interesting to consider to what extent perception can be seen as the sociologist's counterpart of what the economist calls utility. Both agree that they are based on subjectiveness, although 'perception' and 'utility' may be measured by objective standards. The introduction of the concept of perception (and with it of subjective indicators) would seem to stem from a concern for better understanding of societal processes before entering the stage of action. Some might argue that where economists jumped into the water and disturbed all the fish, sociologists want to know more about the fish before feeding them, for instance. But then, the economists were doing the actual planning and they were the ones who had to develop instruments for it, with barely sufficient time to think.

This difference in approach led to considerable criticism of what came to be called objective indicators and sometimes sharpened the discussion between economists and sociologists. This issue is constructively addressed by various contributors to this volume and we can therefore leave the subject at this point for the moment. Meanwhile, it seems useful to keep some differences in concerns in mind. Drewnowski, for instance, has argued that indicators should be limited to observable and measurable phenomena: 'subjective poverty... does not provide any clear guidance for action.... Objective "absolute" poverty is the most relevant concept... which is fit to become a starting point for policies and plans' (Drewnowski 1977a: 206). He observed also: 'concentrating efforts at the measurement of subjective feelings seems to me nothing but retreading of old paths which have proved to lead nowhere' (Drewnowski 1977b).

VII Social indicator research, whether for purposes of understanding or of action, is severely limited by the existing data base, and not only in developing countries. When changes in the various indicators over time are sought, it soon appears that sound data on population do not exist outside census years, and also that census data are not always of the same standard. Data on life expectancy, on the occurrence of disease, on causes of death, exist, but their coverage is often restricted to less than half the population. The same holds for data on income distribution, education, and so on.

The data problem would seem to be indicative of the priority given to social aspects of development, although this is not necessarily so. One might argue that if governments were serious about social development – or about providing more social facilities – they would make available the resources needed to collect data on a regular basis, so that monitoring would be possible. The absence of such facilities, however, may be so glaring that governments feel data collection is not necessary (or desirable!), while to do it would carry the opportunity cost of foregoing a number of clinics and/or primary schools, for instance. This does not detract from a point that has been made by many authors, i.e. that data shortages preclude any thorough description and understanding of various components of development.

Another problem relates to the internal consistency of any given set of data meant to describe the social component of development. An example referring to an enterprise can be used for clarification. Assume that we want to express the performance of the enterprise in a number of key figures, for instance such quotients as output per worker, stocks per unit of output, net profit per unit of output, profit per worker, and so on. If all data were based on the accounts of the enterprise, and the accounts satisfied the condition that they truly reflected what they were supposed to count, *and* if they were made in accordance with best bookkeeping practices, then all key figures calculated from them would be internally consistent. This implies that a change in one of the key figures should result in a series of changes in other key figures, so as to maintain consistency. Applying this criterion to social indicators means thinking not merely in terms of the economic or sociological relationships between indicators, but also in terms of accounting relationships. The latter, of course, are supposed to hold when the social indicators measured all relate to one and the same country. This problem poses itself not only at the moment of measurement, but also at that of deciding upon what action should be taken in this sphere of life. To take this into account would mean that policy-makers must respect the internal logic of the issues at hand. In turn, this implies that they should not decide to do just anything, even though it might be politically desirable.

Recognition of this problem seems to be implicit with the development of social accounting matrices (SAMs). As shown elsewhere in this volume, SAMs constitute an extension of the national accounting systems that were developed in the years between 1935 and 1955. Although most SAMs are still in an experimental stage, they are sufficiently developed to clarify issues related, for instance, to income distribution; with an extended use of supporting tables, they could show how a great number of social indicators could be placed in a coherent whole.

VIII Stemming from a concern with action in fields that in common language are identified as social policy, social indicator research is seen by many as instrumental to that policy. Concerned not only with what are termed social facilities, but also with social security, the stimulation of certain types of group and individual behaviour, and relations between groups, social policy is undergoing quite basic reconsideration in many countries. While some of the issues related to social indicator research still await solution, it seems that the policy problem itself is being re-defined, if not in many developing countries then at least in some parts of Europe and in the United States.

This redefinition is related closely not only to the effects of social-economic policy-making in the West (e.g. high economic growth rates, high levels of social facility availability accompanied by lower levels of social responsibility and higher levels of alienation), but also to the economic crisis of the past few years and to a concentration in thinking on the essentials of society and what policy-making has done to prevent or stimulate them. Booth (1982) shows that one main reason for the poor state of social planning in Britain today lies in the subordination of social to economic objectives, as caused by the failure to define social goals and the relatively neglected state of social indicators in contrast to the sophistication of economic statistics, despite the recent 'Social Trends' reports. He argues that this is no accident but a result of the belief that social progress depends on economic growth and on the fallacy that social and economic issues can clearly be distinguished.

Thus we return to the problem of definition, this time to that of the field of social policy and how its goals should be specified. We also return to the issue of 'economism', a matter to which various contributors address themselves.

IX Although one can largely subscribe to Booth's analysis, further clarification would seem to be found in the observation that, while policy-making processes in the West implicitly subordinated social objectives to explicitly stated economic ones, policy-makers mostly stated explicitly that economic goals are not subordinated to social ones. This would seem to be related to the form that social policy has taken, especially social welfare planning.

In the welfare states of Northwest Europe, social welfare policy has been concerned very largely with social work and social security. Eventually, it also came to include services such as housing, health, education, social and cultural services. Various groups, which partially overlapped, became the object of special focus: the old, the young, the disabled, widows, the unemployed and so on. Of late, the (political) right of individuals and groups to participate in public decision making has also become an area of social policy. The preparation and execution of such policies has put a considerable claim on public resources and has caused consumption to go up at the expense of investment, even though social policy systems are partially financed by a redistribution of income. Thus in the Netherlands, for example, while the number of people working for central government increased from 114,500 to 174,700 between 1958 and 1978, those among them who functioned in the ministries directly involved with social policy increased from 17,500 to 41,700 (CBS various years), raising their relative weight from 15.3 per cent to almost 24 per cent. In the period after the first oil crisis (1973-78), this group of civil servants increased by 17.5 per cent, while the total population grew from 13.4 to 13.9 million, that is to say by 3.7 per cent over the five-year period. De Kok (1981) reports that in 1980 some 100,000 man-years were spent on social services alone; while in health care (275,000), education (265,000) and other services (60,000) some 600,000 man-years were employed. The benefits for social protection alone totalled 96.3 billion guilders in 1980, or 33.5 per cent of net national income.

It would be outrageous to suggest that these data are typical. On the contrary. However, when national income is low and governments have the tendency to centralize as many social services as possible (health care, education, social housing), as is the case in most developing countries, it is understandable that a relationship between the objectives of economic development (growth of income per capita, balance of payments equilibrium, etc.) and those of social development should be given primary consideration. The generation of resources and, on this basis, of government revenue, is obviously pre-conditional for the expenditures needed to reach such objectives. Economic development, in this sense, is instrumental to social development or, better said, to the increase in social facilities. But also, government expenditure for social objectives can only partly be considered as expenditure that might lead to the generation of resources. In other words, there is a trade-off: the more that is spent on social objectives, the less can be spent on generating additional resources. Here the national welfare function returns to our discussion. The history of Northwest Europe seems to indicate that policy-makers have preferred to give higher priority to objectives of economic development, and that only after a certain level of these had been achieved, could social development objectives obtain more priority. The majority of Third World countries may or may not exhibit similar value systems: many people speak of 'another development'. Yet visitors to Europe and the United States from what are called 'developing countries' frown upon the loss of many social values that are still present in their own societies: individual responsibility for the socially weak, the extended family, the importance of interpersonal relations and of leisure, and a greater interest in history, to mention but a few.

X There is no doubt, however, that social indicators have played an important role in identifying areas of concern for social development, especially in the sphere of social facilities. They have awoken many governments to the bitter fact that various groups – as differentiated by income and location – have little or no access to education, public health, shelter or employment. In many countries, indicators made to identify poverty have been adopted officially as a means with which to focus policy intended to ameliorate the life of the poor; as such, the social indicator movement has had a directly beneficial effect. The World Bank will use such indicators in deciding on the nature of the loans it provides, and in bilateral development co-operation more and more countries have adopted the poverty criterion as one of the most important for the allocation of grants, loans and technical assistance.

XI Whereas in the debate on the subjectivity of 'objective' indicators (the problem of weights) the role of the national state is being raised, whether implicitly or explicitly, it is becoming increasingly clear that this role is much influenced by foreign states and by supra-national organizations. With the re-thinking of social development objectives in particular and those of development in general, the role of the state is similarly being questioned. This occurs partly on the basis of dissatisfaction with the welfare state in which so much responsibility is monopolized by the state, and partly from the vantage point of those who prefer to work with (objectively measured) subjective indicators that are based on the concept of perception. The contribution by Koskiaho in this volume is a particularly thought-provoking example of this type of questioning.

XII Finally, this volume is divided into three parts. The first deals with problems and approaches to measurement in social indicator research. The second concerns problems of social development and social policy, to which social indicator research can play the role of handmaiden. In fact, of course, the two have areas of overlap, as will become clear from reading the various papers. In the third part, a bibliography on social indicator research and social planning is provided.

References

Baster, N. (1972) 'Development Indicators: An Introduction', in N. Baster (ed.): *Measuring Development* (London, Frank Cass), 1-20.

Bauer, R.A. (1966): 'Detection and Anticipation of Impact: The Nature of the Task', In R.A. Bauer (ed.): *Social Indicators* (Cambridge, Mass., MIT Press), 1-67.

Bayless, M. & S. Bayless (1982): 'Current Quality of Life Indicators: Some Theoretical and Methodological Concerns', in: *American Journal of Economics and Sociology*, Vol. 41, No. 4, 421-37.

Booth, T.A. (1982): 'Economics and the Poverty of Social Planning', in *Public Administration*, Vol. 60, No. 2, 197-214.

Carley, M. (1981): *Social Measurement and Social Indicators* (London, Allen & Unwin).

Centraal Bureau voor de Statistiek (various years): *Statistisch Zakboek* (The Hague, CBS).

Chartered Institute of Public Finance and Accountancy (1979): *Community Indicators* (London, CIPFA).

De Kok, A.C.M. (1981): 'Present State and Prospects of the Welfare State', in C.A.O. van Nieuwenhuijze (ed.): *The Quest of 'Another Development', A Social Approach?* (The Hague, Institute of Social Studies, 145-156; mimeographed).

Drewnowski, J. (1974): *On Measuring and Planning the Quality of Life* (The Hague, Mouton, for the Institute of Social Studies).

— (1977a): 'Poverty, Its Meaning and Measurement' in *Development and Change*, Vol. 8, No. 2, 183-208.

— (1977b): Review of B. Strumpel (ed.): *Economic Means for Human Needs: Social Indicators for Wellbeing and Discontent* (Ann Arbor 1976), in *Social Indicators Research*, Vol. 4, No. 2, 241-245.

FAO (1949): *Essential of Rural Welfare* (Rome, FAO Agricultural Studies No. 27).

Fitzsimmons, S.J. & W.G. Lavey (1976): 'Social Economic Accounts System (SEAS) Toward Comprehensive Community-Level Assessment Procedure', in *Social Indicators Research*, Vol. 2, 4, 389-452.

Gross, B.M. (1966): 'Preface: A Historical Note on Social Indicators', in R.A. Bauer (ed.): *Social Indicators* (Cambridge, Mass., MIT Press), ix-xviii.

Land, K.C. (1975): 'Theories, Models and Indicators of Social Change', in *International Social Science Journal*, Vol. 27, 7-37.

— (1981): 'Identification of Socio-Economic Indicators for Use in Integrated Social and Economic Planning', in *Socio-Economic Indicators for Planning* (Paris, UNESCO), 25-69.

Land, K.C. & M.M. McMillen (1980): 'A Macrodynamic Analysis of Change in Mortality Indexes in the United States, 1946-1975, Some Preliminary Results', in *Social Indicators Research*, Vol. 7, 1-46.

Liu, B. (1978): 'Variations in Social Quality of Life Indicators in Medium Metropolitan Areas', in *American Journal of Economics and Sociology*, Vol. 37, No. 3, 241-60.

OECD (1973): *List of Social Concerns* (Paris, OECD).

Sinden, J.A. (1982): 'Application of Quality of Life Indicators: Policy Evaluation for 26 Australian Towns', in *American Journal of Economics and Sociology*, Vol. 41, No. 4, 401-420.

Stone, R. (1973): 'A System of Social Matrices', in *The Review of Income and Wealth*, series 19, 143-66.

Tinbergen, J. (1956): *Economic Policy; Principles and Design* (Amsterdam, North Holland).

UN (1954): *Report on International Definition and Measurement of Standards and Levels of Living* (New York, United Nations; E/CN: 3/179; E/CN: 5/299).

— (1961): *International Definition and Measurement of Levels of Living; An Interim Guide* (New York, United Nations; E/CN: 3/270/RW.1; E/CN: 5/353).

— (1963): *1963 Report on the World Social Situation* (New York, United Nations).

UNRISD (1968): *Annual Report* (Geneva, UN Research Institute for Social Development).

— (1970): *Contents and Measurement of Socio-Economic Development* (Geneva, UNRISD).

UNSO (1971): *A System of Demographic Manpower*, and *Social Statistics Series, Classifications and Social Indicators* (New York, United Nations Statistical Office: ST/STAT/49).

— (1974): *System and Social and Demographic Statistics* (New York, United Nations Statistical Office: E/CN/3/450).

PART ONE

LEVEL OF LIVING INDICATORS

INTRODUCTION

I Part One of this volume contains four papers: the first, by Baster, provides us with a review of recent social indicator research and the issues it raises; the second by Apthorpe, on the subjective versus objective discussion, is followed by Ellis's application of Quality of Life indicators and then by a paper by Van Heemst on Social Accounting Matrices (SAMs) and their relationships to social indicators. These four papers discuss some of the basic problems in social indicator research: that of objective versus subjective indicators; of the coherence of social indicators; and of measurability.

Before attempting to focus these three aspects of the debate, it seems relevant to mention one particular aspect which causes considerable frustration: what have social indicators to do with sociology or economics and who, therefore, has the right to lead the movement. Various authors hold that there is nothing about social indicators that is conducive to a better understanding of what is social, and say that this is because economists were among the first to formulate such indicators. Others complain that social indicators have been called so because they refer to non-economic phenomena, implying that anything non-economic would therefore be social. Yet others, e.g. Apthorpe in Chapter 3 and Koskiaho in Chapter 10, argue that the distinction social-economic is artificial because there is basically nothing in society that is either purely economic or purely social. For relative latecomers to this field this discussion is somewhat surprising. It might be asked what would have happened if social indicators had been given a different name to begin with, e.g. 'indicators of public consumption'. Would sociologists then have asked more of them than economists ask of business cycle indicators, for instance? Of course, business cycle theory, which is used to help the selection of indices that make up a business cycle indicator, is relevant. A discussion about such theories is useful and may bring us closer to an understanding of reality. In the same way, other theories will be used in the composition of social indicators and these also are open to debate. But to argue on the basis of the word 'social' that the theory behind social indicators should be sociological or economic or whatever, would seem to miss the point that social indicators were developed to provide information for the decision-making process.

Since those who write about the subject seem to agree that there is nothing purely social about the phenomena that social indicators are expected to describe, it would seem that the expression 'social indicators' is a misnomer. Had they been called, as suggested, 'indicators of public consumption', then another group of social scientists might have appropriated the field – for instance, welfare economists who specialize in the field of public consumption or public goods and who theorize, for instance, on why decision-makers allocate public goods in a particular way. Social indicator research might then have moved in another direction – for instance, towards finding a closer connection with SAMs which link expenditure on social services to groups, and to earnings and production by sectors and factors of production.

II Van Heemst, who writes about this possible link-up in Chapter 5, shows that little progress has been made in this direction. He also shows, however, how powerful an analytical tool planners would have if the supporting tables of SAMs were expanded to include a series of social indicators implicit in the figures of the SAM proper, and if the SAM itself were given additional entries. Although, for instance, income group-specific expenditure by government on certain social services might not easily be given in SAMs, conceptually it would be possible in the same way that spatial disaggregation has proved feasible.

Van Heemst's paper continues from where Baster leaves off in Chapter 2. Whereas Baster explains a number of the principles, Van Heemst shows how these principles might be put into practice and what kind of difficulties are likely to emerge.

III In the General Introduction to this volume, we have tried to show the importance of the debate on subjective and objective indicators. Various authors in this volume refer to it: Baster, Apthorpe, Ellis and Koskiaho. Whereas Koskiaho doubts the significance of indicators that are based on opinions and assessments by individuals, Ellis considers that it is possible to derive meaningful quality of life indicators for specific groups in society. It is interesting to note that some of the most important indices which enter into Ellis's quality of life indicators are closely associated to what Koskiaho thinks should be studied in more detail, namely, access to resources by different groups and individuals. Thus, whereas there is agreement on the relevance of variables that should be taken into account, there is disagreement on whether a meaningful indicator could be made.

Leaving aside the problems of measurement and of the weights to be attached to individual components of overall indicators, the problem of objective versus subjective indicators is in essence one concerning their relevance for both analysis and policy-making. The problem, in our view, is primarily one that concerns the validity of *evaluations* based on the outcomes of these measurements; *a priori*, there is no reason to assume that the evaluations will differ depending on who makes them in order to provide arguments for action, whether by government or by one or more of the groups involved. This would only be the case if the evaluators had different value systems.

What we have in mind may be clarified as follows. Assume that two regions in a given country prove to have perfectly identical 'scores' on 'objective' social indicators. Assume, furthermore, that a survey of various population groups in the two regions indicates that in one region the level of living is perceived as providing a low degree of well-being, whereas in the other it is perceived as providing a high degree of well-being. This reduction of the problem seems to be useful in two ways: first, it draws attention to the question that undoubtedly will arise in the minds of planners and policy-makers as to what to think about these results and what to do about them; secondly, it draws attention to the problem of what the role of the state would have to be in this regard.

The answer to the first question may be that the remarkable difference in outcome for the two regions can be ascribed to differences in culture, and that further research will be necessary to test this hypothesis. The query as to what should be done may be answered in this way. This is not altogether satisfactory, however: if the hypothesis is not refuted by the facts, the problem is back on the tables of the policy-makers who will have to decide whether they will or will not do anything about it. As always, value judgements now start to play a role. Thus, if the policy-makers are of the more progressive variety who feel that access to material sources of level of living should be spread equitably, for instance, whereas the region scoring low on perceived well-being is one with a large share of population who have lost access to such resources for the benefit of others on the basis of commensurate policies, the policy-makers may consider that nothing should be done. Bringing about a higher score of perceived well-being would imply going back on earlier policies. In other words, perceptions of well-being may be low in certain groups precisely because 'objective' indicators have been equalized. Therefore, evaluation of the score on the indicator on the basis of government objectives seems to be relevant here. The meaning of the score on an indicator in terms of the action it prompts thus seems to arise from the values that inform the action and the legitimacy of those who have the power to act.

This brings us to the role of the state which social indicator research seems to take as given and therefore does not explicitly discuss. In Part Two of this volume this issue is approached more directly, for instance by Van Nieuwenhuijze; but even in this first part it comes into the discussion in Ellis's contribution on Ciskei. Ellis does this implicitly and explicitly: implicitly by selecting his components of an overall indicator of quality of life as indicators of the barriers that prevent particular groups from attaining the goals they see as important for themselves, thus seeming to assume that the state should enable each particular group to attain its objectives. Explicitly, Ellis raises the issue by taking into account the group's access to power. Specialists will judge whether Ellis's contribution manages to overcome the dichotomy between objective and subjective indicators. Whether he succeeds in this regard or not, however, what he and his collaborators found in Ciskei constitutes a socio-politically most relevant document on the effects of *apartheid*.

The discussion on objective-subjective in level of living indicator research is closely related to the debate on economism and the mechanistic view that some economic planners have or may have had of societal change. In his subtle paper, Apthorpe explores the extent to which the various dichotomies can also be construed as relative, suggesting that peace between the battling parties could be a more rational outcome of the debate. Some differences, he infers, are at best gradual and not really of a fundamental nature.

IV Some basic points of the problem of measurability have been indicated in the general introduction to this volume, and need not be repeated here, the more so since Baster's exposition in the following chapter deals with it extensively.

2 SOCIAL INDICATOR RESEARCH: SOME ISSUES AND DEBATES

Nancy Baster

This is necessarily a partial and selective review,[1] written from the point of view of someone whose main interest has been in the uses of social indicators in the context of social development and social planning in developing countries, and also from the point of view of someone interested in the applied rather than the more theoretical end of research, even if in practice it is difficult to separate the two.

What I have tried to do is first to present a very general overview of recent work on social indicators, and then to discuss a limited number of particular issues, including the debate about different approaches to the measurement of levels of living, or quality of life, the question of an appropriate framework for integrating social indicators with economic and other aspects of development, and problems of distribution and disaggregation. These are only a few of the topics that could be selected, but they are all topics which bear a direct relation to Jan Drewnowski's work, and they raise issues which are as alive today as they were ten years ago. They will serve, I hope, to set his contribution in a wider context.

I An Overall Picture of Recent Work on Social Indicators

Table 1 represents in summary form some of the directions of recent work on social indicators. It was originally used to provide a summary of discussions at a seminar on statistics for social development held at the Institute of Development Studies at the University of Sussex, but it can also be used to provide a starting-point for the present discussion on social indicators.

The centre column in Table 1 reflects what seems to me to be the dominant trend in the development and use of social indicators at the present time, that is the development of indicators relating to central social policy concerns such as levels of living, basic needs, distribution, poverty, integration and structural change in the context of national

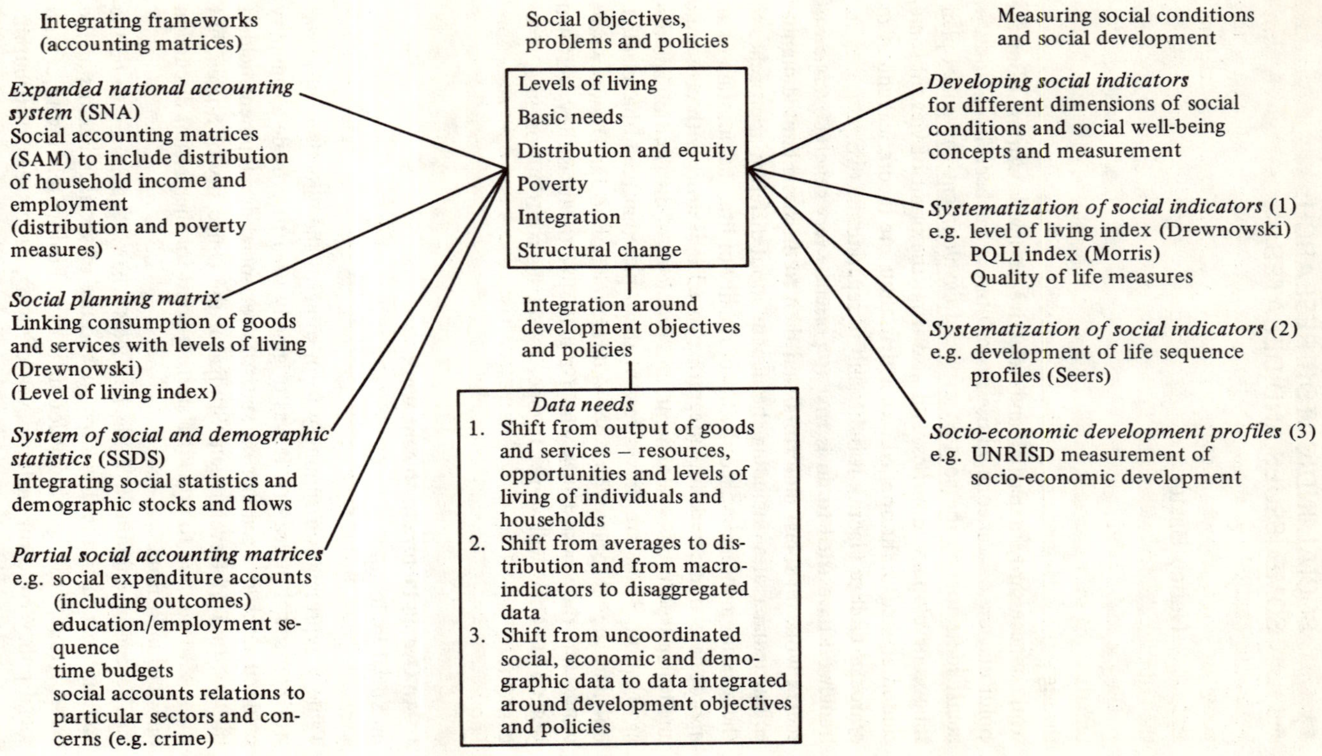
Integrating frameworks
(accounting matrices)
Social objectives,
problems and policies
Measuring social conditions
and social development
Expanded national accounting system (SNA)
Social accounting matrices (SAM) to include distribution of household income and employment
(distribution and poverty measures)
Social planning matrix
Linking consumption of goods and services with levels of living
(Drewnowski)
(Level of living index)
System of social and demographic statistics (SSDS)
Integrating social statistics and demographic stocks and flows
Partial social accounting matrices
e.g. social expenditure accounts (including outcomes)
education/employment sequence
time budgets
social accounts relations to particular sectors and concerns (e.g. crime)
Levels of living
Basic needs
Distribution and equity
Poverty
Integration
Structural change
Integration around development objectives and policies
Data needs
1. Shift from output of goods and services – resources, opportunities and levels of living of individuals and households
2. Shift from averages to distribution and from macro-indicators to disaggregated data
3. Shift from uncoordinated social, economic and demographic data to data integrated around development objectives and policies
Developing social indicators
for different dimensions of social conditions and social well-being concepts and measurement
Systematization of social indicators (1)
e.g. level of living index (Drewnowski)
PQLI index (Morris)
Quality of life measures
Systematization of social indicators (2)
e.g. development of life sequence profiles (Seers)
Socio-economic development profiles (3)
e.g. UNRISD measurement of socio-economic development

development goals, and the strengthening of the social information and statistical base in order to articulate these concerns more adequately, and to facilitate analysis of significant interrelations. However, this policy-oriented research depends on more basic research on concepts and measurement, and some of the directions of research are listed on the right and left-hand sides of Table 1.

On the right-hand side are listed some of the efforts made to systematize the measurement of social conditions and social development through the development of social indicators. The first item covers work on the development of indicators of particular aspects of social conditions and social change. Examples would be indicators of employment, crime, nutrition, poverty, status of women, social mobility. The list would embrace a wide range of social concerns, such as those included in the well-known volume by Sheldon and Moore on *Indicators of Social Change* (1968), which contained sections on the demographic framework, on structural aspects of social change, which included economic growth, labour force and employment, knowledge and technology, politics, family change, religious trends, and on 'distributive' features, such as consumption, leisure, health and education. The same wide approach is reflected in most national reports on social trends, and in the United Nations guidelines on social indicators (United Nations 1978). A great deal of current research on social indicators is concerned with efforts to improve the measurement of significant aspects of social conditions and social change, a circular process involving the clarification of concepts and definitions, selection of relevant and reliable indicators, improvement of the statistical base, and empirical validation. The development of widely accepted indicators of a particular social phenomenon is necessarily a slow process, calling for expert knowledge and close experience of the area concerned.

Work on indicators more directly related to individual welfare or levels of living, forms a subset of this wider range. The main search has been for better measures of the outcomes of social processes and social policies in terms of individual well-being and distribution over the population. The social indicator programme of the Organization for Economic Co-operation and Development (OECD 1976) represents one major effort to clarify concepts and to develop indicators in this field, and indicates the general direction of research in member countries. The earlier United Nations report on the international definition and measurement of the levels of living (United Nations 1954) was the first attempt to develop indicators and measures of levels of living in the context of developing countries. Much of the recent research on indicators of levels of living and social well-being has been influenced by these two basic reports.

The next three items on the right-hand side of Table 1 illustrate various efforts that have been made to develop an integrated set of measures of levels of living, or quality of life. The first of these is the level of living index developed by Jan Drewnowski (1974), outlining a methodology for aggregating indicators and components of levels of living into a single level of living or quality of life index. We shall come back to this later. Another more recent, and less sophisticated example is the PQLI (Physical Quality of Life Index) proposed by the Overseas Development Council (Morris 1979). The PQLI index is based on three social indicators, literacy, infant mortality rate, and expectation of life at age 1, and is intended to provide a simple measure of social development for comparison with aggregate measures of economic growth, and for making comparisons over time. Omitted here, but discussed later in the paper, is the development of an integrated measure of quality of life using subjective, or perceptual indicators.

Another rather different approach where research is still at an early stage (the third item on the right-hand side) is the use of life expectancy or life-cycle profiles to develop an integrated set of social indicators (Seers 1977). This involves the extension of demographic matrices to provide a picture of the distribution over the population of various characteristics relevant to social policy, such as education, health, employment, classified by age, sex, place of residence, etc., and to facilitate the development of a set of social indicators based on transition ratios.

The fourth item listed on the right-hand side is different from the first three in that the emphasis is put on developing an interrelated set of social and economic indicators for measuring socio-economic development. One of these is the measurement of socio-economic development developed by the United Nations Research Institute for Social Development (McGranahan et al 1972), which is based on sixteen closely-related development indicators, economic, social and structural. Country profiles based on correspondence points can be mapped and compared with the average or 'expected' profile based on international comparisons. A body of data is being built up to facilitate the analysis of time series. Other examples could be given of efforts to develop measures of socio-economic development for comparisons between countries, and between regions within countries, using a variety of methods, ranging from simple ranking to the use of component analysis and other forms of multivariate analysis.

One of the criteria of a social indicator is that it should form part of a wider system of relationships, or frame of reference, and a major effort over the last decade has been put into the development of different social accounting systems,[2] reflecting different conceptual models of the interrelation between economic, social and demographic variables. We shall return to these later in the paper, and only refer briefly here to the items on the left-hand side of Table 1.

Item 1 includes recent work on social accounting matrices (SAM). These accounts incorporate both employment and distribution of household income in an expanded system of national accounts, making it possible to trace the complex linkages between production and distribution of household income. These social accounting matrices reflect an analytical model which has provided the basis for much of the current research on employment and distribution of income in the International Labour Office and elsewhere. Item 2 includes Drewnowski's social planning matrix as an example of a social accounting matrix where the main focus is put on the links between the output of goods and services and levels of living, measured in physical units, links that are central to much of the current research on basic needs.

The third item on the left-hand side represents the main alternative (or complementary) system developed over the last decade for the integration of social and demographic statistics. The core of the system of social and demographic statistics (SSDS) consists of the demographic stocks and flows which link together the different social states or social concerns in a number of life sequences. These include the learning and earning sequence, family groupings and their changes, health conditions, and the sequence relating to delinquency. The transition matrix representing demographic stocks and flows (basically a demographic input/output matrix) provides a basis for analytical work establishing linkages between different life sequences. For example, the education/earning sequence is a familiar ingredient in employment and education planning. The SSDS does not in itself reflect an analytical system in the way that the system of national accounts does, although as indicated later, it can be seen as part of a wider social systems or social change approach to development.

Finally, on the left-hand side, an item is included labelled partial social accounting matrices. These correspond to what, in the French planning system, have been called satellite accounts, i.e. accounting systems including both quantitative data relating to particular sectors or policy issues, such as social service accounts which facilitate the functional analysis of social expenditure, including the distribution of benefits. The satellite accounts are linked with, but separate from, the conventional accounting systems. They reflect an analytical approach to the development of social indicators, and can be seen as part of a goal-oriented approach to development analysis and planning.

II The Measurement of Social Welfare and Quality of Life

The definition and measurement of social well-being and quality of life has provided one of the main themes of work on social indicators, both in developed and developing countries. Three different approaches can be found in current research, each with their own advantages and limitations, and each with a number of conceptual and methodological problems which have been widely debated in the literature. The three approaches are distinguished by their underlying rationale, and by the use of different kinds of indicators and units of measurement, and can be divided into those involving the use of monetary measures of GNP and its various components, those involving the use of measures of social conditions (sometimes called objective social indicators), and those involving the measures of people's perception or assessment of well-being (sometimes called subjective social indicators).[3]

GNP and Related Monetary Measures

A variety of monetary measures derived from national accounting concepts are commonly accepted as useful if incomplete indicators of economic welfare or material well-being. These include various measures of income, output and consumption, per capita and per household. Per capita national income has the advantage of providing a summary measure which has an underlying rationale in economic theory and is part of a consistent national accounting framework, and which can with some reservations (relating particularly to price changes and exchange rates) be used for making comparisons over time and between countries. However, reservations about the adequacy of per capita GNP as a measure of even economic welfare have steadily increased since the days of Pigou's example of the social costs of smoke from factory chimneys, with the result that there has been an increasing volume of research both on improving the measure within existing boundaries, and on ways of modifying the concept to include various aspects of welfare at present excluded.

A good deal of work has gone into improving existing measures within the conventional boundaries of national accounts, for instance by incorporating estimates of output and consumption in the informal or household sector of the economy, by combining private and government expenditures attributable to households to provide a measure of total consumption, and by experimenting with different weighting systems for taking into account changes in the distribution of income.

A number of ambitious efforts to incorporate additional benefits and disbenefits in a global measure of net national welfare have been made (in the USA and Japan for example). This would include aspects such as changes in leisure time, environmental pollution, other household activities, particularly activities of housewives. However, problems of deciding what should be included or excluded from a measure of net national welfare, and the difficulty of imputing values to activities or situations outside the market, has meant that this research has remained largely exploratory and is unlikely to affect present measures of national income for some time to come.[4] But it does lead to an increasing overlap between work on monetary measures of welfare and work on social indicators covering areas of common interest.

Objective Social Indicators

The development of indicators of levels of living or social well-being represents one of the main themes of social indicator research. To a large extent this work reflects a response to the limitations of economic measures of welfare, and the need to go beyond economic measures of resources and output of goods and services to focus more directly on changes in social well-being and quality of life. Such measures are needed to describe the situation and direction of change, to analyze interrelations between changes in social well-being and other aspects of development, to quantify social objectives, and to monitor progress towards these goals.

The general direction of international research over the past twenty years can be illustrated by taking four examples, the report of the UN expert group on the international definition and measurement of the levels of living (United Nations 1954), Jan Drewnowski's work on the measurement of levels of living and welfare (Drewnowski 1974),[5] the OECD research programme on the measurement of social well-being, and Lisk's categories of basic needs (Lisk 1979), reflecting the orientation of the programme launched by the International Labour Office in 1976 (ILO 1976).

In all four examples levels of living, or social well-being, is defined in fairly general terms, with reference to the satisfaction of needs. The UN report refers to levels of living in terms of living conditions, particularly the satisfaction of needs and wants, including physical well-being, material elements of consumption, and non-material needs, or human freedoms. Jan Drewnowski defines the level of living in terms of the satisfaction of human needs. The OECD programme speaks of 'identifiable and definable aspirations of fundamental and direct importance to human well-being', while the ILO programme is by definition oriented towards the satisfaction of basic needs.

All four studies propose that levels of living or social well-being should be measured indirectly through the identification of different aspects or components, and the identification of appropriate indicators under each component. It is in the selection of components and indicators that the concept is really defined. It can be seen from Table 2 that a number of components are common to all four lists – health, education or learning, housing and physical environment (either separately or together). These, together with nutrition, which is not included in the OECD list, make up the most commonly-used 'core' components. Income and employment are excluded from the Drewnowski and Lisk lists, included, if only as background information, in the others. Personal security, or law and order, is included in the Drewnowski and OECD lists. Leisure and use of time are included in these two lists, excluded in the others. Finally, there are those components, human freedoms (UN), social environment (Drewnowski, OECD), social opportunity and participation (OECD), and participation and equality (Lisk), which are much less clearly defined, and which do not fit easily into the component structure, partly because they are more closely related to political and social processes, and to some extent cut across the other components. A closer look at these components shows that they cover a wide variety of concepts, with an emphasis on participation and equity as common factors.

Work on clarifying these concepts has proceeded in a number of directions. One has been to consider participation in terms of distribution and equity, cutting across all substantive components, or aspects of well-being. Another direction, following Maslow's psychological theory of human needs,[6] is illustrated by Allardt's exploratory analysis of dimensions of welfare in Scandinavian countries (Allardt 1973a), which emphasized the 'loving' and 'being' dimensions of welfare, as distinct from the material, or 'having' aspects. His 'loving' would include primary and secondary attachments, while his 'being' would include participation in decision-making and political processes. Similar ideas have been explored in the World Indicators Programme at the Univer-

Table 2. Levels of Living: Categories/Components in Selected Studies

International definition and measurement of levels of living (United Nations)	Drewnowski's level of living and welfare	OECD: measuring social well-being: social concerns	Categories of basic needs (lists)
Health	Level of living	Health	Food
Consumption and nutrition	Nutrition	Individual development	Clothing
Education	Clothing	through learning	Housing
Employment and conditions	Shelter	Employment and quality	Health
of work	Health	of working life	Education
Housing	Education	Time and leisure	Clean water supply
Social security	Leisure	Personal economic situation	
Clothing	Social security	Physical environment	
Recreation	Social environment	Personal safety and ad-	Participation
Human freedoms	Physical environment	ministration of justice	Equality
Background components	Level of welfare	Social opportunity and	Quality of working life
Population and labour force	Somatic status	participation	
Income and expenditure	Educational status		
Communications and transport	Social status		

sity of Oslo, and in the UN University programme on development indicators.

The crux of the component/indicator approach to the measurement of levels of living or well-being lies in the validity of the indicators that are selected and the reliability of the statistical measures used. Indicators have been proposed under most of the components in the four lists, covering different aspects of the components, including in some cases indicators of inputs (e.g. expenditure and facilities) as well as outputs, both flow and stock indicators, and indicators of 'access'. For measuring levels and trends in levels of living and social well-being emphasis has been put on a balanced and comprehensive coverage of components, on the use of a limited number of indicators covering the different aspects of a component, and on indicators reflecting 'outcomes' rather than 'inputs', points which were strongly stressed in Drewnowski's study as well as in the OECD programme. In practice the range of indicators is limited by the lack of agreed operational definitions for many of the components (e.g. learning, health, security), the lack of correspondence between the indicator proposed and the condition to be measured, which applies particularly when indicators of services are used as proxies for outcomes, the use of partial measures, such as measures of registered unemployed rather than measures of underemployment, and above all, by the lack of reliable data. There is a continual process of revision and experimentation, for example, in the use of anthropometric measures as indicators of nutritional status.

Some of the questions which arise can be illustrated by taking one or two examples. In the case of health, the UN short list included expectation of life and infant mortality rate, as well as crude death rate and facilities (doctors and hospital beds) per head of population. All these are widely used indicators, and the first two would be widely accepted as valid indicators of changes in health status. But the relation between an increase in hospital beds and doctors and an improvement in health is questionable, and the crude death rate is clearly affected by the age structure and is not a reliable indicator of changes in health status. Yet these may be the data most readily available. The OECD, which has been primarily concerned with defining concepts rather than the availability of data, has proposed indicators to cover four different aspects of health: expectation of life, morbidity (measured through disability days), quality of health care, and access to health care. Drewnowski distinguished in his scheme between flow (level of living) indicators and stock (welfare status) indicators. His suggested health (flow) indicators included access to medical care (an ordinal indicator), proportion of deaths from infectious and parasitic disease, and the proportional mortality rate. Yet data on the first are not easily available, and data on the second are likely to be unreliable in countries where registration of deaths by cause is confined to only a small section of the population.

It is clear from this that there is no consensus about *a* set of indicators of levels of living or welfare, just as there is no agreement about a comprehensive set of components, although there is a growing area of agreement around components of what have come to be called basic needs, and experimentation with indicators within each component. The main problems relate to methods of comparing or summarizing aspects of levels of living measured in different physical units, to the measurement of distribution and dispersion, and to the availability of data. We shall return to these questions later, after looking at the third approach to the measurement of social well-being.

Subjective Social Indicators

The third approach to the measurement of quality of life is through the use of subjective social indicators to measure the degree of satisfaction of people with their lives as a whole, and with various aspects or domains. This has now become a major focus in social indicators research. Work on perceptual or subjective social indicators is more closely linked with psychological theories of human behaviour, and to this extent has an underlying rationale which work on objective social indicators has often lacked. To some extent the work can be seen as a critique of the adequacy of objective indicators as indirect measures of the quality of life, but at the same time it both complements and extends this work.

The main objective of the now considerable research effort in this field has been to develop sets of items which will provide an efficient means of assessing perceived life quality in a number of different domains making up people's general satisfaction with their lives. In one major study carried out at the University of Michigan it was found that fifty per cent of total life satisfaction could be explained by the level of satisfaction in twelve life domains, which included work, health, family life, environment, income, leisure time, housing, and satisfaction with government (Andrews & Withey 1976). One effect of the work on subjective indicators has been to widen the concept of well-being beyond the conventional level of living components. It provides a way of exploring the links between changes in objective conditions and people's satisfaction with these changes, and raises questions such as the effect of rising aspirations on the quality of life, and the possibility, for example, that people may feel relatively 'poorer' even though conditions may be improving.

On a more limited scale subjective or perceptual indicators are used as a check on the adequacy and relevance of objective indicators, or as alternative measures where objective indicators have not been developed. The OECD social indicator programme, for example, includes an indicator of satisfaction under each of the major social concerns, satisfaction with the availability of medical care, with educational experience, with working life, etc. Some programmes in developing countries have also experimented with perceptual indicators where objective indicators are inadequate. The Malaysian programme on socio-economic indicators, for example, includes an indicator of the percentage of household heads who perceive their income status as poor or very poor, and the percentage of those falling in the poverty group who perceive they are poor. The Philippine programme experimented with subjective indicators evaluating political participation, and the perceived degree of social mobility.

Research is continuing on establishing the stability and comparability of both domains and indicators, and the validity of measures of satisfaction, but it is clear that work on subjective indicators has already widened the debate in fruitful directions,[7] and is closely linked with efforts to give more weight in the development of indicators to people's own perception of their needs, priorities, and aspirations. But compared with the established use of indicators of levels of living in the developed countries, the role of perceptual indicators is still relatively untested.

A Composite Measure of Levels of Living?

Jan Drewnowski's work on the measurement of levels of living and welfare belongs to the mainstream of work on objective social indicators, building on the earlier UN work on the definition and measurement of levels of living. Writing at UNRISD in the late 1960s he gave shape to the concept of the social aims of development, and tackled head-on and in characteristic way the methodological problems involved in constructing a comprehensive measure of levels of living that would be useful for development analysis and planning. He proposed solutions to a number of problems which are widely debated today. One may agree or not with the solutions proposed, probably the problems are too complex for simple solutions, but they represented at the time a major contribution to the debate. This can be illustrated by looking at two of the methodological problems involved, the problem of aggregation, and the problem of distribution.

The question of comparable units of measurement does not arise in the case of the first and third approaches to the measurement of social well-being, where welfare is measured either in monetary units or along a scale of individual satisfaction, but in the case of objective indicators, measured in different physical units, some common scale is needed if changes in different components are to be compared and, if desired, aggregated. Scaling and weighting are two different but related problems. A number of different solutions are possible to the scaling problem. Indicators may be converted to a common scale by a process of standardization using the mean and standard deviation of each indicator. This method has been used for example in the UNESCO work on human resource indicators. Scales may be based on 'correspondence points' derived from cross-national comparisons as in the UNRISD work on the measurement of socio-economic development (McGranahan 1972). Scales may also be constructed by determining 'critical points' on the distribution of each indicator. Drewnowski followed this third approach, and constructed a normative scaling system with reference to three 'critical points' – the 'intolerable' point (where needs were not satisfied at all), the 'minimum requirement' point, and the 'affluent' point. The resulting indices could then be used to measure changes over time and to make comparisons between indicators and components. Clearly a large element of judgement is involved in selecting the critical points, particularly the 'minimum requirement' level, but this is a problem which underlies much of the present discussion of poverty lines and minimum levels of adequacy.

The question of aggregation into a single index, which has probably been the most debated aspect of Drewnowski's work, now appears of less importance. Problems of weighting are not insurmountable, provided the assumptions underlying different weighting procedures are made clear. For most purposes a set of disaggregated but comparable indices is more useful than a composite index. More weight would now be given for purposes of comparison to the development of a limited number of representative or 'proxy' indicators for each component, or an overall measure of welfare, such as the expectation of life, or weight-for-age of children, or literacy rate.[8]

Such an overall measure would correspond in part to Drewnowski's level of welfare (Table 2). This concept was overshadowed by his level of living index, but the idea of expectation of life (or an elaboration of this) as a unifying concept, closely associated with changes in levels of living, has been developed in a number of studies. The same idea lies behind the PQLI, although the composition of the index has been criticized on a number of grounds.[9]

Distribution, Disparities and Disaggregation

Distribution is a central element in work on social indicators, and reflects the different approaches discussed above. Work on distribution of income has become a major research area, and increasing use is being made of aggregate measures of inequality, such as the Gini coefficient, and of monetary measures of relative and absolute poverty, such as the ratio between the income shares of the top 20 per cent and lowest 40 per cent of income earners, or the proportion of households with incomes below an agreed poverty line. There is a large and expanding volume of methodological and empirical research, and also an awareness of the limitations of these measures as indicators of welfare, both because of problems of definition and data, and also because too often available data on incomes exclude individuals and households both at the top and bottom ends of the income range.[10] This problem arises particularly in countries with large informal or semi-subsistence sectors, where data on monetary income have relatively little meaning. In spite of these limitations, in countries where data on household incomes are reasonably complete, the cross-classification of the size distribution of household income by socio-economic groups, by rural/urban population and other functional breakdowns, provides a basis for indicators of disparities which can be supplemented with additional information on resources and levels of living. This is also needed for any structural analysis of the factors affecting distribution.

The measurement of distribution and dispersion of indicators of levels of living or 'basic needs' raises rather different problems. Ideally one would like to have for each of the key indicators an indication of the distribution over the population in such a way that one could calculate mean and dispersion, and could say that such and such a proportion of the population fall below or above defined cut-off points or critical levels with respect to nutrition, health, education, housing etc. This would correspond to Jan Drewnowski's proposal that each indicator index in his level of living index should be weighted by a coefficient derived from a Lorentz-type curve, which would be drawn from data on the proportion of the population falling within ranges defined by the critical points on his scale. Increasingly, international discussion is moving along these lines, using cut-off points based on the range of cross-national data. However, it is not so easy to move from averages to distribution over the population within countries, since many of the measures used are measures of collective rather than individual or household conditions. There are some indicators where there is a built-in distributional element, such as literacy rates or enrolment rates, but which cannot be expressed as a range. There are other indicators where average rates may be based on measures which, because of the way they are constructed, cannot provide data on distribution over the population (e.g. calorie intake from food balance sheets), and where different measures have to be found. There are other indicators, such as access to health care, where data depend on household or locality data. Comprehensive data on the distribution of levels of living over the population would require both comprehensive household surveys of levels of living[11] and possibly a different range of indicators.

Many of the indicators lend themselves more easily to the measurement of differences or disparities between groups and communities, between men and women, between socio-economic or occupational groups, between rural and urban populations, or regions. The OECD social indicator programme for example, has put a great deal of emphasis on this kind of disaggregation (OECD 1977). Average levels for different groups can be compared with each other or with the national average, and changes over time noted and compared with other social and economic indicators. Indicators of co-variation, or the correlation between levels of living and other socio-economic characteristics of the population, have been stressed in the social indicator literature. Again the difficulty arises that this kind of disaggregation requires comprehensive surveys. Normally at the present time indicators of disparities or differences are obtained by drawing on a patchwork of data from different sources, using different definitions and with partial coverage, which means that measures are very approximate and difficult to compare over time.[12]

Partly because of the many difficulties in obtaining regular information on the distribution of levels of living from such comprehensive household surveys, there is considerable support for a different kind of disaggregation which would not start from the disaggregation of national average indicators, but which would start by developing indicators of levels of living relating to particular social or occupational groups, or particular localities. Much of the current research on indicators relating to particular policy areas, such as health, low-income urban and rural groups, or children, involves research at a locality level. The difficulty is to link these micro-studies to provide an overall picture of differences and trends.

One of the more systematic studies in this field is the UNRISD project on the measurement of development at the local level (Matthew & Scott 1980). The major focus in this project is on the measurement of levels of living in 'representative areas', drawing on both formal and informal sources of information. The components covered correspond approximately to those already discussed, but there is more scope for experimentation with different indicators in the light of local conditions and needs, and with different kinds of data collection. It is also possible to look at distribution within these localities, and within particular occupational or social groups. If carried out on a continuing basis such reporting systems could provide information on changes over time, and on the relation between economic, demographic, and other changes in levels of living. The extent to which information at this level can or needs to be aggregated at a higher level is left open to question.

III Integrating Frameworks

One of the criteria of a social indicator is that it should be seen as part of a broader system of interrelations. The debate about different approaches to the measurement of welfare are parallelled by the debates about appropriate integrating frameworks. The possibility of developing social accounting frameworks, both comprehensive and partial, has been a major interest in social indicator research since the mid-1960s, and is at present a rapidly expanding field. It is not possible in a few pages to review these developments in any detail, but only to indicate what seem to be rather basic conceptual or theoretical differences underlying different social accounting systems, partly again with the purpose of looking at Jan Drewnowski's social planning matrix against a wider background. Three underlying approaches, or frames of reference, will be distinguished, which may be labelled for convenience an expanded economic model.

Expanded Economic Model

The emphasis over the past decade on employment and the reduction of inequality and poverty as development goals, has focussed research on the interrelation between these goals and economic growth, and on the expansion of conventional economic growth models to take into account employment and the distribution of household income and expenditure. The joint study by the World Bank and the Institute of

Development Studies at the University of Sussex, *Redistribution with Growth*, and the reports of the country employment missions organized by the International Labour Office, reflected this shift of emphasis.

The model (as developed for example by Pyatt & Thorbecke 1976) is intended to bring out the linkages between the living standards of different socio-economic groups and the structure of production on the one hand, and between production activities and the distribution of household income on the other. The key link is between the distribution of factor incomes, and the distribution of this income among households, depending on the structure of employment and assets. The distribution of income between households and other institutions also affects savings and investment, both public and private. The model focusses attention on the relation between the pattern and structure of economic growth and distribution of income, on the factors affecting employment and distribution, and on the trade-off between economic growth and equality. The conceptual model has been developed in the form of social-accounting matrices (SAM), which have been tried out in a number of developing countries.

Models which incorporate aspects of distribution, employment and household consumption focus attention on areas where economic and social aspects of development are closely interwoven. The focus on household consumption and living standards, disaggregated by socio-economic group, makes it possible to incorporate monetary measures of welfare, distribution and poverty into the analysis. In particular, the disaggregation of household income by socio-economic groups, which is a feature of the SAM, can be combined with additional information on consumption and levels of living of these groups. However, the model remains a demand-oriented economic growth model, the economic system remains the main focus of the model, and the selection of key variables and significant relations reflects a particular theoretical approach. As with the measurement of economic welfare discussed earlier, many aspects of social welfare and quality of life are excluded.

A Welfare-Oriented Approach

Jan Drewnowski's social planning framework, elaborated in the late 1960s, was intended to illustrate an approach where an improvement in levels of living was seen as the final aim of development, and economic growth or the output of goods and services, was seen as an intermediate aim. One purpose of his model was to create an awareness of the interdependence between economic and social factors in development, and to show that an improvement in social welfare depended as much on what happened in the economic sectors as in the social 'sectors' more narrowly defined. His model was in some sense an 'expanded economic model', and his social planning matrix was set out in the form of a social accounting matrix, but he went much further in specifying the social aims of development, and in spelling out the links between the flow of goods and services, and levels of living, in real terms.

This was done in the form of an input-output matrix, or interdependence table expressed in physical units, which was made up of three blocks. The first block indicated the links between the factors of production and the output of goods and services; the second stage referred to what is called welfare generation, that is, the impact of the flow of goods and services on the levels of living (a flow concept), and thence on the level of welfare (a stock concept) of the population. A third stage allowed for the feed-back effect of the state of welfare on the quality of labour, and hence on productivity.

The planning model based on this interdependence table was a linear programming model in which the objective function (the level of living) represented the final aim of the plan, and the economic resources needed to achieve these aims were expressed in the form of constraints. The Drewnowski model, like the global Bariloche model with which it has much in common, was never intended to be an operational model, but was intended to illustrate a new 'social approach' which would provide an example for more detailed models. It is difficult to imagine such an optimizing model being applied in practice on a comprehensive basis, although a number of examples could be given of partial approaches along these lines. Level of living targets and consumption norms have always played an important part in planning in socialist countries, where both incomes and physical consumption norms are centrally planned. A similar approach is used elsewhere in defining objectives and targets in public sector programmes, such as education, health and housing. Some of the approaches currently suggested in the context of a 'basic needs' strategy contain elements of Drewnowski's model, with norms and targets defined in terms of levels of living, or basic needs. Much of the current research on human development, for example in the 1980 *World Development Review*, is concerned with exploring the links between the output of goods and services and levels of living (health, nutrition, education and fertility), and the interrelation between these, which is the central focus of Drewnowski's matrix.

Social Systems Models

Since Gross's (1968) essay on social systems accounting in Bauer's well-known collection on *Social Indicators*, a number of generalized social systems models have been proposed as broad frameworks to guide the development of social indicators (Land, Land & Felson, Allardt). Their significance lies in the fact that they combine measures of social change with policy output indicators, and link the analysis of the actual patterns of social change or development with policies and programmes designed to change the situation. They shift the weight of analysis from policy and programmes to changes in the social structure. They provide a framework for partial analytical models which include structural as well as policy and output measures.

The generalized model proposed by Land (1975) provides an example. In his model social policy output variables (the social welfare function) are linked both with policy instrument variables and with social system (non-manipulable) variables. In addition, provision is made for 'side-effect' variables which reflect the indirect or second-order effect of policy goals as well as of social system variables. The social system is broken down into four broad categories, or subsystems, corresponding to types of activity: family, economy, government and religion, knowledge and technology. With minor differences these correspond to the structural categories of social change included in Sheldon and Moore's *Indicators of Social Change* referred to earlier: economy, labour force and employment, knowledge and technology, politics, family, religion.

Land's approach is not intended to provide a global model of social change, but a frame of reference for guiding the development of indicators, for exploring interrelations, and for developing partial models relating to particular policy areas.[13] These might include broad areas of social change, such as the impact of technological innovation on the structure of employment and levels of living of different social groups, or the effect of rural-urban migration on conditions in rural areas and in the shanty towns, or analysis relating to particular policy areas, such as the factors affecting fertility, nutrition, or the status of women.

One such framework which specifically links the main elements of social structure with the satisfaction of individual needs can be found in Allardt's welfare model for selecting indicators of national development (Allardt 1973), in which the social structure is seen as the mediating factor between societal allocations through the main social institutions (economy, political system, integrative system, and knowledge), and output in terms of societal goals and individual needs satisfaction.

The distribution of needs satisfaction and disparities between regions and social groups are also indicators of the distribution of resources resulting from these processes. The dynamics behind this distribution call for analysis in terms of institutional, structural and historical factors. Increasingly, differences in levels of living between socio-economic groups, between formal and informal sectors, or between regions, are seen in the context of this wider structural framework, with more emphasis on structural, or socio-economic parameters and indicators.[14]

IV Integration Around Development Objectives and Policies

Without an agreed framework, much of the current work on social indicators is focussed around generally-agreed development objectives (the central column in Table 1), drawing where relevant on on-going research. Much of this work is related to particular policy areas such as employment, population and fertility, food and nutrition, health, education and learning, or to the situation of particular social groups, such as children or women. Systems of indicators have been developed in each of these areas for the purpose of assessing the situation and trends, for developing programmes and monitoring results, involving research at both macro and micro level. Research on fertility, for example, covers both the analysis of global trends and interrelations with other development indicators, and the analysis at the community and household level of factors related to changes in fertility. Research on food and nutrition has involved the use of indicators at the global level to assess the world food situation and to monitor changes, and the development of indicators in relation to policy and programmes, both at the national and local level. Probably the greater part of social indicator research, both national and international, has been related to the development of indicators within these and other policy areas, and the links between them.[15] At a sectoral or programme level emphasis has been put on the development of sets of indicators for defining targets and for monitoring outputs and performance (Imboden 1978).

At a more strategic or integrated level, the emphasis on international development goals relating to basic needs and poverty has provided a focal point for the development of social indicators. Again, research ranges from rough global assessments of the proportion of the world's population living in poverty, or below defined levels of adequacy with respect to basic needs, to the more detailed analysis of the factors related to different patterns at the country level, and increasingly to the analysis of distribution and disparities within countries. This has involved both the use of a limited number of basic needs indicators – nutrition, health, literacy – and the more detailed analysis of a wider range of indicators relating to particular population groups, such as rural small farmers, or urban low-income groups. It has also involved widespread discussion on methodological problems of measuring poverty, raising many of the issues discussed earlier in this paper.[16]

One of the main limiting factors in the development of social indicators is the availability of relevant, reliable and timely data on even the 'core' indicators of levels of living. Much of the needed data is inadequate or unreliable, for example vital statistics, and figures on deaths by age or cause of death. Estimates of malnutrition may have to rely on small-scale micro-studies, or ad hoc nutrition surveys. Data from the census, such as literacy rates, will only be available at infrequent intervals, and often after long delays. Data on incomes and employment are notoriously misleading in countries with large informal sectors. Data on access to services depend on special surveys or mapping. As suggested earlier, a wide variety of measures have been proposed and tried out to improve the quality of information available on levels of living, ranging from integrated programmes of household surveys, or specially-designed level of living surveys, to building up a continuous monitoring system at the local level. There is also widespread support for the development of social indicators in a programme and community context, e.g. in relation to primary health care or rural development programmes, and for making greater use of locally-trained informants, and of data collected in the course of implementing programmes. This is associated with pressure for a more 'participatory' approach to the selection and use of indicators, which is reflected in the social indicator literature,[17] and which represents a challenge to over-reliance on a limited number of macro indicators. This dialogue, or dialectic, between a more centralized 'consensus' approach and a more diversified and participatory approach to the development of social indicators is one of the major issues that arise in considering Jan Drewnowski's contribution.

Notes

1. I have drawn partly on a more substantive review made for the United Nations University a few years ago (Baster 1978).
2. The development of more comprehensive social accounting matrices is a rapidly-expanding area of research, and the whole field is reviewed in a book to be published shortly (Juster & Land, eds., forthcoming).

3. These labels are not entirely satisfactory since there is a good deal of overlap, just as there is with the terms welfare, levels of living, social well-being and quality of life.

4. For a review of these issues see United Nations (1976).

5. Reference is made throughout to the 1974 publication, but it has to be remembered that this is largely an up-dated version of studies which were written over the period 1966-70 and appeared as United Nations Research Institute of Social Development (UNRISD) reports.

6. Maslow (1954) established five categories of human needs, ranked in ascending order: (a) survival and safety, (b) security, (c) belongingness, (d) esteem, and (e) self-actualization.

7. For a recent collection of comparative studies of quality of life see Szalai & Andrews (1980).

8. These questions have been discussed in a paper by Hicks & Streeten (1979).

9. See, for example, the critique by Larson & Wilford (1979).

10. Some of the limitations of existing statistics on economic distribution, particularly from the points of view of international comparability, have been discussed in a recent UNRISD publication (McGranahan 1979).

11. There has been a good deal of discussion of household living surveys in connection with the OECD social indicator programme (just as there was twenty years ago in the report of the UN expert group), and the UN Statistical Office has been promoting household survey capability in developing countries, but there is still a good deal of discussion on how best to use this capacity to build up sets of data on levels of living and changes over time.

12. Many examples could be given of efforts to bring together indicators of income and levels of living by relevant socio-economic groups in countries with inadequate data. See for example Elliott on Zambia (1976) and the 'basic needs profile' of Kenya in Ghai, Godfrey & Lisk (1979).

13. Although Land and his collaborators at the University of Illinois have been developing a number of macro-dynamic social indicator models for the USA using demographic accounting techniques (Land 1981).

14. This point of view has been strongly put by Cadman Atta Mills for example, who argues that 'the socio-economic *and* political organization of society and strategic development targets should be the object of the Social Indicator Movement', rather than social welfare indicators (Mills 1981: 113).

15. Illustrations of research on cross-sectoral linkages can be found in the chapter of the 1980 *World Development Report* dealing with 'Human Development: Policies and Issues'. Much of the research cited in that chapter is concerned with analysis of the interrelation between incomes, education, health, nutrition and fertility, both as means and aims of development. Other examples relate to particular social groups, such as women (UNESCO 1981), or children (Singer & Baster 1981).

16. See for example the discussion of alternative poverty measurements in Scott (1981).

17. This concept of participation and dialogue is reflected, for example, in the programme of the United Nations University on development indicators. It is also found in much of the literature on evaluation and monitoring, for example, in Soon Young Yoon (1980).

References

Allardt, E. (1973a): *About Dimensions of Welfare: An Exploratory Analysis of a Scandinavian Study* (University of Helsinki Research Group on Comparative Sociology, Research Report No. 1).

— (1973b): 'A Welfare Model for Selecting Indicators of National Development', *Policy Sciences*, 4, 1, 63-74.

Andrews, F.M. & S.B. Withey (1976): *Social Indicators of Well-being* (New York and London, Plenum Press).

Baster, N. (1978): 'Work on Social Indicators by National Governments, Research Institutes and Individual Scholars: A Selective Review and Discussion of Issues and Problems', in Rao, Porwit & Baster (1978).

Drewnowski, J. (1974): *On Measuring and Planning the Quality of Life* (The Hague, Mouton, for the Institute of Social Studies).

Elliott, C. (1976): 'Four Indicators of Distribution in Zambia: A Diachronic View', in UNESCO (1976).

Ghai, D., M. Godfrey & F. Lisk (1979): *Planning for Basic Needs in Kenya* (Geneva, International Labour Organization).

Gross, B. (1966): 'The State of the Nation: Social Systems Accounting', in R. Bauer (ed.): *Social Indicators* (Cambridge, Mass., MIT Press).

Hicks, N. & P. Streeten (1979): 'Indicators of Development: The Search for a Basic Needs Yardstick', *World Development*, 7, 6, 567-580.

Hopkins, M.J.D. & O.D.K. Norbye (1978): 'Meeting Basic Human Needs' (Geneva, International Labour Office, World Employment Programme, Economic and Social Policy Synthesis Programme, Working Paper No. 13).

Imboden, N. (1978): *A Management Approach to Project Appraisal and Evaluation* (Paris, Development Centre of the Organization for Economic Co-operation and Development).

International Labour Office (1976): *Employment, Growth and Basic Needs* (Geneva, ILO).

— (1980): *First Things First: Meeting the Basic Needs of the People of Nigeria* (Geneva, ILO).

Juster, E.J. & K.C. Land (eds) (forthcoming): *Social Accounting Systems: Essays on the State of the Art* (New York and London, Academic Press).

Land, K.C. (1975): 'Theories, Models and Indicators of Social Change', *International Social Science Journal*, XXVII, 1, 7-37.

— (1981): 'Identification of Socio-Economic Indicators for Use in Integrated Social and Economic Planning', in UNESCO (1981).

Larson, B.A. & W.T. Wilford (1979): 'The Physical Quality of Life Index: A Useful Social Indicator?', *World Development*, 7, 6, 581-584.

Lisk, F. (1979): 'Indicators of Basic Needs-Oriented Development Planning', *Labour and Society*, 4, 3.

McGranahan, D.V., et al. (1972): *Contents and Measurement of Socio-Economic Development* (New York, Praeger).

McGranahan, D.V. (1979): *International Comparability of Statistics of Income Distribution* (Geneva, UNRISD).

Maslow, A.H. (1954): *Motivation and Personality* (New York, Harper).

Matthew, N.T. & W. Scott (1980): *A Development Monitoring Service at the Local Level: Socio-Economic Observation Areas in Kerala* (Geneva, UNRISD).

Mills, C.A. (1981): 'Identification of Social Concerns and Social Indicators Relevant to Development Planning in Africa', in UNESCO (1981).

Morris, M.D. (1979): *Measuring the Condition of the World's Poor* (New York, Pergamon).

Organization for Economic Co-operation and Development (1976): *Measuring Social Well-Being: A Progress Report on the Development of Social Indicators* (Paris, OECD).

— (1977): *Basic Disaggregations of Main Social Indicators* (Paris, OECD).

Pyatt, G. & E. Thorbecke (1976): *Planning Techniques for a Better Future* (Geneva, ILO).

Rao, M.V.S., K. Porwit & N. Baster (1978): *Indicators of Human and Social Development: Report on the State of the Art* (Tokyo, United Nations University).

Scott, W. (1981): *Concepts and Measurement of Poverty* (Geneva, UNRISD).

Seers, D. (1977): 'Life Expectancy as an Integrating Concept in Social and Demographic Analysis and Planning', *The Review of Income and Wealth*, Series 23, No. 3.

Sheldon, A. & W.E. Moore (1968): *Indicators of Social Change: Concepts and Measurements* (New York, Russell Sage Foundation).

Singer, H.W. & N. Baster (1980): *Young Human Resources in Korea's Social Development* (Seoul, Korean Development Institute).

Soon Young Yoon (1980): *A Score for Development* (Bangkok, UN Asian and Pacific Development Institute and UN Children's Fund).

Szalai, A. & F.M. Andrews (eds) (1980): *The Quality of Life: Comparative Studies* (London, Sage).

United Nations (1954): *Report on the International Definition and Measurement of Levels of Living* (New York, United Nations).

— (1976): 'The Feasibility of Welfare-Oriented Measures to Complement the National Accounts and Balances' (New York, Economic and Social Council, E/CN 3/477).

— (1978): *Social Indicators: Preliminary Guidelines and Illustrative Guidelines* (New York, UN, Statistical Papers Series M No. 83).

UNESCO (1981): *Women and Development: Indicators of Their Changing Role* (Paris, UNESCO, Socio-Economic Studies 3).

3 DEVELOPMENT INDICATORS: SOME RELATIVITIES OF SUBJECTIVITY AND OBJECTIVITY

Raymond Apthorpe

The labels 'subjectivity' and 'objectivity', and 'social' and 'economic', live in the standard literature on development indicators and methods and techniques in development studies for the most part as received attributions. Yet the strongest tendency is for such attributions to be understood and adopted as if no actual process of attributing were involved, as if no particular interests and options were available or at stake, either in the literature from which they have been received, or in the new work building on this. The conventional wisdom about methods and techniques in development studies is: these are tools, just tools. Hurry along and get on with the job of putting them to work.

The aim of this essay, which could be described as looking into some discursive aspects of research methods politics, is to take a broader view of 'tools' than is customary. This view will be discussed on the basis of the debate that has been going on in the literature on social indicators. Some relativities as well as binarities will be identified as well worth examining in further work. Unlike the present essay, which is introductory only, further work could go on to look into the research status of selected substantive areas of development policy and then review actual policies accordingly.

Development Indicators and Development Studies

Development indicators[1] differ widely in character and purpose. Some are 'economic', 'social', 'environmental' or whatever. Some point to aggregate and others to distributional features. Some have been devised specifically for planning purposes, others not. The development indicators literature is far from uniform in its scope and orientation.

In consequence, while looking at one area or part of the field, there is a natural tendency either to ignore the rest or to subsume the whole under generalizations which fit only part of it. For instance, to neglect or misrepresent work on economic indicators, while looking only at social indicators, leads easily to under-estimating the depth and extent of controversy in the field as a whole. Some central issues in indicators studies and methods are deeply controversial.[2] That, indeed, may be why they are central. At all events, it is the main argument in this paper that to displace questions of subjectivity and objectivity, and of binarities and relativities, from the field of development indicators as a whole to that on social indicators alone, does justice to neither.

Our subject, then, while being partly that of some aspects of social indicators in particular must also be that of some aspects of development indicators in general.

Another complexity for development indicators studies is: some of the subjectivity-objectivity problems about indicators are about 'development' and 'planning' as well as measurement and indicators *per se*. It is easy to overlook this double nature of the matter in preoccupations only with technical and instrumental exercises and applications.

It could be said with some justification, therefore, that most work with development indicators is atheoretical in a sense. This observation is much less true of the thinking that went into engendering and constructing the idea of social indicators in the first place, such as the writings of Jan Drewnowski. The point is rather that the theory which went into the building of these foundations becomes neglected or is unknown to those who proceed on the basis of them. Few studies of such methods and techniques in social and development studies, of indicators, *simultaneously* identify theoretical (and philosophical) and technical (and instrumental) issues. Few seek to put them all on one agenda. The aim of such a conjoined approach would be that one dimension would not just be subsumed under, not mistaken or substituted for the other. At the same time it would of course be counterproductive to lose a focus, and a legitimacy, altogether. That is the rub.

A Note on History

It was in the mid-1960s particularly that 'social indicators', 'social accounting', 'social reporting', 'monitoring social change' were considered in some development studies discourse to lie on the frontiers of new thinking. Sheldon and Parke said this emphasis

> ... emerged from an awareness of rapid social change, from a sense of emerging problems with origins deep in the social structure, and from the ambience of the early Johnson Administration which encompassed a commitment to the idea that the benefits and costs of domestic social programmes are subject to measurement and to the belief that each newly perceived, albeit ancient, inadequacy in the

society should and would call forth a corrective response from a federal government whose efficacy would be assisted by social measurement, planning and new management analytical techniques....
Economists... saw a role for their skills as theorists and measures of welfare, sociologists ... saw the relevance of their own research tradition in the measurement of social trends, political scientists ... sought ways to rationalize government programmes, [and there were responses also from] social workers, public administrators.... Out of this emerged ... 'the social indicators movement', an apt description in that, as in all movements in their initial stages, the participants were ill-defined as to membership, had little organization, and shared few specific objectives, but sensed great needs and opportunities for change, celebrated shared but necessarily ambiguous symbols, and were led by able and articulate idealists (1975: 693).

By the middle 1970s what were called 'subjective' indicators had become prominent in various investigations into the quality of life. Among other things they were thought '... to provide "direct" measures of individuals' evaluations of their well-being, as opposed to "objective" indicators which may mean different things to different people' (Buttle et al. 1977). It was to this particular direction in social indicators studies that, for instance, Jan Drewnowski took the strongest exception. In a review in the journal *Social Indicators Research* he said he felt moved fundamentally to question

... the usefulness of the very concept of subjective well-being. Seen from the point of view of economic theory subjective well-being is indistinguishable from the well-established concept of individual utility. After a century of discussion we all know for sure that utility is non-measurable, non-comparable as between persons, and non-summable. There is no point in continuing to argue about that.

He turned also to what he said was

... the core of the problem of social indicators ... the basic role social indicators ought to play is to provide an alternative to the traditional measures of welfare oriented towards an evaluation of the subjective feelings of individuals.... Social indicators are based on the assumption that the well-being of individuals depends on the degree of satisfaction of their needs. These needs can be expressed in physical units of a sort. There is of course a value judgement involved in the establishment of the list of needs, but both the needs and the degree of their satisfaction are observable facts.... Thinking along these lines is methodologically more satisfactory and also more relevant for the solutions of practical problems, i.e. for policies and planning. Concentrating efforts on the measurement of subjective feelings seems to me to be nothing but retreading of old paths which have been proved to lead nowhere (Drewnowski 1977a).

One could scarcely wish for a clearer statement of a macro-planning economist's and statistician's stance *against* 'feelings' and 'perceptions', coupled with a correlative case *for* 'needs' and 'satisfactions'. This is, however, a position taken about planning and policy in general as well as macro-economics and statistics in particular. Yet displacing attention in this way from, as it were, the signifier to the signified, permits of seeming innocence of any such thing. It does not leave both 'our' (expert) and 'their' (target group) subjectivity on the wayside but only 'ours'. This presents 'professionals' as being without (other than professional) values, as if experts were solely judges of the values of others. In this way, an entirely unnecessary – and no doubt usually unintended – 'obstacle' to 'objectivity' arises. This is a common subject in many discussions in social studies which are unapplied to problems of public policy, which address simply some general questions about error, bias and accuracy of science and observation. (Some sections of Jacques Maquet's 'Objectivity in Anthropology' and its 'CA Treatment' in *Current Anthropology*[3] published in the mid-1960s are in point here.) Whole volumes of criticism about value-free social science and its opposite could be cited as well. In applied social and development studies there is often virtual suspension of all this self-awareness, as if theory and analysis were the very antithesis of practice and action. Such in effect 180 degree turns can occur in the work of an outstanding contributor to both. For example who pondering the operative premisses of Gunnar Myrdal's *Asian Drama* (1968) would have expected them to have come from the author of *The Political Element in the Development of Economic Theory* (1953) and *Value in Social Theory* (1958)? It is totally inadequate so to construe 'experts' as to make believe that while their dicta may be 'methodologically unsound' or fall at times into 'technical error', they would nevertheless, in that capacity, always be objective in some sense, never subjective.

Another matter is that of misplaced applications of input-output thinking. Indicators for example of educational facilities and their uses, of numbers of teachers and schools, of levels of education and attendance, are commonly sought in the area of education research as social indicators of inputs into education. Usually in this area it is perfectly well-recognized that these are not also indicators of such skills and other ultimate results as the policy involved aims to bring about. But, are these 'final outcomes' well-conceived as 'outputs' at all, whether of these particular inputs or of others? (Cf. Apthorpe 1978). Would, for example, catalyst effects, whether educational or social or economic for that matter, be well described in terms of manipulations of input-output matrices? Rote-learning has its place in many kinds of educational programmes. But is rote-learning ever the principal stated property or aim of any public educational policy – even of rote-learning?

Unfortunately a great deal of the standard work on development indicators of various kinds falls between both stools – theory and practice – even if it does end up on a technically or statistically highly polished floor. The indulgent aim of the present essay is to sit firmly on both stools, to satisfy both theory and practice. To facilitate this balancing act it relates (a) to relative as well as binary subjectivity-objectivity, and (b) relative as well as binary social and economic conceptualization. It will find some of the social indicators debate to be at the same time both somewhat less and somewhat more controversial than recent contributions have suggested.

'Social' and 'Economic' as Binaries

Despite two decades of supposedly interdisciplinary and problem-oriented effort in social and economic development studies, a basically binary economic/non-economic distinction still provides the fundamental underpinning of most of them. So, even a specifically social indicators discussion should not focus altogether on so-called social in isolation from so-called economic indicators. Social indicators as we now know them were engendered by development economics to assist macro and national planning economists in their preoccupations. At first these were more or less solely with international aid and economic growth, if that state of innocence ever really existed. Later, macro and national economic development planning diversified to include concerns with redistribution.[4] Originations as entrances are important. Economic planners wanted distributive indicators to complement the aggregative indicators they already used and 'to handle' and 'service' new areas as well as the new aims in which they engaged.

Economists' influence was responsible also for '... the dominance of the imagery of the national economic accounts in discussion about social indicators' (Sheldon & Parke 1975: 695). Development economics described this broadening of its terms of concern and discourse about economic laws and factors as bringing in important but what nevertheless it dubbed non-economic considerations. It continues in some schools to be these non-factors that development economics likes to call 'social', holding the social aspects of this and the economics of that to be substantially and fundamentally different dimensions of both general laws and particular facts alike.

One problem with this, as many critics have suggested, is indeed that of the homogeneity implied of 'social' as 'residual' in this sense. There is very little such homogeneity in actual practice. For instance, my terms of reference under a UN social development assignment on social planning proved, in one country, to refer mainly to the construction of physical infrastructure in a strategy called community development. In another country and assignment they proved to be about re-centralization of personnel in a strategy there called regional development. In yet a third the task turned out to be about subsistence and non-monetary 'incomes' in a strategy called nationhood building.

Fewer critics have found the imagined lack of heterogeneity of economic factors and relations to be the problem. Fewer still are criticisms which have explicitly addressed general distinctions 'between indicators measuring a general level of living reached by society at a particular moment but which have no immediate link with government policies or plans at this time, and those aimed specifically at measuring levels reached in relation to these policies and plans'.[5] Those which are available tend to proceed either dichotomously under binary social-economic signs or by treating social indicators as if they stood alone.

Drewnowski said in his 1966 foundation paper (1966: 4)[6] that his concerns with indicators were 'not with all of them, but only with those that are most significant for the process of development', normally meaning by 'the process of development' the planning of development or perhaps the process of planned development. At the outset he said 'social' and 'economic' should be treated as a distinction of aims not means, and in relation to sectoral planning. His point was that any means will always have to be both social and economic.

An UNRISD 'Social Planning Study Group Meeting' in 1967 took this discussion further. Its conclusion was that if 'social' and 'economic' were considered as different 'sectors' in 'development', then cross-sectoral were on the whole more significant than inter-sectoral factor correlations. It followed that a sectoral approach to social (or for that matter also economic) planning could not be recommended. 'All final aims are essentially social. All economic targets are essentially means. But all means are not economic and all social aims are not final.' Drewnowski looked for a way of approaching his problem of social and economic considerations which would 'put an end to the muddle resulting from the alleged "impossibility of drawing a clear-cut division between economic and social aims" and to the faulty practice of judging the value of social improvement by its contribution to economic growth instead of the other way around' (Ibidem: 14).

The general principles chapter in his *On Measuring and Planning the Quality of Life* (1974) is about 'social variables ... as counterparts of economic variables'. It is common in this context for a major attribution of objectivity – to economic – and a major attribution of subjectivity – to social – indicators to be made. The broadest context of this could be said to be an over-arching binarity deeming 'objective' and 'economic' to be hard and measurable, and oppositely, 'subjective' and 'social' to be soft and unmeasurable. Of course, this is not always consistently implicated in this work, of which social qualification is after all a principal stated purpose. Nonetheless the discussion in his 1966 paper of 'the need and the possibility of quantification' is of social concepts only. Some of these social concepts, he said, are quantitative and directly measurable by definition. Of others, some seemed 'not ... to be amenable to useful quantification at all. They mostly concern institutions (e.g. family, social class). Even if some measurement can be applied to them (size of family, numbers of people belonging to a social class), these measures will not bring out the essential elements of the role of the concept in society. For example, the size of the family is not a decisive element in explaining the role of the family in society' (Ibidem: 16-17).

This and similar positions hold the core problem of social indicators to be 'the objective-subjective indicators debate' (despite and at the same time because of efforts to take a determined stance in favour of a unified approach). The challenge of social indicators for this kind of approach is presented as that of measuring the unmeasurable, objectifying the subjective, making the soft hard. Success in this would make it possible to mix social indicators on an equal footing with economic indicators. The challenge of economic indicators is to measure the measurable.

Often social planning is similarly understood and tackled. For instance in Taiwan a factory manager once put it to me – with some vigour – that there was no need for social planning in times of economic prosperity because: 'with full employment you do not need social development planning.' He went on: 'even if you had unemployment you would not need social development planning. Unemployment means there is always a queue of people at the gates of the factory looking for work.' As the line of people at the gates was of men not women looking for full-time work, yet the factory had been planned with a part-time female labour force in mind, fortunately there was an obvious topic to take up. Whatever else social means it also means sexual, gendered. That helped!

Planners who subsume the social in the economic in their approaches to redistribution and basic needs in effect adopt a similar position. However, unlike the vision of the social as encompassing of the economic, as in Drewnowski's early paper already cited, we find here the different view of the social as 'a corrective' to economic planning. Some other approaches similarly regard the social as external and irrelevant (or internal but an obstacle) to the economic in good old utilitarian and neo-classical fashion.[7] More facilitative for the purposes of the present paper is a different order of approach which does not begin with an economic-social divide and then seek some sort of integration across it. It is not necessary – or best – always to project subjectivity and objectivity as a split only in the social indicators field.

There are useful alternatives to necessarily subsuming 'subjective development' under 'subjective indicators' and thus conflating feelings and immeasurability with preferences, interests and behaviour.[8] It was consistent with Drewnowski's *premisses about planning and statistics* that, wanting to break with tradition in respect of 'measurable welfare ... as essentially a substitute for "the concept of soical utility" in welfare economics', he did not find it needful to distinguish subjective indicators from subjective development. It would be inconsistent with other premisses not to take other points of view.

'Subjective' and 'Objective' as Either/Or

An indicator binarily tends to be dubbed objective rather than subjective when it is held to represent a given fact, condition, problem or even a process, to which a policy is or is to be addressed. It is in this way that 'problems' can be treated as givens, 'policies' not, by a form of reification as in commonsense or lay conceptions of problems and of policies as causal remedies.[9]

Oppositely, indicators which are not held to represent these very things themselves but only factors (not facts) said to be contributory to them, will tend to be given another status and not classified as objective. Drewnowski's splitting of indicators studies into '... two distinct branches, one on measuring people's ideas about their conditions and one measuring ... different conditions of life (themselves)'[10] provides us with an example of this. If objectivity is assumed of the latter, subjectivity will be attributed to the former. You could almost say that in this approach this must be so, for the peace of mind, the mental sanity, of its practitioners.

This same tendency in allocating a high-valued concept of objectivity is even stronger where it is less the aims than the means of implementation of the envisaged policy which is held to be its main distinguishing feature. Once a substantive area has for some reason been deemed to lie beyond the reach of the planning in mind, it is unlikely that any indicators known for that area would be graced as objective. But if new plans are made which are believed to have powers of reaching parts and problems which the others could not reach, that which earlier had seemed to be a hard and fast binary line comes to run and dissolve a bit.

Another common basis for attributing objectivity in a highly-valued and binary (to subjectivity) sense is when indicators are said to comprise an irreducible overview of the situation or problem to which a policy is to be addressed.

Correlatively, in some contrasting circumstances the tendency is to allocate a highly-valued subjectivity. Indicators of perceivedly non-economic standards in perceivedly non-economic areas can be highly-valued as subjective while nevertheless being felt to be resistant to measurement. If a policy is found not to have worked out in practice as expected and defects of ideology, for example, are blamed for this poor performance, what earlier may have been regarded as subjective and not highly-valued may still be treated as subjective but now highly-valued. This tendency is even stronger where development planners focus on target groups whose own development objectives seem to them to be opposed to those which they – the planners – have set.

But 'subjective' and 'objective' need not always be allocated binarily. Relativity can be discerned as well, for instance if we bring the frame into the picture (or enlarge the picture to take in the frame). What previously was a hard dividing line between concerns and indicators appears now to be much less so. That a perception of poverty has been deemed unmeasurable does not mean that development planning must necessarily be adjudged to be subjective in other regards too. In fact, subjectivity is graced (or disgraced) with objectivity as soon as it is treated, whether statistically or not, as a form of source of resistance to the planned change proposed.

There is also the matter of the relativity of objectivity in respect even of listing the technical properties of indicators. An example of this comes from a brief comparison of 'some practical indicators of health and nutrition' in a WHO document (1974). This compares and contrasts a number of indicators with regard to the information they reflect. Objectivity is listed as one criterion for this exercise. Others are ease of collection, adequacy of coverage, specificity and sensitivity. From a table given (reproduced as Table 1) one can then read how, for instance, 'good' objectivity is not necessarily also 'good' coverage (or 'good' specificity, or 'good' sensitivity, etc.).

Different Kinds of Policy Orientation

A further avenue for exploration relates to the particular kind of policy orientation for which indicators are sought. It is common for work on indicator construction and selection to argue that they should be useful

Table 1. A Comparison of Some Practical Indicators of Health and Nutrition

Indicator	Reflection of	Objectivity	Ease of Collection	Adequacy of Coverage	Specificity	Sensitivity
1. Mortality						
(a) Age specific, 1-4	Severity of PCM in children	Good	Easier at national than local level	Good	Good when rates are high; poor when low	Good when rates are high
(b) proportion of all deaths under 5 years	Severity of PCM in children	Good	Easy	Good	Affected by changes in population structure as well as nutrition conditions	Good when proportion is high
2. Proportion of low birth weights	Existing malnutrition in adult population; earlier malnutrition during development	Good	Variable depending upon location of births and adequacy of record system; probably easier in urban areas	Variable depending upon proportion of births recorded	Reasonable	Moderate when proportion is high; decreasing as proportion decreases
3. Height at age 7 (or school entry age)	General malnutrition persisting over several years and affecting physical development	Good	Relatively easy; may require institution of a recording program	Good (if representative schools studied)	Good if secular trends followed or a comparison made within same genetic population	Good on basis of secular trends
4. Age of menarche	General malnutrition persisting over several years and affecting functional development	Fair to good	Fair; direct interview needed	Variable depending upon accessibility of population (e.g. school-leaving age)	Good if followed on basis of secular trends and if delayed in the population under study	Good if menarche is delayed

Source: WHO (1974).

tools for planning. In development studies as a whole, however, it is more common for different kinds and purposes of policy-orientedness to be only very poorly articulated if, that is, they are articulated at all. In this way one kind of policy-orientedness comes unnoticed to be confused with another.

It is not necessary to go so far as to argue that each and every technical property of indicators – viewed in isolation from other considerations – is use-specific in order to show that some are (cf. Apthorpe 1979: 236). 'Ease of collection' for example, 'validity' and 'replicability', could be said to be requisites of indicators for all purposes. Similarly, all indicators should be based on 'readily available' data, although the precise nature of such availability may vary widely. Life expectancy can be calculated from a population census. But if such a census is carried out only once every ten years, and it takes a further two or three for actuarial calculations to be made, the practical value of this indicator will be negligible if it is required rapidly and for a recent period. Other rather constant desiderata are 'specificity', 'coverage' and 'scalability'. All indicators should be 'reliable', that is not subject to measurement errors due to extraneous features including indeterminacies in the method of measurement itself. And so on.

On the other hand, that indicators should be 'appropriate for action' is not entirely a matter of their technical properties. The significance of the possible action envisaged is to be taken into account including its level or form of organization or institutionalization. If, say, a municipal body is the agency required to take the action concerned as regards a particular topic, for which indicators are not available on a municipal basis, they will not be of great practical value to municipal councils. Similarly, a per person condition or problem will (at least) require indicators constructed on a per person basis, per hectare conditions call for per hectare indicators, and so forth. Profiles of, say, agricultural productivity on a per agricultural manpower basis, and profiles of 'the same' agricultural productivity on a per unit of area basis, may differ considerably. (That there is perhaps never a one-to-one relationship of indicators and their indicata, however close the proxies obtained, is another issue altogether.)

Relative (or even binary) use-specificity of indicators for different kinds of policy analysis may among other things relate to the amount and kind of data which the indicartors in question encompass. The predictive power attributed to individual indicators may reflect this particularly. For example, expectation-of-life-at-birth summarizes survival rates at all ages and thus provides a simple and convenient measure of what conventionally in population statistics passes for a general state of health. But while expectation-of-life-at-birth is useful as a summary indicator it is obviously too summary to serve as an objective. For an evaluation, say, of medical policy in any particular area it cannot serve as a diagnostic device for any practical purpose of problem identification. Obviously, too, it gives no 'quality of life' information.

For another example we may think of the property 'sensitivity' and, taking an 'economic' indicator, contrast its value for prescription on the one hand and description on the other. Is sensitivity necessary for all purposes of statistical exactitude and policy planning? Not always. General stocks and share prices, for instance, may well offer a sensitive *descriptive* indication of a state of market which is apt to change even from hour to hour. For the description of such volatility such sensitivity might be essential. However, general prices are poorly *predictive* of changes of that market. What might be a good guide for buying might be a bad guide for selling. What might be an aid to an instrumental purpose of management in a given situation might be no aid at all to diagnosis (cf. Mukherjee 1981).

An early and brief but pertinent social indicators contribution (Carlisle 1970) adverted in its own way to the variety and relativity of particular purposes for which indicators might be needed (though classifying actually the indicators rather than their purposes as informative, predictive, evaluative etc.). An effort of my own (Apthorpe 1979: 239-257) found it necessary to distinguish descriptive, predictive, diagnostic, prognostic and evaluative casts of policy-orientednesses. A recent longer listing[11] includes the following areas: cognition, analysis, conceptualization, projection, orientation, operationalization and direction, planification and targetting, monitoring and retrospective analysis. Conjurers may be able to pull single – however integrated or complex and whether social or economic – indicators out of hats instead of rabbits as the 'best' or the most 'comprehensive' indicator of 'development in general'. Such tricks are not without value when they are audacious and well done. Yet unfortunately a supposedly all-purpose indicator, even of a carefully delimited concern, is more likely to be a no-purpose indicator.

As for other legitimacies there is the perennial GDP. Despite its alleged dethronement as an indicator of national development following diversification from growth into growth and distribution goals, no Director of a National Economic Development Authority worth his office would ever fail to continue to plead a GDP 'score', if, that is, he could find any percentage rise in this to report. This may be legitimate enough for governmental functions of administration and planning. One can also resort to the GDP in a chill advice, when a dousing is called for.

This may only be economically unconstitutional! Attributions of binarities and relativities may very much depend on the particular kind or aim of policy orientation at the time, in respect even of 'the same' phenomena. Now they are subjective, now objective, now highly-valued, now not. Unaware of this one is caught in contradictions of purposes. Aware of this one is in a better position to manoeuvre. What prognosis dubs subjective may have an objective role to play in diagnosis. What is objective and basic in a policy package for prescription may be the very opposite for description. If it can be presented that only 'social' or subjective indicators are full of woe, 'economic' and objective indicators can then conveniently go unscathed.

In thus addressing these remarks only to relativities, as if they were completely different from binarities, the wrong impression may be given that subjectivity and objectivity are always reversible. This really would be to misrepresent the point of the present exercise. Worse, it would leave us stranded with, not actively in search of, a method. This would be to be left, as it were, without method at all, like having a ration of methodological thinking but not a productive supply (Sartre 1963). If critical rejection of something which was originally put forward in a carefully delimited and qualified way forgets or is unaware of this, it will misrepresent its quarry and thus misfire (even though by chance it may find some other bull's-eye instead). What may be practical and fruitful for the most generalist of national and international comparative development studies is unlikely to be so for more particularistic and local studies.

The chief net benefit for criticism to slip into relativities, if only to slip out of them and back into binarities later, before slipping out of binarities once again (and so on), is that head-on critical analysis of primary postulates, identification and contemplation even, tends sometimes to be almost too difficult to cope with. If you look directly at the sun you will go blind. Sideways-on approaches may have fewer side-effects. Each social science discipline in its various ways confronts its own dilemma of subjectivity and objectivity. No discipline addresses itself to measured considerations only. Probably none neglects these entirely either. Much depends, whatever the discipline, on particular topics and tendencies. Some problem-oriented research in development studies and on development indicators, for instance in Taiwan and the Philippines, has laid stress on social analysis. However, at the same time it was at pains *not* to propose a 'development sociology' to offset, correct or complement the dominant 'development economics'. Such a 'partnership' (of the rider and horse) would have had little to do with the nature of most development problems that development studies pretend to address.

Whatever else most development problems are besides, they are existential problems, that is not solely – or dually – economic, or sociological or political or whatever (cf. Apthorpe 1980). And, if there is something unproductive about ideas of the social in dichotomous formulations there must also be something unproductive about such ideas of the economic as well.

Cross-cutting unfortunately almost all approaches is the prevalence of what Richard Titmuss called 'the public burden model of welfare'.[12] In effect this does nothing but bolster dichotomous social and economic – and to some extent also subjective and objective – distinctions. In turn, these are all further reinforced by thinking about social policy as being just what economic policy can afford.

This brings me again and finally to 'subjective development' rather than subjective indicators. Some approaches in development studies do not find it necessary to distinguish subjective development as a problem for policy and planning from problems for which subjective indicators have been sought or denied. By 'subjective development' I mean something phenomenological, something invested with internal or self-meaning and not simply a purpose of a function. Indicators of such subjective development could – in either Drewnowski's or Strumpel's senses – be either objective or subjective, or, for that matter, neither. Some of the current – and eternal – debate about 'development from below', 'felt needs' and 'popular participation' is, in fact, about subjective development. 'From below' solutions are not necessarily solutions to 'from above' problems.[13] Two (sub-)universes of discourse figure here, not one; so there is also a discontinuity to explore and not continuity only.

Notes

1. Cf. Apthorpe (1973). The present essay is part of larger work on patterns of thought, word, will and strategy in development studies.

2. For example compare two articles in *Development and Change*, by two authors with, after all, institutionally very similar affiliations: Jan Drewnowski (1977b) and Wolf Scott (1979).

3. *Current Anthropology* 5: 47-55 and Vol. 7, no. 3, June 1966, pp. 361-366.

4. On 'growth' and 'distribution' as the central theoretical and practical topics for classical economists see R.P. Wolff (1982). By 'redistribution'. I am referring to reformist redistribution with (or after) growth.

5. This was taken up by W.L. Kendall in an ECAFE advice which among other things influences the UN Secretary-General's report, prepared largely by Jacques Bardot, *Social Indicators* (E/CN, 5/518, 2 January 1975). For a detailed discussion and elaboration of 'historical systems', 'systems of intervention', 'and levels' see Gerard Martin (1976a & b).

6. I read his phrase 'the economic concepts that are also significant in development', as implying differences of economic concepts on this footing, but this is not developed.

7. On neo-classical approaches in this vein see Villamil (1979).

8. Useful recent discussions of subjectivity, objectivity, behaviourism, voluntarism and related issues are: Burrell & Morgan (1979), and Andriaansens (1980).

9. Cf. Schaffer (1981), and my 'Agricultures and strategies' to be published in Clay & Schaffer (1984).

10. Drewnowski (1959: 274); we may recall here the situations in the citations at the outset of this essay.

11. By W. Zapt in work cited by Horn (1980: 432).

12. Cited by Booth (1982: 210). Cf. also recent work on economy and welfare in the USA by Martin Rein and Lee Rainwater.

13. I draw here from discussions with P. Kuperus.

References

Adriaansens, H.P.M. (1980): *Talcott Parsons and the Conceptual Dilemma* (London, Kegan Paul).

Apthorpe, R.A. (1973): *Development Indicators* (Manila, University of the Philippines, National Development Research Center).

— (1978): 'Answers in Search of Questions in Social Studies of Public Policies: Some Food for Thought' (The Hague, Institute of Social Studies, *Dies Natalis* address).

— (1979): 'Social Indicators and Social Reporting in Papua New Guinea', in W. Scott (ed.): *Measurement and Analysis of Progress at the Local Level*, Vol. III (Geneva, UNRISD), 227-275.

— (1980): 'Distant Encounters of a Third Kind: Problems of Generalism in the Teaching of Development Studies', *Bulletin* (IDS, Sussex), 11, 3, 25-33.

— (1984): 'Agricultures and Strategies', in E. Clay & B.B. Schaffer (eds): *Room for Manoeuvre: An Exploration of Public Policy Planning in Agriculture and Rural Development* (London, Heinemann).

Booth, T.A. (1982): 'Economics and the Poverty of Social Planning', *Public Administration*, 60, 197-214.

Burrell, G. & G. Morgan (1979): *Sociological Paradigms and Organizational Analysis* (London, Heinemann).

Buttle, F.H., E.A. Wilkening & O.B. Martenson (1977): 'Ideology and Social Indicators of the Quality of Life', *Social Indicators Research*, Vol. 4, 3, 353-369.

Carlisle, E. (1972): 'The Conceptual Structure of Social Indicators', in A. Shonfield & S. Shaw (eds): *Social Indicators and Social Policy* (London, Heinemann).

Drewnowski, J. (1966): *Social and Economic Factors in Development: Introductory Considerations on Their Meaning, Measurement and Interdependence* (Geneva, UNRISD).

— (1974): *On Measuring and Planning the Quality of Life* (The Hague, Mouton, for the Institute of Social Studies).

— (1977a): Review of B. Stumpel (ed.): *Economic Means for Human Needs: Social Indicators for Well-being and Discontent* (1976), *Social Indicators Research*, 4, 2, 241-245.

— (1977b): 'Poverty: Its Meaning and Measurement', *Development and Change*, 8, 2, 183-208.

— (1979): 'Basic Needs and Social Indicators: A Suggestion for an Integrated Approach', *Labour and Society*, 4, 3.

Horn, R.V. (1980): 'Social Indicators: Meaning, Methods and Applications', *International Journal of Social Economics*, 7, 8, 421-460.

Martin, G. (1976a): 'The French Experience of Social Planning', in UNESCO: *The Use of Socio-Economic Indicators in Development Planning* (Paris, UNESCO), 121-160.

— (1976b): 'A Methodological Outline for Social Model Building', in UNESCO (1976), 255-282.

McLachlan, H.V. (1981): 'Is Power an Evaluative Concept?', *British Journal of Sociology*, XXXII, 3, 392-410.

Moser, C. (1970): 'Measuring the Quality of Life', *New Society*, 428, 1042-1043.

Mukherjee, R. (1981): 'On the Use of Social Indicators for Planning', *Social Indicators Research*, 9, 2, 183-195.

Sartre, J.-P. (1963): *Search for a Method* (New York, A.A. Knopf; trans. H.E. Barnes).

Schaffer, B.B. (1981): 'Recapturing Public Policy for Politics' (Sussex, Institute of Development Studies, mimeographed).

Scott, W. (1979): 'Poverty Monitoring in Developing Countries', *Development and Change*, 10, 3, 445-459.

Sheldon, E.B. & R. Parke (1975): 'Social Indicators: Social Science Researchers are Developing Concepts and Measures of Changes in Society', *Science*, 188, 16.

Villamil, J.J. (1979): 'Planning for Self-Reliant Growth', in J.J. Villamil (ed.): *Transnational Capitalism and National Development: New Perspectives on Dependence* (Brighton, Harvester).

World Health Organization, Nutrition Unit (1974): 'Review of Currently Available Indicators in the Field of Health and Their Use in Nutrition Activities', *Protein Advisory Group Bulletin*, IV.

Wolff, R.P. (1982): 'Pierro Sraffa and the Rehabilitation of Classical Political Economy', *Social Research*, 49, 1, 209-238.

4 AN OVERALL FRAMEWORK FOR QUALITY OF LIFE EVALUATION SCHEMES WITH APPLICATION TO THE CISKEI (SOUTH AFRICA)

G.F.R. Ellis

This article presents an overview of the different Quality of Life components that can be measured (including the State of Welfare, Level of Living, and subjective aspects), and so provides a framework (a) for developing particular measurement schemes, and (b) for comparing the coverage of different QOL estimation schemes. The proposal is based on a reasonably precise concept of the nature of Quality of Life; however, there are many ways in which the broad proposal could be implemented. In particular, one could aim at developing it in a simple, broad-brush way, or in much more complex detailed measurement schemes. To illustrate the ideas underlying the proposal, we give a simple application to the South African situation.

While this article gives the main outlines of the framework proposed, it omits discussion of many of the detailed points that arise; these are considered in a more extensive exposition of the proposal in Ellis (1980). One can find use of the basic framework as an aid in examination of aspects of the South African situation in HAP (1981a, b). There are of course various other valuable and interesting articles that present overall frameworks for QOL assessment.[1] The ideas presented here are consistent with many of those other approaches; however, the present proposal has been developed from a particular viewpoint which gives it a particular shape. In addition, while the proposal presented is an overall framework, it has – as for instance in the case of Drewnowski's work (1974, 1978) – been developed in sufficient detail (see Ellis 1980) to indicate how it would be applied to many specific situations. This enables its implications to be compared with those of some of the detailed QOL measurement schemes that have been developed, and with proposals such as those for estimating the satisfaction of Basic Needs.

I Welfare and the Function of Society

The problem of defining the welfare of a particular group in society is obviously a very thorny one. While certain aspects of welfare (e.g.

physical health) may be relatively clear, determination of the more sociological and psychological aspects raises considerable methodological problems. In particular, certain aspects one would want to evaluate would be highly value-laden, and different observers might assess the situation quite differently; as an example, some population sections might feel severely deprived if there were no mosques in the locality, while for others the requisite might be a Catholic church. Clearly the aim should be a welfare measure that avoids such sectarian views. This implies obvious problems in choosing the variables that might enter a Quality of Life assessment function, and applying measures to them.

Given that one does not wish to incorporate particular aesthetic, social, religious, and other value judgements in one's assessment, how should one proceed? The key feature one can focus on is, instead of setting measures which in effect prescribe goals for the members of society, to consider *the barriers that prevent them from attaining the goals they see as important for themselves*. In effect, while welfare is difficult to measure, what is relatively easy to determine is the nature of many of the factors that affect welfare, and some consequences that follow from a lack of welfare. Thus these aspects should be featured explicitly in a useful evaluation scheme. Essentially, instead of evaluating directly the group's immediate welfare, one attempts to evaluate their ability to attain their desired goals and to deal with any problems or difficulties that may face them.

The clearest way to introduce this is to focus on the fact that – through carelessness, error, accident, misunderstanding, or whatever – problems will inevitably arise in society. A crucial feature, then, is: does the capacity exist for correcting the errors that arise, and how efficiently does the error-correcting mechanism function? This approach is useful because the theory of error-correcting mechanisms is well-understood. The fundamental mechanism is that of feedback control (Milsum ed. 1968), often studied under the name 'Cybernetics' (Wiener 1973), which is the basis of control *inter alia* of biological systems including the human body (Milsum 1966), engineering control systems (Harrison & Bollinger 1969; Graham & McRuer 1971), and organizations (Beer 1974), enabling them not merely to maintain equilibrium in the presence of disturbances (the process of homeostasis), but also purposefully and effectively to attain set goals. In each of these cases, the regulation of disturbances takes place by the process of (a) comparing the desired state of things with the actual state, and (b) if necessary, sending information about a perceived discrepancy to appropriate control mechanisms, so that they can take action to make the actual state approximate more closely to the desired state.

It is reasonable to suppose the same general principles apply in social systems: for 'the heart of social problem solving has to do with the regulation of disturbances' (Dunn 1974). Thus one may conceptualize society as a cybernetic system in which there are many feedback loops whose function is to correct errors and to solve problems that arise in the functioning of the system.[2] As in the other examples mentioned above, the feedback control loops in society also act to enable and facilitate the normal functioning of the social system.

Adopting this viewpoint, one may then claim that the success of a particular social system in carrying out this error-correcting function will determine the quality of life for people in that society. This view is explored in the remainder of this paper. The model of society outlined above is developed further in the following section, and its relation to the Quality of Life concept is explored in later sections.

II The Nature of the Feedback System

We consider a particular group of people within the context of a particular social system. The concept we use to order the scheme is that of levels of control, where the welfare status of the group at each level is determined by factors at the preceding levels (Figure 1).

Figure 1

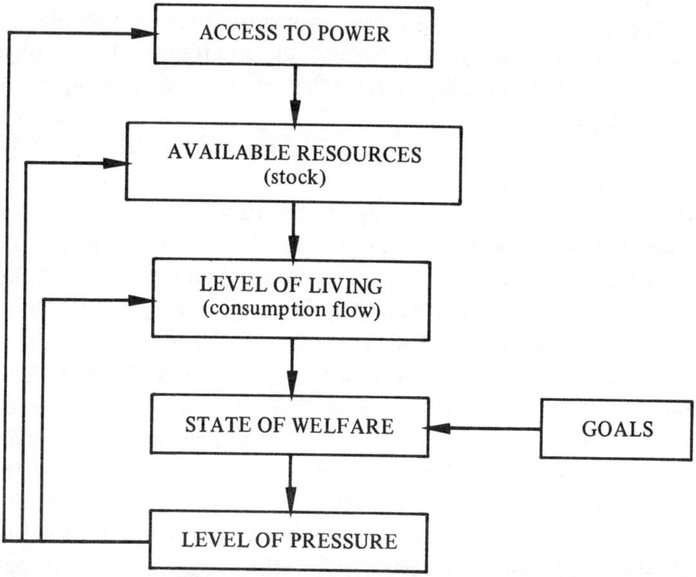

The basic level is that of the *State of Welfare*; we call this Level 0. This is a state of the group at a particular instant of time, and is the quantity we are ultimately concerned with. It can be considered as consisting of two major components, one concerned with material well-being and one with socio-cultural well-being. As mentioned above, it is in the main very difficult to assess (although some components, e.g. 'Somatic status' [Drewnowski 1974] are relatively straightforward).

It is easier to measure aspects of the first level of control, namely the *Level of Living* (Level 1). This is concerned with the deployment of the available flow of resources and amenities which make possible the maintenance and improvement of the State of Welfare. Thus one would find here, for example, the way available income is used in expenditure on food and medical services, on rental payments to maintain shelter, and so on. However, the concept of resource-usage implied here is not a narrow financial one; it encompasses all resource usage leading to increased welfare, using the term 'resource' in its widest sense to include, for example, clean air and quiet, unspoiled countryside, sonnets and symphonies. The definition of a resource, therefore, will be taken to be any quantity or feature whose use or deployment can be controlled to improve the group's welfare directly. Thus an art gallery is a resource which I use ('enjoy' or 'consume') if I visit the gallery; a beach or wilderness park is a resource I am able to 'consume' if I am able to visit it. Again, both 'organization' and 'knowledge" are resources which can be used or 'consumed'. Overall, this level is concerned with all ways the flow of available resources is used to increase the group's welfare;[3] the main four categories of such resource use are: resource use for physical welfare and safety, for security, for 'higher' needs, and for organizational purposes.

What can be achieved by choices at this level is determined by the total flow of resources available to the group. The second level of control is therefore that specifying the quantity and nature of *Resources Available* to the group. We can consider these resources as divided into natural resources, human resources, economic resources, technological resources, and enabling resources. Resources may be convertible to other resources at some 'exchange rate' or 'terms of trade' (e.g. by a manufacturing process or by trading). Because of the convertibility of money, it is one of the most important of resources, and so personal incomes are clearly one of the major components of the 'financial resources' section. Each available resource can be 'consumed' in various ways at the 'level of living' level to increase immediate welfare (e.g. personal income can be used for buying clothes, for entertainment, for food, etc.); or can be saved in various ways.

The resources available to the group are in turn determined by the group's access to the power structure in the society. Thus the third level of control is that of *Access to Power*. By definition, 'power' consists of those features of the social system which can lead to allocation of new resources to the group's benefit. Such power can be exerted by virtue of coercion, trust, standing or authority in the community, or other essentially political mechanisms. The access to power need not be direct, as long as it is effective. Institutional forms and controlling regulations are particularly important organizational resources in modern society, so the ability to control these features – which to a considerable degree determines the effective resource availability to the group (imposed restrictions may prevent 'available resources' from being 'usable available resources') – is an important aspect of power. The basic aim at this level is to characterize those communication channels through which the group can influence or change the allocation of resources in society (whatever those channels might be).

The three higher levels so far discussed ('access to power', 'resource availability' and 'level of living') each control the level below, and so determine the zero-level (the 'state of welfare'). The final level in the main set is the 'minus-one' level, which lies below the state of welfare, and will be called the *Level of Pressure*. This is the level manifesting the results of either a good state of welfare, or the lack of it. The two main kinds of pressure are what one might call 'consequential' pressure (automatic results of a state of welfare, e.g. a high death rate following from a poor health situation), and 'societal' pressure, which may act through institutionalized channels, or in other ways (e.g. protests may be sent to officials, or complaints laid 'through official channels'; public protests may be held; or general discontent may exist and be manifested in opinion polls, or features such as high crime rates). We find at this level the subjective indicators of happiness.

The final element in the main set of feedback loops, is what will be called the *Goals* of the group. This comprises those factors acting as the reference signal for the system, determining the direction in which the group wishes to influence events. Comparing this desired state with the actual state results in control signals (evidenced in the 'level of pressure') which flow through the three major feedback loops to the top three levels of control, and thereby attempt to direct the group's future in the desired direction (cf. Milsum ed. 1968, Krendel 1970, 1971).

Although this is not necessarily the way in which they will actually function, it is convenient to think of the three main feedback loops as operating sequentially. An example will make this clear. Suppose the parents and headmaster of a school agree that smaller classes are desirable for the pupils. First, the pressure generated (meetings with the headmaster, Parent-Teacher Association meetings, and so on) will result in feedback to level 1, where it is considered whether the need can be met by revised use of the existing flow of resources (a room can be converted from a storeroom to a classroom; teachers can be asked to teach extra classes, instead of doing library duty; and so on). If this proves not to be a feasible method of solution of the problem, the second feedback loop (to level 2) is activated. That is, it is considered whether other resources from the stock of resources available to the school might be brought into play to provide the extra teaching needed, if necessary through appropriate conversion of the form of these resources (e.g. funds set aside in a development fund are used to build a classroom; school buildings are rented out at night, creating extra income which can be used to pay salaries; and so on). Suppose it is not possible to meet the need this way, because the school has already (within the possibilities allowed by the institutional framework) allocated all its resources. Then it is required, in order to solve the problem, that new resources be made available to the school. The third feedback loop is activated; the authority controlling the relevant power (the local education authority) is asked if it will make more resources available to the school. This department will in turn consider action through the main three feedback loops; it will consider if it can re-allocate its existing flow of resources to deal with the problem (actions are considered that are 'without financial implications', e.g. teachers are transferred from another school); it may bring into play unallocated resources (e.g. it may allocate funds in hand to pay new salaries); or it in turn may apply to its relevant resource-providing authority (perhaps the local authority executive committee) for further funds needed. That body in turn may go through the same three steps. Obviously there are not just one but many feedback loops of each kind that might be called into play: if a direct request to the executive committee to make more money available for education fails, for example, then perhaps a public meeting might be called to air the situation. In general, the third level feedback takes on a 'political' nature.

To complete the overall picture of the feedback system, three further significant features should be mentioned (see Figure 2). First, an important mode of resource consumption is the use of a resource flow to build up further resources. That is, *Investment* may take place. This covers many broad ranges of activity where a resource flow is not used for immediate improvement of the state of welfare, but put to uses which will build up resources (at the second level) and so will later on be capable of increasing welfare.[4] For example, pupils are trained to

Figure 2

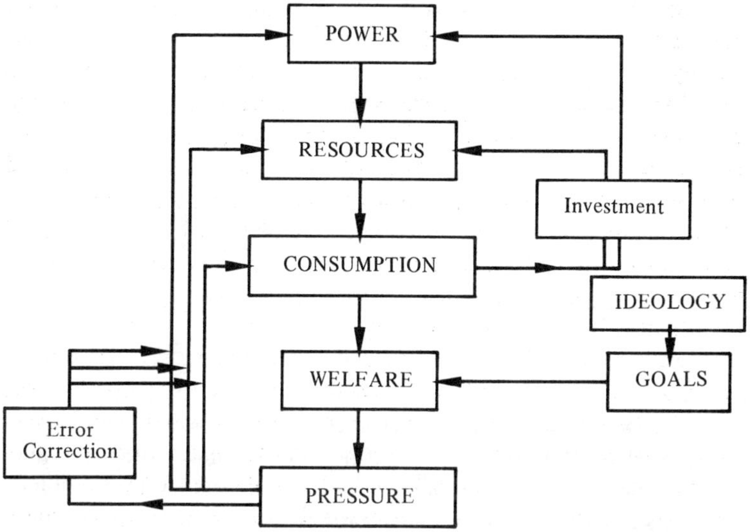

become teachers by use of resource flows which could have been used for more immediate benefit – for example, the instructors could have been manufacturing transistor radios instead – in order to build up a resource that will pay off in the long term, namely, a supply of qualified teachers. In particular, this covers production and exchange processes; it also covers most of the usage of resources for security, i.e. to ensure the continued functioning of the group in the future. Investment may also take place through a flow of resources from the first to the third level, representing political investment (e.g. expenditure on a political campaign or on union officials).

Second, when obvious malfunctioning occurs in any of the three major feedback loops, action may be taken to correct the situation through specific *Error Correction* mechanisms in society. These operate through review boards, appeals procedures, and so on; in general, they have the nature of a 'legal' process, acting back on the feedback loops themselves. Because this level can in principle control aspects of the political process, we call it level 4.

Third, the goals that are set by the interest group, or that are implied by their actions, are influenced by a variety of factors; they partly depend on the group's welfare situation, but also reflect psychological, ethical, ideological, and other features. It is clear that this influence is of significance in the functioning of the overall system. However, we do not wish to commit ourselves to some particular view as to the nature

Figure 3. The Effect of the Perceived Situation on the Chosen Goals

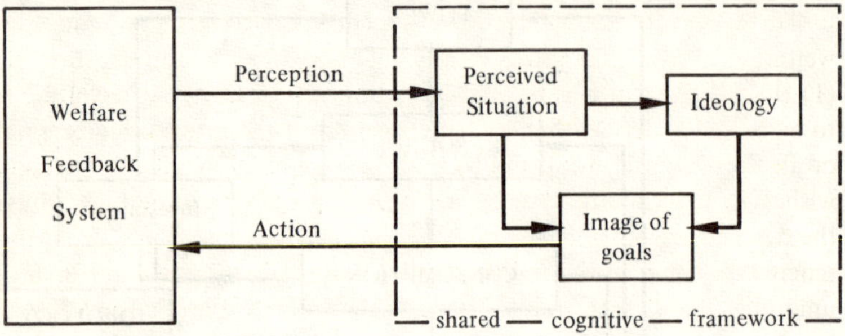

of these influences at this stage; accordingly, all such influences have been lumped together under the label *Ideology* (which is just a symbolic label for them). Inclusion of this label reminds us that the functioning of the system – probably even the perceived levels of welfare – can be altered by changing these features (e.g. through propaganda or by an advertising campaign). The causal links by which they are altered are schematically represented in Figure 3; they depend on perception of the situation by the group and will be influenced by many variables. As they have the general nature of psychological action, it will in general be difficult even to decide what these variables are, let alone to characterize the nature of the interaction. In the proposal presented here, these interactions will not be modelled explicitly; this is equivalent to stating that we consider the welfare of a group with a given outlook on life, and do not explicitly take into account the fact that one can alter perceived levels of welfare by altering the group's ideological or psychological stance. This is not to say that such effects are unimportant; but rather that what we primarily wish to characterize is the responsiveness of the social system to the group's needs as they perceive them, rather than its ability to mould those perceived needs anew. Modelling these aspects will be more difficult than the rest of what is attempted here, and can legitimately be left to a later stage of development of this proposal. It would be easier to model explicitly the variables entering the 'Goals' section of the system, and to consider how they are altered by 'perception' and their influence on the Level of Pressure; this is where one can consider such features as the effects of rising expectations or depressed expectations on levels of satisfaction. However, even this will not be advocated at the present stage of development of the current proposal. Significant progress has been made towards identifying the relevant variables (see e.g. Michalos 1980,

McKennell & Andrews 1980) and can be taken into account in further development of the system.

To obtain a clear picture of the feedback system determining the welfare of a particular group, one should make a clear identification of, (1) the society which is the context within which the group's welfare is to be considered; (2) other groups in that society significantly affecting, or affected by, the group's welfare;[5] (3) the level of detail at which one wishes to describe the group's situation and the time-scale over which the description will hold. Given such choices, the suggestion[6] is that the scheme outlined above (and depicted in Figure 2) will give an essentially unique causal classification of the different feedback loops operating to improve the welfare of the group; and that what actually determines the group's welfare at a particular time and place, is the functioning of this feedback system in its given environment at that time and place. This seems a reasonable hypothesis, as the model proposed is in fact a simple representation of the chain of cause and effect determining the group's welfare.

III The Quality of Life Concept

The proposal that overall welfare can be evaluated in terms of the barriers to obtaining desired objectives, can now be given a more precise formulation: it is suggested that *the quality of life situation of a particular group in society can be estimated in terms of the efficacy, within reasonable limits, of the welfare feedback system (outlined in section II and depicted in Figure 2) in attaining the group's desired goals*. In more detail, it is to be estimated by seeing how effective that system has been in creating a good 'state of welfare', in enabling the optimal use and redeployment of available resources, in obtaining new resources where needed, and in dealing with malfunctions of the feedback system itself, within the constraints imposed by the natural environment and taking into account the needs of other groups in the social environment. We shall consider the overall thesis in this section, and in the next shall turn to a discussion of the kinds of useful quantitative measurements that correspond to this concept.

The first point is that the concept presented here includes the measurable variables that are usually regarded as directly affecting the 'quality of life',[7] but (in principle) completed to include all such variables; and categorized by causal level. The concept of resource implied is, by definition, any quantity that can be controlled or deployed to the group's advantage; as well as obvious material and financial resources, therefore, the concept will include for instance such features as goodwill, knowledge, abilities, institutions, and so; and they may occur as negative quantities (liabilities) as well as positive quantities. It is through this breadth of definition of the concept 'resource' that the scheme proposed acquires its satisfactory logical basis; the difficulties in meaningfully utilizing the scheme are thereby shifted from the problem of definition, to the problem of exploring the consequences of the chosen definition. Similarly each of the consequences of the state of welfare (and so in particular, subjective measures of QOL) will be included; thus the contention is that each of the normally proposed QOL and basic needs measures will find a place in the scheme, but completed and categorized by causal level.

The second point is that the proposed organizational scheme of 'levels of control' is not just a convenient framework for presentation of factors affecting overall welfare; more than that, it is an arrangement of these quantities into a scheme that enables one to estimate measures of the group's freedom to act; and this is precisely the application proposed. In doing so, it explicitly incorporates one of the major features of concern in considering the quality of living; this freedom not only constitutes a concept carrying its own intrinsic merit, but may also be claimed to be a basic condition for full human development.

Queries about the use of the proposed concept as a measure of 'quality of life' may conveniently be focussed on two questions: does it omit features it ought to include, and does it allow features it ought to exclude?

As regards the first query, we explicitly exclude from the assessment framework attempts to evaluate the 'ideological' or 'goals' aspect of the system; correspondingly, we do not advocate attempts to evaluate the group's 'spiritual' state as part of the evaluation of the 'state of welfare'. The primary resulting concern is that the scheme constructed may be 'too materialistic', particularly as it omits attempts at evaluating that higher side of life within which the ultimate concept of the meaning of living is contained. For example, according to Frankl (1962), 'Man's main concern is not to gain pleasure or to avoid pain, but rather to see the meaning of life.' The response to this is twofold. On the one hand, it does not seem possible to attempt evaluation of such aspects (which could be incorporated in an extension of the present proposal, where one explicitly modelled the features we have labelled 'Ideology' and 'Goals' in Figure 3) without adopting very particular ideological stances; but this is precisely what we are trying to avoid, because of the divergences of opinions on such topics. It would not seem possible to obtain a generally agreed evaluation of these aspects. On the other hand, we are able to consider the developmental conditions which might lead to psychological and spiritual satisfaction (for example, we can evaluate the availability of peace and quiet for meditation, communication possibilities with others of similar persuasion, etc.), and the 'pressures' resulting from the presence or absence of such welfare (e.g. widespread movements seeking for new faiths, expressed satisfaction or dissatisfaction with old faiths, and so on). Thus the proposed scheme probably allows as close an approach to an 'unbiased' operational evaluation of the prospects for developing such welfare as one can attain. The suggestion, therefore, is that the scheme is not too narrowly based; one could extend it into these further areas only at the cost of introducing value judgements that would prejudice the degree of agreement on measures resulting from the scheme, and hence its possible useful application.

As regards the second query, 'quality of life' has essentially been defined in terms of control over one's siutation; the implication is that the more control one has, the better. But might it not be that after a certain level of control is attained, this is no longer true; in fact that thereafter, greater control over one's situation implies a worsening of welfare? (Is there not a limit to reasonable consumption levels? Is it really a boon to be able to consider genetic manipulation, or the destruction of cities by nuclear bombs?) There are basically two responses to this. The first is to claim that control is of the essence in developing human capabilities and responsibilities, and that the risks inherent in developing responsibility do not detract from the quality of life of the group involved. The further implication would be that if this responsibility were misused, this would be manifested on the one hand in the current evaluation of the situation by other groups in society (who might experience oppressive circumstances through the effects of this control on them); on the other hand, it would be manifested in later evaluations of the situation of the group concerned: if bad effects did not show up at a later stage, then the situation did not produce negative results and may therefore be adjudged to have not been a bad situation after all!

The second response would be to agree that the availability of too much control is bad; in fact, one might suggest that evaluation functions of all QOL variables will exhibit a maximum associated with an 'optimal' value of the relevant quantity (below the optimum value, 'more is better', but above it, 'more is worse'). Then in each case when evaluating the 'good' associated with a QOL variable, one would have to estimate this 'optimum' value of the variable, corresponding to the maximum utility. We could in this case understand the reason we are so accustomed to thinking 'more is better' is that in the usual situations of imperfect communication and scarcity of resources, the optimum cannot be obtained, for it lies outside the 'feasibility boundary'. In fact, if this optimum value of the welfare variable is high enough, we may never be in danger of achieving it, and in this case the two approaches to the problem merge.

In terms of setting up an overall framework for schemes, we do not have to choose between these two viewpoints; it is sufficient to note that they are both available for consideration when a particular scheme is set up.

The conclusion one may derive from these considerations is that the proposed criteria do indeed give a reasonable way of measuring a concept that may suitably be called the 'Quality of Life' of the group concerned.[8] It has the merit of being to a considerable degree ideology-free. For example, in considering the feedback to the third level, we do not worry whether the political system in operation is given the label 'capitalist', 'socialist', or whatever; we simply consider what the response of that system is to a request from the group for some change in the situation. This response can be monitored and measured independent of ideological labels.

IV Measures of Quality of Life

Given the overall framework developed above, one can assign measures to the Quality of Life of a group in one of four related but different ways; by adopting modelling, indicator, qualitative, or empirical approaches. We shall here consider only the indicator approach (for discussion of the others, see Ellis 1980).

The aim of this approach is to obtain indicators (a) of the values of the QOL variables at each of the six main levels in the welfare feedback system (cf. Figures 2 & 4), and (b) of the efficacy of the feedback channels themselves; to derive suitable normalized indices from the indicators; and possibly to combine indices in ways that throw particular light on the situation considered. The general methods of measuring social indicators, deducing QOL indices from them, and aggregating such indices have been widely discussed in the literature, so we shall not deal in depth with these aspects, but rather will concentrate on those features specific to the particular framework proposed here.

The crucial feature to be established is, what are the components of welfare for which indicators are needed in a complete QOL assessment scheme. A suggested classification according to the overall frame-

Figure 4. The Different Levels in the Main Feedback System, and the Corresponding quantities Represented

Levels	Quantities considered
Level 4	Error correction (Legal Access)
Level 3	Access to power
Level 2	Available resources
Level 1	Level of living
Level 0	Physical welfare
Level –1	Distress symptoms

work outlined in the previous sections is given in Table 1, and is elaborated in Ellis 1980: Appendix A. The suggested classification of components of welfare is essentially obvious, except that the 'State of Welfare' variables have been chosen according to Maslow's scheme (1954); some other suitable set of components could be substituted when setting up particular QOL evaluation schemes if appropriate.[9] Having identified each component of welfare that will be taken into account in a specific scheme, measures of its quantity, quality, and equality of distribution are needed; these should then be re-expressed, through suitable evaluation functions, in terms of normalized indices assessing the degree to which the corresponding need is fulfilled. Choice of the 'critical levels' which convert the indicators to indices (cf. Drewnowski 1974, 1978) will imply a choice of standards which will have to be set relative to what is possible and what is acceptable – and this relativity of measurement is inevitable.

Where possible one will use cardinal indicators, but in many situations one will have to use ordinal indicators instead (cf. Ibidem). There may be some aspects of the welfare levels that cannot reasonably be quantified even by an ordinal indicator; this will occur when one cannot produce a set of criteria for 'better' or 'worse' situations that would be generally agreed upon; that is, one cannot obtain agreement on the normative implications of the associated indicators. In this case, that aspect should be explicitly kept in the evaluation scheme but labelled 'N.I.' (*No Indication*). One might, for example, use this categorization for the 'Self-actualization' aspects of the State of Welfare. In addition, when a detailed scheme is adopted but there are some aspects of the situation for which data (while in principle attainable) is in practice unavailable, that aspect should be explicitly kept in the evaluation scheme but labelled 'N.A.' (*Not Available*). In addition to evaluating the indices corresponding to the variables in the different control levels, one should evaluate indices indicating directly the quality of

*Table 1: Components and Aspects of Levels of Welfare**

ERROR CORRECTION

(1) Administrative correction procedures
(2) Legal corrective procedures
(3) Correction of legal proceedings
(4) Legal freedom

ACCESS TO POWER

Direct Political Power	Direct Economic Power	Indirect Power	Persuasive Power	Coercive Power	Political Freedom
(i) National Government	(i) Employer's power	(i) Influence on national government	(i) Legitimation	(i) Local	(i) Political action
(ii) Local government	(ii) Employee's power	(ii) Influence on local government	(ii) Moral	(ii) National	(ii) To organize
(iii) Specific Utilities and organizations	(iii) Producer's power	(iii) Indirect economic power	(iii) Standards	(iii) International	(iii) Expression
	(iv) Consumer's power	(iv) Indirect international power	(iv) Charisma (v) Motivation		

AVAILABLE RESOURCES

Natural Resources	Human Resources	Economic Resources	Technological Resources	Enabling Resources	Economic Freedom
(i) Land resources (ii) Non-renewable resources	(i) Population (ii) Labour	(i) Personal income (ii) Group income	(i) Energy (ii) Information	(i) Stability (ii) Information	(i) Ownership (ii) Work choice
(iii) Renewable resources	(iii) Management	(iii) Capital	(iii) Transport	(iii) Assessment and adaptability	(iii) Trade and manufacture
	(iv) Recruitment (v) Skills (vi) Leadership	(iv) Borrowing power (v) Goodwill	(iv) Coercive (v) Production (vi) Technocrats	(iv) Motivation (v) Initiative	(iv) Training (v) Information

Physical Welfare	Safety	Economic Investment	Political Investment
(i) Nutrition	(i) Police protection	(i) Education	(i) Political activity
(ii) Clothing	(ii) Unofficial groups and security expenditure	(ii) Community processing, distribution and maintenance	(ii) Coercion
(iii) Dwelling	(iii) Fire, ambulance	(iii) Other resource processing and distribution	(iii) Persuasion
(iv) Utilities	(iv) Rescue, emergency	(iv) Resource investment	
(v) Health	(v) Environmental control	(v) Trade and export	
(vi) Environment		(vi) Persuasion	

'Higher' Needs	Organization	Loss of Resource Flow	Social Freedom
(i) Facilitating resources	(i) Community organization	(i) Resource loss	(i) Freedom of action
(ii) Community resources	(ii) Economic organization	(ii) Resource decay	(ii) Freedom of association
(iii) Self-affirmation	(iii) Public organization	(iii) Inefficiency	(iii) Freedom of expression
(iv) Recreational and cultural		(iv) Ineffectiveness	(iv) Freedom of communication
(v) Living environment			(v) Religious freedom
(vi) Religious resources			

STATE OF WELFARE

Physiological Welfare	Safety	Belongingness	Esteem	Self-Actualization
(i) Nutritional status	(i) Environment	(i) Family life	(i) Morale	
(ii) Health status	(ii) Violence and accidents	(ii) Community life	(ii) Group status	N.I.
(iii) Bodily state	(iii) Existence	(iii) National acceptance		
(iv) Physical fitness	(iv) War	(iv) International acceptance		
	(v) Vulnerability			

LEVEL OF PRESSURE

Physiological Response	Social Pressure	Economic Pressure	Political Pressure
(i) Death rates	(i) Social action	(i) Economic action	(i) Political action
(ii) Disease	(ii) Social protest	(ii) Work pathology	(ii) Political protest
(iii) Medical action	(iii) Social pathology	(iii) Market pathology	(iii) Political pathology
(iv) Surveys	(iv) Subjective indicators	(iv) Subjective indicators	(iv) Subjective indicators

* Also shown are the 'freedom' aspects which directly reflect important aspects of the functioning of the main feedback loops.

operation of the major feedback channels themselves. In the first place, one should indicate which channels are available to the group at all; that is, one should consider the group's freedom of action in using the available channels, and what channels are simply not available. Further one can consider the quality of the system response (does it make the appropriate kinds of response to signals of distress and do they have the correct sign, i.e. do they actually tend to improve the situation?); the lag in response (how long one must wait for a reaction to occur?); the quantity of the response (is it sufficient in magnitude to appreciably affect the situation?); and the distribution of the response (does it act to increase or decrease inequalities of welfare?). In many cases these aspects can be evaluated directly (e.g. one can evaluate the time delay and nature of the response to a planning application submitted to a local authority; cf. Krendel 1970, 1971).

An indicator approach based on the framework presented here can provide a viable way of systematizing and presenting to the decision-maker data representing the current state of welfare of the group concerned. The particular realizations of the overall scheme will clearly be rather non-unique in their details; in particular one could implement the scheme at many different levels of detail, as one has considerable choice in the number of indicators chosen and the level of aggregation used. The process of classification can be carried out to an arbitrarily detailed level; for example, expenditure on nutrition (at the 'Level of Living' level) could be detailed in terms of total expenditure, or expenditure on carbohydrates, sugars, protein, and so on. The art of correct choice lies in selecting a scheme which gives the right amount of detail for the purpose at hand (that is, which will give the needed information to a decision maker, but will not overburden him with excess detail); which is closely related to the causes of increased welfare; and if possible, which emphasizes aspects of the situation that can relatively easily be quantified. It is suggested that in measuring overall Quality of Life a choice of indicators should be made so that at least some index measures each of the major aspects indicated in Table 1, rather than having very detailed and elaborate measurements in some area of concern at the expense of completely missing out others. Obviously this could lead in general to very complex schemes. This is not surprising; one would expect an overall framework to allow very elaborate measurement schemes, for QOL is a complex subject. However, for practical usage two features are important in allowing one to use simpler representations that nevertheless can convey most of the desired message.

First, one can *aggregate indices* to give overall measurements for some areas of concern from more detailed measurements in those areas. This enables one to construct a simpler picture of the situation from complex measurements; however, it also raises all the usual problems about the choice of the aggregation function (which is most often chosen to be linear) and the weighting of the different factors entering that function. It could be done in quite sophisticated ways, for example, to allow for conditional ranking (such as that implied in Maslow's hierarchy of needs, or implied by the concept of a resource 'bottleneck') in determining the overall indices. Second, one can reduce the measurement problem greatly by choosing *representative indices* in each area of concern; then instead of measuring a large number of indices and aggregating them, one would only have to measure the few representative indices, and accurate indications would be obtained provided the representative indices had been skilfully chosen so that they were in fact representative of the other indices not actually measured. In thinking of these possibilities, there is perhaps one minimum criterion one should set: namely, that *any particular scheme chosen should make at least some attempt to represent the situation at each of the six main levels in the welfare feedback system* (Fig. 4). Using an indicator approach, this implies that at least one indicator should be chosen at each of these levels. The further criterion to aim for if possible, is that *at least one indicator should be used to represent the quality of functioning of each of the main feedback loops* as well. In any case, if indicators are not chosen or are not available for any of these features, it is strongly suggested that this should be made clear; so that the user can explicitly bear in mind that there is an area of concern for which he ought to have data, but which is not represented in the available QOL indices.

The scheme presented here provides a framework within which one can look at the coverage of welfare aspects by any particular proposed choice of QOL indicators; it can be used to highlight particular areas of concern that are not represented by the chosen indicators (two examples of this use are given in Ellis 1980: Appendix B). It can be used either in a general (overall) application, or in considering specific domains of concern (e.g. quality of health care or quality of housing). In each such application, use of the overall framework as a guide in setting-up specific schemes should help ensure an adequate coverage of aspects of welfare by the chosen indicators; for example, it will ensure that in setting-up indicators for housing, one considers the 'political' question of how a housing project is to be controlled – which is crucial to measuring the quality of living of those in the project. In a full assessment of QOL, one might anticipate using a particular QOL Index

Scheme that fits into the framework outlined above, on the one hand, and in-depth evaluation of particular aspects of the situation (micro-studies based on interviews) on the other. That is, it is not claimed that the QOL indices by themselves will be completely adequate for assessing the situation; but that when used in conjunction with interview techniques, an adequate overview should be attainable.

V The Quality of Life of the Ciskei and Its Relation to Nyanga (Cape Town)

In a series of events centred in August 1981, the South African authorities evicted from 'bachelor' quarters in Cape Town a considerable number of Black men, women and children, the majority of whom had originally come to town from the Transkei and Ciskei (however, many had been in town for a considerable number of years, and some were born there). These people erected temporary dwellings on open ground in Nyanga, and lived there for some time (with many of the men and women going off to work each day, returning to their squatter shanties in the evenings). Eventually the authorities demolished the temporary dwellings, leaving the people concerned exposed to wind, driving rain, and bitter cold. They were provided with blankets and plastic sheeting by some of the citizens of Cape Town, but these too were taken away by the authorities to ensure that no shelter at all was available (even branches of trees used as shelters were removed). Despite this the people stayed on living on the bleak open ground, until eventually they were arrested in a massive police exercise and deported to the Transkei in buses; many families were completely split by these proceedings, with babies and children separated from distraught parents for weeks (at the time of writing, there are still children who simply do not know where their parents are and women who do not know where their husbands are). Symptomatic of the situation is one eight-month old child who has been in jail three times and in the drip room at the Red Cross hospital twice. While in jail, the only food provided for this infant by the police was (absolutely literally) bread and water.

The actions by the authorities before the final arrests were quite deliberately designed with the purpose of reducing the Quality of Living of the Black people concerned. The aim was to reduce their QOL to such a degree that they would leave the area (the official vision is that they should return to 'where they came from'). This can be seen as the continuation of a long-standing policy of influx control involving both direct controls enforced through continual policing activity (particularly taking the form of 'pass raids', often involving armed officials invading hostels or houses at about 4 a.m. to demand identity papers) and such features as restricting the provision of housing for blacks and limiting amenities in their townships (local finances are arranged so that the major source of income for the local Administration Boards is revenue from township beer and liquor sales). A major feature of this policy is that 'migrants' are not allowed to have their wives or children with them, and so are expected during their entire working lives to be satisfied with contact with their families limited to about one month a year (if they do not agree with this and bring their families to town, the full weight of the law is used against them; so one finds men arrested for 'harbouring their wives').

Despite this policy, many of the people concerned have determinedly remained in the area. In some instances they have always lived in town; in other cases they have left the rural areas long ago, and have no home there. However, some have left these areas (the Transkei or Ciskei) quite recently; the question is why they do not return there, given the pressure that is being exerted on them to do so?

It is here that relative Quality of Life measurements come in. One must presume that 'homeland' blacks come to Cape Town in order to increase their present or future expected Quality of Life.[10] Thus one may immediately obtain some sort of estimate of what homeland conditions must be like: people would not come to Cape Town and endure the prevalent urban conditions unless Homeland conditions were significantly worse. Considering the treatment they receive in Cape Town, this is a somewhat startling conclusion. However, it can be checked by directly estimating the QOL in the rural areas from whence they came. The rest of this paper aims to use the QOL framework established in previous sections, as a basis for estimating QOL in the Ciskei (cf. HAP 1981). It may be expected that the situation in the Transkei will be very similar.

The procedure used was the simplest that could give an estimate of the Quality of Life of ordinary Black people in Ciskei rural areas, based on the framework introduced above. The aim was to give a global view of the Welfare Feedback System for these Ciskei inhabitants. In order to do so, a panel of experts was set up and asked to indicate their estimates of the various welfare indices, relying on a knowledge of local conditions obtained through extensive reading, statistical research, and direct knowledge of the area. This procedure is clearly not as satisfactory as a detailed survey of local conditions specifically aimed at obtaining data for a QOL estimate; but the contention is that it nevertheless provides a good first estimate of the overall situation. Others may disagree with details of this estimate; it at least provides a reasonably exact statement of what the problem areas are, according to the understandings of the panel, instead of vague general comments that cannot be proved or refuted by more detailed studies.[11] Anyone who claims the situation is otherwise will have to concentrate on these aspects and produce counter-evidence related to them.

The panel was chosen on the basis of detailed knowledge of recent conditions in the rural Ciskei. It comprised Dr Francis Wilson, Director of the South African Labour and Development Research Unit at the University of Cape Town (SALDRU), and author *inter alia* of *Migrant Labour in South Africa*; Dr Charles Simkins, Senior Research Fellow at SALDRU and author *inter alia* of *South African Unemployment: A Black Picture* (1978), *The Distribution of the African Population of South Africa by Age, Sex and Region-Type* (1981a), and *The Demographic Demand for Labour and Institutional Context of African Unemployment in South Africa: 1960-1980* (1981b); Ms Pippa Green, Research worker at SALDRU; and Dr George Ellis, Chairman of the Western Cape Branch of the Quaker Service Fund and author *inter alia* of *On Understanding the World and the Universe* (1974), and *The Quality of Life Concept: An Overall Framework for Assessment Schemes* (1980) and the present article. To give a specific focus to the study, they were asked to concentrate on conditions in the Keiskammahoek area (which was the subject of an intensive study in 1952, see Hobart Houghton & Walton 1952). The task was to produce an ordinal indicator for present conditions in this area relative to each of the major Quality of Life aspects represented by a block in Table 1. While a more detailed study would have given a Quantity Index, Quality Index and Distribution Index for each of these aspects, this was not attempted; rather an overall QOL indicator was given for each aspect. It was decided to use an ordinal index scale of from 1 to 7, rather than the scale from I to IV proposed by Drewnowski (1974); it was felt the latter scale was a bit too coarse, while the scale from 1 to 7 seemed to give a reasonable and usable range of indicators.[12] The normalization chosen was: 7 is a state of total affluence; 4 is the Minimum Effective Level (i.e. state when the corresponding need can be considered to be just met at a very minimum level); 3 is the Poverty Datum Level or Minimum Living Level (at and below this level, one is living in a state of real deprivation); and 1 is a state of complete destitution (below this survival should not be possible).[13] According to reasonable norms, state 3 is the lowest level that should be considered tolerable, and state 4 or above should be the goal of planning policy.

The resulting indices are as follows (with very brief indications as to the indicators used to derive them):

Level 0: State of Welfare

Physiological Welfare Index, 2 (indicators, occurrence of Kwashiorkor and Marasmus; weight-for-age scale). Safety Index, 5 (although the crime rate is rising, the area is still relatively safe). Belongingness Index, 2 (although the population feel strongly attached to their rural homes and community, there are severe problems due to family break-up by migrant labour, no national acceptance, no international acceptance). Esteem Index: 3 (dependence and uncertainties are hallmarks of the area). Self-Actualization Index: No Indicator.

Level 1: Level of Living

Physical Welfare Expenditure Index: 2 (expenditure is strictly limited by the income levels in the area; the major source of income is migrant remittances which are rising in real terms but presently averaging about R13 per person per month and with a badly skewed distribution; and the cost-of-living in rural areas is much higher than in urban areas). Safety Expenditure Index: 3 (safety is largely established by social networks rather than by expenditure on safety services; however, ambulance services are inadequate and beyond the means of most locals). Education Expenditure Index: 3 to 4 (large numbers of children are at school, but expenditure per child is low and the quality of teaching is poor; very few facilities are available for technical training). Investment Rate Index: 4 to 5 (because investment is very difficult for Blacks in the cities, migrants are investing in houses and cattle in the rural areas to a significant degree). Political Investment Rate Index: 1 (political expenditure on Party membership is obligatory if pensions are to be obtained, work is to be available in many spheres, etc.; because this is not voluntary, it has been regarded as a negative feature of the local scene. Almost no channels for political investment are available for locals who wish to change the direction of local or national politics). Higher Needs Expenditure Index: 3 (the Church has facilities everywhere, and there still are self-help organizations of various kinds in operation; few other facilities exist). Organization Expenditure Index: 5 (levels of public expenditure are relatively high). Loss of Resource Flow Index: Not Available (the panel did not wish to assign a value, although there are various indications of substantial losses, e.g. by soil erosion on the one hand, and such features as pensions which are theoretically available not actually materializing, on the other). Social Freedom: 1 (owing to the overall structure of the country, the people concerned cannot choose where to live, nor can they choose to have their wife or family with them if they move to areas where jobs are available at reasonable wages).

Level 2: Available Resources

Natural Resources Index: 1 to 2 (no mineral resources, unreliable water availability, and land area quite inadequate relative to the population; this is reflected in a high degree of landlessness of the local population). Human Resources Index: Population, 6; Management and Skills, 3; Leadership, 4 (potentially there are considerable skills available in the population, but many of the most able leaders are in jail or banned). Economic Resources Index: Personal Income, 2; Other Resources, 2 (unemployment is very high and local wages very low, so there is almost total reliance on migrant remittances for cash income; agricultural productivity per capita is very low; while income available for public expenditure in the Ciskei is not unreasonable, little of it accrues to the benefit of the local population). Technological Resources Index: Energy, 1; Other, 3 (lack of fuel is a serious problem; availability of telephones, transport, etc. is limited and too expensive for many of the population). Enabling Resources Index: 2 (the result of political pressure is a scarcity of stable institutions, as groups that do not toe the Party line are stamped on; motivation and initiative are heavily damped, again for political reasons – it is dangerous for an individual to show any substantial independence). Economic Freedom Index: 1 (the whole Labour Bureau structure is explicitly built to prevent freedom of choice in seeking work).

Level 3: Access to Power

Direct Political Power Index: 1 (the locals have no access to political power in the wider South African scene, and very little chance of influencing the local scene either). Direct Economic Power Index: 1 (although workers sometimes belong to trade unions when working in town, they are liable to arbitrary arrest or detention if they play an active union role). Indirect Power Index: 1 (the only influence available is at the local level, and this has marginal impact because of other overriding power structures). Persuasive Power Index: 1 (although some of the leaders have the needed abilities to a considerable degree, they have no access to media enabling them to influence a constituency, and public meetings are by and large not permitted). Coercive Power Index: local, 2; national and international, 1. Political Freedom Index: 1 (opposition is completely restricted by the South African and Ciskei security police; the detention of political opponents of both the central and the local authorities is common).

Level 4: Error Correction

Error Correction Index: 1 (while institutions exist that in principle allow corrective measures, in practice they are unavailable to any Black person without the backing of substantial money and a White lawyer; thus in the rural areas, *de facto* no redress is available).

Level -1: Level of Pressure
Physiological Pressure Index: 2 (mortality rates are very high). Social Pressure Index: 3 (pathologies such as drunkenness, mental illness and suicide are better indicators than protest, as the latter is mainly latent because of repressive measures in force). Economic Pressure Index: 2 (again protest is largely latent rather than actual although some trade union activity is evident; the major indicator is large-scale illegal economic activity which provides the only means of support for many families). Political Pressure Index: 2 (protests are latent rather than actual, but pathologies are evident in the many detentions).

The above estimates are summarized in Table 2. The indices provide a broad overview of the situation, which can clearly be seen to be largely below a tolerable level; thereby providing an understanding of the strong 'push' to migrate to the urban areas. This overview needs to be supplemented by in-depth studies of particular aspects of the situation; in general such studies confirm the view outlined above (see e.g. Thomas 1973, Clarke & Ngobese 1975, Westcott 1977, HAP 1981b, and others). One point to note here is that there is a considerable flow of information through various South African Government run or financed organs (particularly the South African Broadcasting Corporation) presenting a quite different picture, and that information obviously needs to be compared with the assessment given here. Inspection will reveal that a major feature of those presentations is that they often give data on resources supplied (houses built, job opportunities provided, etc.) but not on resource needs – they do not consider the relation between supply and demand. In particular, figures for expenditure are mainly given overall (e.g. total expenditure on education) but not as per capita figures; but the latter are what are mainly relevant to QOL estimates. A further major feature is that these presentations will normally be very partial in their coverage; for example, they will not present data on such aspects as infant mortality rates, freedom of movement, and freedom to seek work unhindered.

While we are reasonably confident of the broad picture presented by the indices listed above and in Table 2, more detailed studies should be undertaken to verify their accuracy; and comparative studies (both in time and relative to other locations) should be undertaken to put this gloomy picture in a proper geographic (cf. CSO 1976) and historical[14]

Table 2: Ciskei QOL Indices: a first estimation, on a scale from 1 to 7

CISKEI QOL INDICES

Index Scale	1	2	3	4	5	6	7
	Destitute		MLL	MEL			Affluent

Level 4 : Error Correction					
Error Correction Index : 1					
Level 3 : Access to Power					
Direct Political Power Index: 1	Direct Economic Power Index: 1	Indirect Power Index: 1	Persuasive Power Index: 1	Coerceive Power Index: Local, 2 other, 1	Political Freedom Index: 1
Level 2 : Available Resources (Stocks)					
Natural Resources Index: 1.5	Human Resources Index: Population, 6 Skills, 3 Leadership, 4		Economic Resources Index: Personal Income, 2 Other, 2	Technological Resources Index: Energy, 1 Other, 3	
Enabling Resources Index: 2	Economic Freedom Index: 1				
Level 1 : Level of Living (Expenditure Rate Indices)					
Physical Welfare Exp. Rate Index, 2	Safety Exp. Rate Index, 3	Economic Investment Rate Index: Education, 3.5 Other, 4.5	Political Investment Rate Index: 1	Higher Needs Exp. Rate Index: 3	
Organizational Exp. Rate Index: 5	Loss of Resource Flow Index: N.A.	Social Freedom Index: 1			
Level 0 : State of Welfare					
Physiological Welfare Index: 2	Safety Index: 5	Belongingness Index: 2	Esteem Index: 3	Self-Actualization Index: N.I.	
Level –1 : Level of Pressure					
Physiological Pressure Index: 2	Social Pressure Index: 3	Economic Pressure Index: 2	Political Pressure Index: 2		

perspective. It is likely that the view obtained of conditions in many other of the South African Black 'Homelands' will be quite similar; and one may note that conditions in some cases are still dramatically declining, owing to continuing 'resettlement' schemes (cf. AFRA 1981).

Notes

The Author would like to thank Drs Francis Wilson, Charles Simkins, Mary Roberts, and Ms Pippa Green for their assistance in developing this assessment.

1. See, for example, Gerson 1976; Shin & Johnson 1978; Mitchell, Logothetti & Kantor 1971; Gillingham & Reece 1980; and Bubolz et al. 1980.
2. See Krendel 1970 and 1971 for articulation of an essentially similar view; the general validity of this model is shown by the current widespread use of the word 'feedback' in many social and organizational situations.
3. This emphasis that QOL depends on resource usage is in agreement with various of the other overall frameworks proposed, e.g. Drewnowski 1974; Shin & Johnson 1978; Gillingham & Reece 1980; Bubolz et al. 1980.
4. We believe it is important to include these loops in any consideration of Welfare; they are omitted from other approaches which are in some ways quite similar to the present one (see, for example, Gillingham & Reece 1980).
5. The interests of each competing group in society will be represented by a similar welfare feedback system; cf. Ellis (1980: Fig. 3).
6. See Ellis (1980: 22-24) for further discússion.
7. Consider, for example, the common use of the phrase 'standard of living', and the variables used to estimate 'basic needs' satisfaction.
8. Note that we would not advocate the present scheme for the purpose of measuring the QOL of an individual; the reason is that in that case the psychological variables, which we do not propose modelling when a group is considered, are likely to be dominant.
9. Choice of these as suitable variables does not necessarily imply that one agrees with the hypothesis that they occur in an invariable hierarchy of needs (see, for example, Gratton 1980); that feature would be considered in setting evaluation functions for the variables chosen.
10. The connection between QOL and migration is made in various references, see for example Gillingham & Reece 1980; Liu 1975; Ellis & Matravers 1981.
11. Note that we have not given detailed references to data supporting the evaluation, for to do so would have led to far too lengthy an article. However, for those who would like to pursue the subject further, see HAP 1981a; Selvan 1976; Granelli & Levitan 1977; Davenport 1980, and Kraak 1981, for aspects of the urban situations; HAP 1981b; The Tomlinson Commission Report 1955; Horrell 1973; BENBO 1975; The Quail Report 1980; Nash & Charton eds 1981; Thomas 1973; Clarke & Ngobese 1975; Wilson et al. 1977; Thomas 1980; Claassens 1980; de Wet 1980; O'Connell 1980; Reynolds 1981, for aspects of the rural situation, and Wilson 1972; Simkins & Desmond eds 1978; Simkins 1981a, b; Ellis et al. 1977; Ellis 1974; Perry 1974; Auerbach 1979; Memorandum 1974; Horner 1974; Marchand 1977; Maree & Graaf 1978; Mare 1980; Desmond 1978; Forsyth & Schiller eds 1979; Report to the MASA 1981, for the overall situation and the policy applied.
12. One may bear in mind here psychological evidence that the human mind naturally distinguishes approximately seven grades of variation in a qualitative variable.

13. The methods by which families survive when below the PDL are discussed, for example, by Willsworth (1979, 1980). In cases where the group does not survive – e.g. if genocide were practiced – one would use the indicator value 0.

14. Particularly one should note that before specific legislation intervened in the situation, the QOL for rural Blacks in these areas was much higher; see Bundy 1979.

References

Abrams, M. (1976): *A Review of Work on Subjective Social Indicators 1971 to 1975* (London, SSRC Survey Unit, Occasional Papers in Survey Research).

Association for Rural Advancement (1981): 'Richards Bay and Removals', (Pietermaritzburg, AFRA Reports 12 and 13).

Auerbach, F.E. (1979): *Measuring Educational Development in South Africa* (South African Institute of Race Relations).

Beer, S. (1974): *Decision and Control* (Chichester, John Wiley).

Bubolz, M.M., J.B. Eicher, S.J. Evers & M.S. Sontag (1980): 'A Human Ecological Approach to Quality of Life: Conceptual Framework and Results of a Preliminary Study', *Social Indicators Research*, 7, 103-136.

Bundy, C. (1979): *The Rise and Fall of the South African Peasantry* (London, Heinemann).

Bureau for Economic Research (1975): *Ciskei Economic Review 1975* (Pretoria, Bureau for Economic Research re Bantu Development).

Central Statistics Office (1976): *The Rural Income Distribution Survey in Botswana 1974/5* (Gaborone, Ministry of Finance and Planning, CSO).

Claassens, A. (1980): 'An Assessment of Self-Help Projects in a District of the Transkei', in F. Wilson & G. Westcott (eds): *Hunger, Work and Health (Economics of Health in South Africa)*, Vol. II (Johannesburg, Ravan Press).

Clarke, L. & J. Ngobese (1975): *Women Without Men* (Durban, Institute for Black Research).

Davenport, T.R.H. (1980): *Black Grahamstown* (South African Institute of Race Relations).

Desmond, C. (1978): 'Limehill Revisited: A Case Study of the Longer-Term Effects of African Resettlement' (University of Natal, Development Studies Research Group).

Drewnowski, J. (1974): *On Measuring and Planning the Quality of Life* (The Hague, Mouton, for the Institute of Social Studies).

— (1978): 'The Affluence Line', *Social Indicators Research*, 5, 263-278.

Dunn, E.S. (1974): *Social Information Processing and Statistical Systems – Change and Reform* (Chichester, John Wiley).

Ellis, G.F.R. (1974): 'On Understanding the World and the Universe' (University of Cape Town, Inaugural Lecture).

— (1980): *The Quality of Life Concept: An Overall Framework for Assessment Schemes* (University of Cape Town, South African Labour and Development Research Unit, Working Paper No. 30).

Ellis, G.F.R., D. Hendri, A. Kooy & J. Maree (1977): *The Squatter Problem in the Western Cape: Some Causes and Remedies* (South African Institute of Race Relations).

Ellis, G.F.R. & D.R. Matravers (1981): *Regional Housing Investigation* (University of Cape Town, Urban Problems Research Unit).

Forsyth, C.J. & J.E. Schiller (1978): *Human Rights: The Cape Town Conference* (Juta & Co.).

Frankl, E. (1962): *Man's Search for Meaning* (Boston, Beacon Press).
Gerson, E. (1976): 'On "Quality of Life"', *American Sociological Review*, 41, 5, 793-806.
Gillingham, R. & W.S. Reece (1980): 'Analytical Problems in the Measurement of the Quality of Life', *Social Indicators Research*, 7, 91-101.
Graham, D.S. & D. McRuer: *Analysis of Non-Linear Control Systems* (Dover).
Granelli, R. & R. Levitan (1977): *Urban Black Housing* (University of Cape Town, Urban Problems Research Unit).
Gratton, L.C. (1980): 'Analysis of Maslow's Need Hierarchy with Three Social Class Groups', *Social Indicators Research*, 7, 463-476.
Guyton, A.C. (1972): *Ann Reviews of Physiology*, 34, 13.
Harrison, H.L. & J.G. Bollinger (1969): *Introduction to Automatic Control* (International Textbooks Co.).
Hobart Houghton, D. & E.M. Walton (1952): *The Economy of a Native Reserve* (Vol. III of Keiskammahoek Rural Survey; Shuter & Shooter).
Horner, D. (1974): 'Control of Movement and Employment of African Workers', *S.A. Labour Bulletin*, 1, 2.
Horrell, M. (1973): *The African Homelands of South Africa* (South African Institute of Race Relations).
HAP (1981a): 'SOWETO: An Assessment', *Change Newsletter No. 1* (Johannesburg, Human Awareness Programme).
— (1981b): 'CISKEI: An Assessment', *Change Newsletter No. 2* (Johannesburg, Human Awareness Programme).
Kraak, G. (1981): *Financing of African Worker Accommodation in Cape Town* (SALDRU Working Paper No. 35).
Krendel, E. (1970): 'A Case Study of Citizen Complaints as Social Indicators', *TEEE Transactions on Systems Science and Cybernetics*, Vol. SSC-6, 4.
— (1971): 'Social Indicators and Urban System Dynamics', *Socio-Economic Planning Science*, 5, 387-393.
Liu, B.-C. (1975): 'Differential Net Migration Rates and the Quality of Life', *Review of Economics and Statistics*, 57, 3, 329-337.
Marchand, C.G.J. (1977): 'A Consideration of the Legal Basis and Some Practical Operations of the Labour Bureau', *S.A. Labour Bulletin*, 3, 9.
Mare, G. (1980): *African Population Relocation in South Africa* (South African Institute of Race Relations).
Maree, J. & J. Graaff (1978): 'Men Without Choice: A Sample Survey of Some African Workers in Cape Town 1975-76', *Social Dynamics*, 4, 1.
Maslow, A.H. (1954): *Motivation and Personality* (New York, Harper & Brothers).
McKennell, A.C. & F.M. Andrews (1980): 'Models of Cognition and Effect in Perceptions of Wellbeing', *Social Indicators Research*, 8, 257-298.
Memorandum on the Pass Laws and Influx Control (1974): Sash 16, 4.
Michalos, A.C. (1980): 'Satisfaction and Happiness', *Social Indicators Research*, 8, 385-422.
Milsum, J.H. (1966): *Biological Control Systems Analysis* (New York, McGraw Hill).
— (1968): *Positive Feedback* (Oxford, Pergamon).
Mitchell, A., T.J. Logothetti & R.E. Kantor (1971): 'An Approach to Measuring Quality of Life' (California, Stanford Research Institute).
Nash, M. & C. Charton (eds) (1981): *An Empty Table* (South African Council of Churches).
O'Connell, M.C. (1980): 'Some Social and Cultural Repercussions of the Betterment Scheme in a Transkeian Community' (Transkei and Ciskei Research Society, Proceedings of the 6th Biennial Meeting at Umtata).
Perry, A. (1974): *African Secondary School Leavers* (South African Institute of Race Relations).
Quail Report, The (1980): *Report of the Ciskei Commission* (Pretoria, Conference Associates).

Report to the Medical Association of South Africa by the Ad Hoc Committee Appointed to Consider Certain Ethical Issues (1981) (Supplement to the *S.A. Medical Journal*, 22 August).

Reynolds, N. (1981): *Dairying as an Instrument for Rural Development in the Ciskei* (SALDRU Working Paper No. 34).

Selvan, D. (1976): *Housing Conditions for Migrant Workers in Cape Town 1976* (SALDRU Working Paper No. 10).

Shin, D.C. & D.M. Johnson (1978): 'Avowed Happiness as an Overall Assessment of the Quality of Life', *Social Indicators Research*, 5, 475-492.

Simkins, C. (1981a): *The Distribution of the African Population of South Africa by Age, Sex and Region-Type* (SALDRU Working Paper No. 32).

— (1981b): *The Demographic Demand for Labour and Institutional Context of African Unemployment in South Africa: 1960-1980* (SALDRU Working Paper No. 39).

Simkins, C. & C. Desmond (1978): *South African Unemployment: A Black Picture* (University of Natal, Development Studies Research Group).

Thomas, T. (1973): *Their Doctor Speaks* (M. Wheeldon).

— (1980): 'The Effectiveness of Alternative Methods of Managing Malnutrition', in F. Wilson & G. Westcott (eds): *Hunger, Work and Health* (Johannesburg, Ravan Press).

Tomlinson Commission (1955): *Summary of the Report of the Commission for the Socio-Economic Development of the Bantu Areas Within the Union of South Africa* (Pretoria, Government Printer).

Wet, C.J. de (1980): 'Betterment and Trust in a Rural Ciskei Village', *Social Dynamics*, 6, 2.

Wiener, N. (1973): *Cybernetics* (Cambridge, Mass., MIT Press).

Willsworth, M. (1979): 'Poverty and Survival: The Dynamics of Redistribution and Sharing in a Black South African Township', *Social Dynamics*, 5, 1.

— (1980): *Strategies for Survival* (Rhodes University, Institute of Social and Economic Research).

Wilson, F. (1972): *Migrant Labour to South Africa* (South African Council of Churches).

Westcott, G. (1977): 'Obstacles to the Development of Transkei Agriculture', in F. Wilson, A. Kooy & D. Hendrie (eds): *Farm Labour in South Africa* (Cape Town, David Phillip).

5 SOCIAL ACCOUNTING MATRICES FOR DEVELOPMENT. SOME COMPARATIVE OBSERVATIONS

J.J.P. van Heemst

I Introduction

The development of social indicator research took place alongside with, and in response to, the development of social accounting frameworks of diverse nature. Among these frameworks the construction of social accounting matrices (SAMs) has attracted increasing interest during the last decade. Interest in the compilation of this type of data system stems largely from growing dissatisfaction with the results of growth policies. These disappointing results, especially as regards their distributional aspects, gave rise to questions concerning the processes and mechanisms by which the production of goods and services and their distribution and redistribution related to each other. To examine these questions on an empirical basis data systems were needed that would provide detailed, consistent and coherent information in relation to the various aspects of the economic process. The models that were to be constructed with the help of these data systems were supposed not only to serve a mere analytical purpose, i.e. to shed light on the questions referred to above, but also to be useful in specific policy contents, i.e. as tools for assessing the distributional impact of different kinds of policy. The data frameworks that play a role in this connection, and which usually contain their data in a matrix format, are commonly referred to as SAMs.

SAMs have been constructed for a fair number of countries, and in most cases this has by no means been an easy task. The compilation of a SAM normally requires large amounts of resources of diverse nature together with a certain degree of courage and ambition.

The resulting matrices for those countries for which such an exercise has been undertaken have a number of major features in common, but at the same time differ in several respects. The features they share, among which is the main structure of the SAM, reflect to a greater or lesser extent the fact that they are addressed to the same broad questions. Their differences may reflect differences in the socio-economic structures of the countries the SAMs apply to, but are also often related to varying situations as regards the availability, scope and nature of the basic data needed for the SAM. These differences involve the kinds of classification applied, the kinds of sector, groups' transactions, activities and commodities distinguished, the degree of detail with which this is done, etc.

These various aspects, which characterize a SAM to a large extent, each play an important role in determining the SAM's applicability as a tool for analyzing economic processes and for the formulation of distribution-oriented policies. Given the fact that SAMs are now available for a number of countries, and in view of what has been said above about the differences between them, it is interesting to make a comparative analysis of their particular features. Such an exercise will not only give us an idea of the potential of the various SAMs as tools in the economic process, it will also indicate in more general terms what progress has been achieved in compiling a data framework which features important aspects of the economic process with particular reference to the distributive dimensions.

The purpose of this paper is to contribute to such to a comparative analysis by comparing certain characteristics of SAMs for eleven countries. The conclusions drawn from the analysis that follows should by no means be considered as representative for the existing stock of SAMs in general.

Section II of this paper, drawing on eleven SAMs, presents information on certain aspects relating to the characteristic components that constitute a SAM. This information may give an idea of the potential of individual SAMs. In Section III some evaluative remarks about our findings are made, referring to general properties that a SAM should possess for monitoring and analyzing processes of production, income generation and (re)distribution. Some attention is also given to the meaning of SAMs for the construction of social indicators and to the conducting of policy-oriented analysis based on social indicators.

Before proceeding to the actual analysis, we conclude with a schematic presentation of the characteristic components that constitute an 'average' SAM, thus providing a framework for the discussion in subsequent sections.

Table 1 presents the main structural elements that are typical of a SAM and which are found in most existing SAMs. It also assumes that the format of a SAM is a matrix.

The table basically consists of a set of rows and columns with the same headings, namely Factors of Production, Institutions, Production Activities, Commodities, External Transactions, plus a few headings for some totals. These headings relate to certain aspects of the economic situation that are considered of importance in the analysis of processes of production, income generation and (re)distribution. The concepts referred to in the five headings are of an aggregate nature, however. An actual SAM presents for most or all of these headings disaggregation according to sub-classifications that are assumed to be of analytical significance. Thus, productive activities are divided according to types of activity, as various kinds of agriculture, manufacturing activities, service activities, etc., while various degrees of refinement through the application of different links of sub-classifications may be used. In a similar way, factors of production are presented in a disaggregated form, for example according to different types of labour, of capital, etc. Institutions are usually divided into households, government sectors and enterprises, each being further subdivided, in particular the household sector. As far as commodities are concerned, their disaggregation follows a commodity classification. The various disaggregations outlined here, which typify a SAM, in most cases yield a matrix with a fairly large number of rows and columns.

The numbers presented in the cells of the matrix can be interpreted as the money values of transactions between the units indicated by the rows and columns. As such, the cells can be seen as accounts that can be read in their row context and in their column context. If read in the row context, the figures in the cells are assumed to imply a receipt for the units to which the row headings refer, while at the same time implying an expenditure for the units which relate to the column context of the cells.

From the above, the reader should have a broad idea of the nature and meaning of the data stored in a SAM. Supplementary information is given in the appendix to this paper.[1]

The various components of the 'average' SAM as outlined above can largely be found in most of the SAMs that have been compiled to date. There are variations, however. A number of SAMs do not include separate commodity accounts, while others do not include accounts for factors of production. On the other hand, sets of so-called satellite tables have sometimes been linked to the 'core' SAM, and may provide information on employment in relation to production activities, on the possession of land or other assets in relation to different groups of households, or on other socio-demographic aspects in relation to a certain group of units (i.e. household, productive activities, etc.) as identified in the 'core' SAM.

In addition, there is considerable variation in the number and types of (sub)classifications and (sub)divisions used in the main components of the SAMs, affecting their potential and possibilities for the policy-oriented modelling referred to earlier.

Table 1: Schematic Presentation of an 'Average' SAM

		Factors of Production	Institutions Current Transactions	Institutions Capital Transactions	Production Activities	Commodities	Total Domestic	Rest of World	Total
1. Factors of Production		-	-	-	Factor Incomes from Domestic Activities	-	Allocation of GDP by factors	Net factor income from abroad	Incomes of the factors of production
2. Insti-	Current transactions	Allocation of factor income to Institutions	Current transfers between Institutions	-	-	-	Income of Institutions before foreign transfers	Net non-factor income from abroad	Incomes of Institutions after foreign transfers
3. tutions	Capital transactions	-	Savings	Capital transfers between Institutions	-	-	Aggregate domestic savings	Net capital flows from abroad	Aggregate Savings
4. Production Activitities		-	-	-	-	Supply of Commodities by domestic activities	-	-	Gross outputs

5. Commodities	-	Expenditures on consumption commodities	Expenditures on capital goods	Expenditures on intermediate commodities	-	Total domestic expenditures on commodities	Export of commodities	Total expenditure on commodities
6. Total Domestic	-	-	-	-	Total Domestic supply of commodities	-	-	-
7. Rest of World	-	-	-	-	Imports	Imports	-	Imports
8. Total	Incomes of factors of production	Incomes of Institutions after foreign transfers	Aggregate investments	Gross inputs	Total supply of commodities	-	Total foreign exchange receipts	-

Source: This table is derived largely from Pyatt & Roe 1977: Table 2.6, but has been modified by the present author.

II Some Characteristics of Eleven SAMs

Introduction

In this section we shall present some numerical and qualitative information on the major components of the core SAM referred to above for the following countries: Iran, Sri Lanka, Swaziland, Philippines, Botswana, Fiji, Malaysia, Kenya, Thailand, Egypt and Indonesia.

The information comes from various sources.[2] If the existence of different versions of a particular SAM is indicated, i.e. referring to different levels of (dis)aggregation, the material presented here is based on the most disaggregated version for which the relevant information was available. In this connection it should be noted that on some of the SAMs discussed here, work on more elaborated and more disaggregated versions is in progress.[3] Our conclusions thus have a provisional and conditional character.

The discussion in this section is largely structured around Tables 2, 3 and 4 which relate to more general information for the eleven SAMs (Table 2), as well as to specific information on Factors of Production (Table 3) and Institutions (Table 4). In addition, some details are provided on Productive Activities, Commodities, and a few other features of the SAMs.

General Aspects

Table 2 gives an idea as to whether the eleven SAMs distinguish certain aspects of the economic process and, if so, the degree of detail in which this is done.[4] The aspects ('categories') referred to are Factors of Production, Institutions, Productive Activities and Commodities. The table indicates that Institutions and Productive Activities have been distinguished in all SAMs, although there is much variation in the degree of detail. For Institutions this ranks from three classes (Thailand), to fifty-one (Fiji). In the first case we are dealing with a first attempt at compiling a SAM mainly on the basis of existing national accounting data; in the second case we have a very disaggregated SAM, incorporating a relatively large number of dimensions for the classification of Institutions.

For Productive Activities the variation in number of classes is equally large, ranking from four (Thailand) to forty-eight (Sri Lanka). Not all SAMs refer explicitly to Factors of Production, e.g. Iran and Egypt. The Iranian SAM was among the first to be built. On the basis of this experience, its constructors decided to incorporate a Factors of Production section in subsequent SAMs to be built for other countries. Thailand's SAM uses no further subdivisions.

Table 2: General Information on Eleven SAMs: Major Categories and Number of Classes per Major Category

		(1)	(2)	(3)	(4)
		Main	Categories		
Country	Year of application	Factors of Production	Institutions	Productive Activities	Commodities
Iran	1970	-	14	12	-
Sri Lanka	1970	57	23	48	-
Swaziland	1971/72	9	10	26	44
Philippines	1972	3	5	12	-
Botswana	1974/75	8	13	15	-
Fiji	1977	8	51	38	54
Malaysia	1970	13	11	30	59
Kenya	1976	7	14	26	-
Thailand	1975	1	3	4	4
Egypt	1976	-	9	12	-
Indonesia	1975	3	4	10	-

Source: various publications, see Note 2.

Those SAMs that have a 'Factors of Production' section with further subdivisions, again show considerable variation in the number of classes distinguished, varying from three to fifty-seven. More details on this are presented in Table 3.

It may be noted that seven of the eleven SAMs do not have a separate section dealing with Commodities. This can usually be explained by lack of data on the supply of commodities by the various kinds of productive activities and through imports on the one hand, and on the use of commodities by institutional sectors on the other. In the case of the Sri Lankan SAM a matrix is used which links household expenditure on consumer commodities to activities and imports. However, this matrix is not integrated in the SAM itself. Except for Thailand, the SAMs that include a commodity section use a number of classes varying between forty-four and fifty-nine, in all cases exceeding the number of classes of Productive Activities.

Factors of Production

Table 3 provides more detailed information on 'Factors of Production' for eight of the eleven SAMs. For each of the three main types of factors of production it indicates into how many classes each type is further subdivided, and which criteria have been applied in making these subdivisions. The main types referred to are wage labour (I), self-employed labour (II), and Other (III). 'Other' relates to the operating

Table 3: Some Information on Eleven SAMs Related to 'Factors of Production'

COUNTRIES	Division I. Wage Labour II. Self-employed Labour III. Other	Number of Classes in each Division	Types of Criteria Used: Locational urban-rural distinction	Locational Other	Occupation and/or skill related	Educational Level	Distinction Foreign Domestic	Distinction Private Public	Other
Iran	n.a.	–							
Sri Lanka	I	27	x	x	x				
	II	27	x	x	x				
	III	3						x	
Swaziland	I	1							
	II	4		x					
	III	4					x		
Philippines	I	2	x						
	II	–							
	III	1							
Botswana	I	5			x		x		
	II	1							
	III[3]	2							
Fiji	I	5			x				x[1]
	II	1							
	III[3]	2							
Malaysia	I	7	x	x		x			
	II	–							
	III[3]	6		x					x[2]

Kenya	I	4			x				
	II	1							
	III	2							
Thailand	n.a.	–							
Egypt	n.a.	–							
Indonesia	I	2	x						
	II	–							
	III								
Total	I		4	2	4	1	1		1
	II		1	2	1				
	III			1			1	1	1

1. Distinction regular labour-casual labour
2. Distinction corporate capital-incorporate capital
3. Include row/column for depreciation

n.a. = not available

Source: Various publications, see Note 2.

surplus which encompasses the returns to all production factors not accounted for under I and II. Table 3 indicates in the first place that all eight SAMs with detailed Factors of Production accounts have 'wage labour' as a main sub-category; moreover, five of them have a sub-category relating to self-employed labour. In the other three cases, the data relating to this type of production factor have mostly been incorporated in the operating surplus, i.e. in 'Other'.

In comparing the numbers of classes into which each sub-category I and II are sub-divided, it will be seen that those for I, wage labour, are normally larger than for II and III. In some cases this fact merely reflects data availability and constraints, but in others it reflects a deliberate attempt by the SAM compilers to emphasize, for analytical reasons, a relatively far-reaching disaggregation of the factor labour (cf. Pyatt & Roe 1977: 59-60).

With regard to the criteria used for disaggregating the main sub-categories, Table 3 shows that for wage labour three types of criteria are used in the SAMs of Sri Lanka and Malaysia, but in other SAMs only one or two types are used. This does not mean that each class of a given sub-category (e.g. wage labour) is classified according to all the criteria used in the SAMs in question. It means rather that at least some classes are classified according to one or more of the criteria used. The row 'total' shows that locational criteria and criteria related to occupation and skill are more frequently used in the case of wage labour. The educational level used in the Malaysian SAM comes close to the skill/occupational criteria. The use of the distinction 'regular labour-casual labour' in the Fijian SAM is interesting. It points to a normally neglected dimension of labour demand and supply which may have important repercussions on the income earned during a certain period of time.

As we have said, the number of classes of the sub-categories 'self-employed labour' and 'others' is relatively small in most SAMs, implying that in most cases only one criterion per SAM is used to make some further sub-division. The criteria used in this regard vary, however, among the different SAMs.

It should also be noted that the Factors of Production accounts of the SAMs for Botswana, Kenya and Fiji include a row and column for depreciation, thus including the estimation of the net factor income generated.

In conclusion, Table 3 shows that in most cases the factor wage labour is more disaggregated than the other factors; among the criteria used in this connection is a certain preference for location criteria, especially the distinction urban-rural, and for criteria related to occupation and/or skill.

Institutions

Table 4 has a similar layout as Table 3, presenting similar kinds of information in relation to Institutions[5] as Table 3 does for Factors of Production. The main types of institutions distinguished are: households (A), enterprises (B), and government (C). All SAMs distinguish explicitly between these types, except those for Iran and Egypt which do not distinguish enterprises.

In most SAMs the number of classes subdividing the three main types is the largest for 'households', no doubt reflecting the wish of the compilers to be as detailed as possible (at least in relative terms) on the various groups of institutional units in the economy which are the ultimate subject of distributional analyses and policies, i.e. the households. At the same time, the SAMs show considerable variation as to number of classes distinguished, with a maximum for Fiji of forty-three. Table 4 also indicates that many household classes per SAM are related to a relatively large number of criteria. In the Fijian SAM, for example, eight criteria are used in relation to forty-three classes of households. The use of the urban-rural distinction is rather striking: it is used in ten of the eleven SAMs. Similarly, the income-class criterion is applied in seven of the eleven SAMs and may be considered a proxy for earning capacity, i.e. the economic potential of the household. To a certain extent the use of the 'farm size' criterion (i.e. the size of the farm to which the household is linked), the 'type of housing', the 'employment status/occupation of the main income earner of the household' and the 'subsistence income cash income' criteria may be seen as proxies for 'economic capacity of the household'. This could mean that in nine SAMs a classification is used that tries in one way or the other to characterize households according to economic capacity. In all nine cases this has been done in conjunction with an 'urban-rural' distinction. In only two cases, i.e. the SAMs for Fiji and Malyasia, has ethnicity served as a classification criterion, in both cases in combination with other criteria.

Moving to the second main type of institutions, enterprises, Table 4 shows that six of the eight SAMs which have a sub-classification for enterprises, use the distinction 'private-public' as the relevant criterion. In the case of Swaziland the size of the enterprise is also used. Furthermore, in the Egyptian SAM public sector enterprises are classified under government institutions, while private enterprises are not explicitly distinguished.

As regards 'government', the third main type of institution, three of the four SAMs using sub-divisions for this type make use of the distinction 'central-local'. In the case of Egypt, the three classes used refer to:

Table 4: Some Information for Eleven SAMs Related to 'Institutional'

Countries	Divisions: A-Households B-Enterprises C-Governmental	Number of Classes in each division	Types of Criteria Used: Locational: urban-rural distinction	Locational: Other	Income Class	Ethnicity	Household by farm size	Employment status main income earner	Distinction private/public	Distinction central/local	Other
Iran	A	3	x		x						
	B	–									
	C	1									
Sri Lanka	A	18	x	x	x						
	B	3							x		
	C	2								x	
Swaziland	A	6	x		x						
	B	3							x		x[1]
	C	1									
Philippines	A	2	x								
	B	2							x		
	C	1									
Botswana	A	9	x				x				x[2]
	B	3							x		
	C	1									
Fiji	A	43	x	x	x	x	x	x			x[3] x[4]
	B	5							x		
	C	3								x	
Malaysia	A	9	x	x		x		x			
	B	1									
	C	1									

Kenya	A	10	x		x		x				
	B	2							x		
	C	2								x	
Thailand	A	1									
	B	1									
	C	1									
Egypt	A	6	x		x						
	B	–									
	C	3									x[5]
Indonesia	A	2	x		x						
	B	1									
	C	1									
Total	A		10	3	7	2	3	2			3
	B								6		1
	C									3	1[5]

1. Size of enterprise
2. Type of housing of household
3. Distinction households with mainly subsistence income-households with mainly monetary income
4. Occupation of main income earner of household
5. For explanation see text

Source: Various publications, see Note 2.

(i) public sector enterprises, (ii) conventional government sector activities such as health facilities, education, defence, etc., and (iii) the government trading sector, which is of considerable significance in Egypt.

Thus, as to 'institutions' we may conclude that the majority of the eleven SAMs use the urban-rural criterion for classifying households together with a direct or indirect earning capacity criterion, in some cases complemented by other criteria. For 'enterprises', the 'public-private' distinction is commonly used for sub-classification; the 'central-local' distinction is used in those cases which have more than one government class.

Productive Activities and Commodities

With regard to 'productive activities' we have concluded on the basis of data given in Table 2 that the SAMs show considerable variation in the number of activities distinguished, i.e. in the degree of disaggregation. All SAMs, however, classify their activities mainly on the basis of the United Nations' International Standard Industrial Classification (ISIC), although a few SAMs have sub-classified according to other criteria. To be more precise, four SAMs (i.e. for Iran, Swaziland, Botswana and Kenya) use a sub-division for some of their activities according to the distinction 'modern-traditional'. This applies to the nature of the production technique with which the activity is carried out. In the Fijian SAM some activities are sub-classified according to the distinction 'commercial-subsistence', and others according to the origin of the inputs, i.e. imported vs. locally-produced.

The four SAMs that include commodity accounts classify these along the lines of United Nations' Standard International Trade Classification (SITC). Apart from this kind of classification, which can be applied at various levels of disaggregation, no other criteria are used for further sub-dividing the commodities distinguished according to the SITC.

Other Features

A few other aspects of some of the eleven SAMs are worthy of brief mention.

First, the Malaysian SAM incorporates a set of 'Wants' accounts, whose purpose is to indicate for the various household groups how much has been spent on the satisfaction of certain wants or needs (food, clothing etc.) through private expenditure on different types of commodities. As such, these accounts re-arrange the purchases of different types of commodities in terms of expenditure made to satisfy certain wants categories.

Second, a manpower matrix is associated with the Sri Lankan SAM which gives details of the various kinds of labour employed in the productive activities distinguished in this SAM.

Finally, the compilation of a set of 'consumption accounts' giving details of various groups of consumption items, including calorie and protein intakes, may be mentioned in connection with ongoing work on an elaborate version of the Indonesian SAM: a set of 'land accounts' giving details for various groups of ownership and use of land etc.; a set of 'manpower accounts'; a set of 'durable goods accounts', also related to various social groups; and a set of accounts which provide details on access to schooling by various social groups, in relation to government expenditure in this field.

III Some Evaluative Observations

Introduction

In this section some evaluative observations will be made that indicate the potential and limitations of the eleven SAMs presented above.

Certain requirements have repeatedly been formulated in the literature dealing with the compilation and application of SAMs, namely, the characteristics that a SAM should possess in order to be used effectively as a data system for models aiming at systematic assessment of the economic process with regard to production, income generation, and income (re-)distribution. These characteristics not only concern the various major categories 'factors of production', 'institutions' etc. which should be included, but also the ways in which these main categories should be sub-divided and the kinds of classification systems and criteria to be used in that connection. Our discussion of the eleven SAMs in the light of the general requirements (i.e. of which the applicability can be considered to have general validity) is organized according to the major components/categories constituting the standard SAM. We then go on to discuss the relation between SAMs and social indicator-oriented research.

In making the various evaluative points, we shall abstract from the specific reason(s) for which the eleven SAMs might have been built, while acknowledging that the presence or absence of certain categories, sub-systems, sub-divisions etc., is probably determined largely by data limitations.

Some General Requirements

Factors of Production. The rationale for incorporation in a SAM of accounts for factors of production is to show how the value added generated in various productive activities is channelled to the different kinds of institutions, especially to different groups of households, via the (different kinds of) factor services provided by each institutional group. In view of the significance of this aspect of the economic process, the fact that nine of the eleven SAMs try in one way or the other to make allowance for it should be seen as an attempt by their compilers to satisfy an important minimum requirement.

The factor 'labour' should obviously be among the major types of factors of production to be distinguished. This is the case in eight SAMs because the majority of those earning an income do so through the provision of this kind of factor service. The distinction made in some of the eleven SAMs between wage labour and self-employed labour is a welcome refinement.

Of the various sub-divisions of the factor labour that have been advocated the most outstanding are those according to type of labour (cf. Allen 1981: 6; Ward 1981: 24, 31; Pyatt & Roe 1977: 59-60) and location (cf. Pyatt & Roe 1977: 59-60). The sub-classification according to type, which may be specified by occupation, skill, level of education or a combination of these, is motivated by the consideration that the various kinds of productive activity, as well as the different technologies applied in each, require different types of labour. At the same time, different groups of households provide different types of labour. Thus, changes in activity output levels as well as changes in production techniques may have repercussions on income distribution among the various groups of households. As such, information on the link between income generated in production and income distributed over households will be required for a more penetrating analysis.

The sub-classification according to location, among other things is necessary to throw light on locational differences in remuneration received by (different types) of labour. A minimum distinction advocated in this connection is that between urban-located and rural-located labour.

In view of what has been said above regarding sub-classification for the factor labour, most of the SAMs examined here seem to leave scope for elaboration, at least when the location and type of sub-classifications are to be applied simultaneously. Table 3 shows that only two SAMs (Sri Lanka and Malaysia) do this, although four others apply a locational sub-division and five a sub-division according to type (including the Malaysian SAM which uses the level of education). Needless to say, it is not only the satisfaction of these requirements which indicates the potential of these SAMs, but also the extent to which the necessary degree of detail is met in this respect.

In connection with other major factors of production, it would obviously be desirable to distinguish not only the factor 'capital' but sometimes also 'land' as a separate factor, especially when land distribution is very uneven. From a statistical point of view, however, it is often very difficult to subdivide operating surplus into returns to capital and returns to land. This may be the reason why the distinction is not often made. Only two of the nine SAMs that make allowance for 'factors of production' refer explicitly to 'capital', and only one to 'land'. The majority apparently include the returns to both factors under the entry 'operating surplus' or 'other'.

Among sub-classifications that have been proposed for returns to capital or, in a somewhat wider sense, for the operating surplus, the distinctions between public and private ownership, and between domestic and foreign ownership should be mentioned (Ibidem: 59). The first has been applied in our sample in one case only (Sri Lanka), the second not at all. It might wondered whether these distinctions are of any use in view of the fact that they can equally be applied in connection with the institutional sectors (i.e. enterprises) that receive these factor returns.

Institutions. According to Ward (1981: 31) the institutional accounts should be split broadly into three categories: households, enterprises and government. This seems fairly obvious and is also rather conventional, considering that it had already been proposed in the early accounting systems of the 1950s, e.g. the final version of the United Nations system. It is hardly surprising, therefore, that almost all SAMs use this major subdivision of the institutional sectors.

The classification of households is generally considered to be of crucial importance: it should be comprehensive in the sense that it should not only include target groups from a policy point of view, but other groups as well, since policies dealing with target groups will inevitably have implications for other groups.[6]

Among the sub-classifications that should basically be applied in conjunction with each other in order to arrive at a meaningful disaggregation of households, the following are frequently mentioned: (i) location, incorporating at least the distinction urban-rural; (ii) economic, reflecting earning capacity in terms of wealth, but perhaps also in terms of labour type. In addition, a sociological classification to reflect ethnic or religious differences can be useful in certain circumstances.

The rationale for the sub-classification 'location' in the urban-rural distinction is that it reflects a fundamental dichotomy related to the concept of duality. As such, it catches a dimension of inequality in living standards which *a priori* is considered of great importance. In addition, and in more general terms, it seems justified on the grounds that policy often has a locational element, since the regional fragmentation of income opportunities is often of great significance.

The economic sub-classification, reflecting differences in earning capacity, is necessary in view of the great differences between households with regard to the ownership of factors that determine earning capacity, e.g. capital, land or type of labour, and lead in turn to income differences between households.

Finally, a classification according to ethnic or religious differences may be necessary to reflect differences in income opportunities (e.g. discrimination) or in expenditure habits of households.

We have observed earlier that nine SAMs use a classification which characterizes households in various ways according to their economic capacity; in all nine cases this is done in conjunction with an 'urban-rural' distinction, and sometimes with an even more detailed locational classification. In other words, attempts have been made in most cases to make the SAMs satisfy two crucial requirements related to the classification of households. Nevertheless, it is questionable whether the various proxies used adequately distinguish households according to earning capacity. This applies not only to the use of a classification based on income classes which, as outlined elsewhere (cf. Ward 1981: 48; Pyatt & Roe 1977: 57), suffers from various shortcomings, but also to most other kinds of proxies applied. However, the fact that most SAMs use a classification based on income classes seems indicative of the non-availability of more relevant alternative primary data.

With regard to the institutional category 'enterprises', the use of a sub-classification according to 'domestic control/ownership vs foreign control/ownership' has been recommended (cf. Ward 1981: 31, 50) and seems rather logical in view of a SAM's major objectives. The same can be said about the introduction of the distinction 'private vs public ownership/control' which, as we have seen, is fairly generally applied. Unfortunately the former type has not been applied in any SAM in connection with enterprises, in spite of its analytical importance, thus pointing to another area in which elaboration seems desirable.

Productive Activities and Commodities. With regard to the classification of productive activities, it has been advocated that disaggregation to a fairly fine commodity level should be aimed at, in order to achieve a high degree of homogeneity and activity-commodity correspondence (Ibidem: 24). Homogeneity should not only be aimed at with regard to their input structure, however. Within a given activity input structures may differ due to differences in technology, which has repercussions on the relative use of factors of production. To take this fully into account, it will be necessary to incorporate a technology dimension into the relevant cases in the sub-classification of activities. This has in fact been outlined by various authors (cf. Ibidem: 28, 58; Allen 1981: 12-13). This could be done by simply applying a modern-traditional dichotomy or a size criterion, e.g. large-small, since these may to some extent serve as proxies for the technology dimension.

When looking at the number of activities distinguished in the SAMs (Table 2), it is clear that the activity-commodity correspondence referred to above is usually not satisfied because the number is too small, indicating that the activities are too aggregated. This will affect the accuracy with which the relationship between commodities and activities may be analyzed.

Our earlier remarks on the 'modern-traditional' dichotomy in four SAMs should be considered as an attempt to refine the analysis of the relationship 'productive activity-input use'. This applies also to the distinction 'commercial-subsistence' in another SAM.

The use of commodity accounts in a SAM is advocated not only to explicate the supply of commodities by domestic activities on the one hand and through imports on the other, but also to show the relationship between the various groups of households and their expenditure on different kinds of commodities. As we have seen, only a few of the eleven SAMs incorporate commodity accounts using conventional commodity classifications, thus demonstrating a clear need for further elaboration of the majority.

SAMs and Social Indicators

With the help of appropriate indicators, Social Indicator Research attempts to assess the quality of life of various groups through measuring the various components that constitute welfare (cf. Drewnowski 1974, esp. Ch. 2). In this a 'flow of welfare' as well as a 'state of welfare' are considered, for both of which the satisfaction of their various components is realized in different ways. In the flow of welfare, for example, some components such as nutrition or clothing are satisfied through the consumption of certain goods (food, beverages, clothes, footwear, etc.) which are either supplied through the market or are produced for own use. Other components such as health or education are in most cases largely satisfied through the provision of collective goods by government. Again, other components, e.g. leisure or the social and physical environment, are satisfied through a variety of inputs which are partly of a material and partly of an immaterial nature, the provision of which may be the result of both collective and private activities.

What has a SAM to do with this? A 'standard' or 'core' SAM may contain information, usually in monetary terms, on some of the inputs involved in satisfying certain welfare components. For some of these components this information may be given for each of the household groups identified; for example, data on expenditure by the various household groups on such commodities as food, clothes, footwear, etc. which form the inputs for components like 'nutrition' and 'clothing'. Expenditure going into a component such as 'education' is given only as a total, so that the SAM shows no direct link with the recipient groups. In the case of 'leisure' or 'environment' components, information on inputs into their satisfaction will mostly be lacking in the core SAM, particularly when these inputs are of a non-economic character. Thus, the core SAM may provide information on the inputs that go into some of the welfare components as distinguished in Social Indicator Research, while only part of this information will be specified per group of households.

This is not intended to suggest that such information is meaningless or insignificant in relation to Social Indicator work; on the contrary. It should be realized, however, that it relates only to a subset of welfare components. Moreover, this information, which is mostly in money terms, cannot be interpreted directly in terms of welfare indicators. For this to be possible, a number of steps are necessary:

(i) the transformation from monetary values to physical units, provided the monetary data are in a sufficient degree of detail;

(ii) calculation of physical units per capita or per household for a given group;

(iii) transformation of these physical units into indicator values.

These operations could be performed and presented in an extended SAM framework[7] or in a set of satellite tables, but this obviously requires much additional data. Thus, on the basis of data in the core SAM and with the help of additional data on population, transformation coefficients, etc. it will be possible to calculate certain welfare indicators. This may then constitute a useful link between SAMs and Social Indicators.

Another link would be in connection with the estimation of welfare effect coefficients, as these have been referred to by various authors (e.g. Drewnowski 1974). By matching monetary data from a SAM to (independently estimated) indicator values of satisfaction of a certain welfare component, an idea might be obtained of the impact of changes in expenditure on the levels of satisfaction of certain (basic) needs; a numerical expression may then be found through calculation of a welfare effect coefficient. Once these coefficients have been calculated, the SAM can be used to analyze the impact of alternative policies on the levels of living of certain groups, taking into account the various interdependencies in the socio-economic system as a whole. Once again, however, such links between SAMs and Social Indicators are limited to a few welfare components only.

In the light of these remarks about the relationship between SAMs and Social Indicators, it is useful to examine whether 'our' SAMs have detailed commodity accounts or other kinds of data (either incorporated into the main framework or in satellite tables) which may provide a link with indicators for certain welfare components.

We have seen that only a few of the eleven SAMs provide detailed data on commodity expenditure by various groups of households. If this information is sufficiently detailed it might be used as a basis for further manipulation in the direction of cértain Social Indicators. But this will require additional data, and the sources consulted by us do not make it clear whether those data are actually available.

We have also seen that only a few SAMs cater for accounts, tables, etc. other than those that can be found in the 'average' or 'core' SAM. The 'wants' accounts, as present in the Malaysian SAM, are of some use since they re-arrange expenditure on commodities into expenditure on certain wants (i.e. welfare components). But more transformations and data are necessary if we are to come closer to Social Indicators. The manpower matrix associated with the Sri Lankan SAM is useful for certain purposes, but it remains to be seen how it can be used directly in relation to Social Indicators. Some of the accounts in the Indonesian SAM, now being prepared in connection with ongoing work on an extended version, seem of immediate interest to certain Social Indicators. This is certainly true for 'consumption' accounts, 'durable goods' accounts, and accounts on schooling. The information contained in these accounts seems to come close to what is actually required for the construction of certain Social Indicators.

As far as the majority of the eleven SAMs are concerned, however, we must conclude that they have neither sufficiently detailed commodity accounts, nor other kinds of data that seem of some direct relevance to Social Indicators.

Concluding Remarks

Above, we have evaluated some characteristics of the eleven SAMs in the light of certain general requirements, and have concluded that for the majority some elaboration would be desirable, along the following lines:

- the (simultaneous) use of sub-classification by type and by location for the production factor labour;
- the making of separate distinctions for other major factors of production such as capital and land;
- the use of adequate proxies for a household classification according to economic potential;
- the use of the distinction foreign vs domestic ownership control with regard to enterprises;
- the separate presentation of commodity accounts and activity accounts;
- the use of refined, disaggregated activity classifications corresponding to a commodity classification;
- the use of activity classifications that reflect differences in technology.

Furthermore, while observing in general that SAMs may play some role in connection with Social Indicators associated with certain welfare components, provided that sufficient supplementary data are available, we have concluded that in their present state most of the eleven SAMs do not lend themselves directly to such a role. In most cases considerable elaboration is required, together with additional data collection, processing, and integration into the existing frameworks.

Notes

1. For other detailed descriptions of the general SAM framework and its possibilities, the reader may consult Pyatt & Roe 1977, Pyatt & Thorbecke 1976, or King 1981.
2. The following sources have been consulted for the information presented here on the eleven SAMs: for Iran: Pyatt & Round 1977; for Swaziland: Allen 1981 and Pyatt & Round 1977; for the Philippines: Bull 1978; for Botswana: Allen 1981; for Fiji: Allen 1981; for Malaysia: Chander et al. 1980; for Kenya: Allen 1981; for Thailand: Grais 1980; for Egypt: Eckhaus et al. 1981; and for Indonesia: Keuning 1981.
3. For example, work on a more disaggregated version of the SAM for Indonesia referred to here is still in progress. Also, at the time of writing, a more elaborate SAM for Botswana was under construction.
4. The order in which the SAMs are presented in Tables 2 to 4 follows roughly the order of the years in which they were actually constructed.
5. Our focus of attention here is on the types of institutions distinguished

in the eleven SAMs and not so much on the various accounts included in connection with Institutions. In certain SAMs more than one type of account (i.e. current account, capital account) is presented for the types of institutions distinguished; in such cases the number of accounts relating to institutions will exceed the number of institutional classes.

6. For more discussion on classification principles in general *re* households, see Pyatt & Roe 1977: 56 and Allen 1981: 7, 8.

7. As far as nutrition is concerned, a Food Accounting Matrix (FAM) may be seen as an example illustrating such an extension.

References

Allen, R.M. (1981): 'Classification Systems for the Social Accounting Matrix; The Experience of Studies in Swaziland, Botswana, Kenya and Fiji' (Paper written for the 7th Conference of the International Association for Research in Income Wealth; Gouvieux, France, 16-23 August; mimeographed).

Bull, R. (1978): 'Social Accounts, Social Indicators and Development Planning', *Development and Change*, 9, 4 (October), 613-630.

Chander, R., S. Gnasegarah, G. Pyatt & J.I. Round (1980): 'Social Accounts and the Distribution of Income: The Malaysian Economy in 1970', *The Review of Income and Wealth*, 26, 1, 67-85.

Drewnowski, J. (1974): *On Measuring and Planning the Quality of Life* (The Hague, Mouton, for the Institute of Social Studies).

— (1979): 'Basic Needs and Social Indicators: A Suggestion for an Integrated Approach', *Labour and Society*, 4, 3 (July).

Eckhaus, R.S., F.D. McCarthy & A. Mohie-Eldin (1981): 'A Social Accounting Matrix for Egypt, 1976', *Journal of Development Economics*, 9, 2, 183-203.

Grais, W. (1981): 'Aggregate Demand and Macroeconomic Imbalances in Thailand Simulations with the SIAM I Model' (Washington, World Bank Staff Working Paper No. 448; April).

Keuning, S. (1980): 'An Aggregated Social Accounting Matrix for Indonesia 1975' (The Hague, Institute of Social Studies; mimeographed).

King, B. (1981): 'What is a SAM? A Layman's Guide to Social Accounting Matrices' (Washington, World Bank Staff Working Paper No. 463).

Pyatt, G. & A. Roe (eds) (1977): *Social Accounting for Development Planning, With Special Reference to Sri Lanka* (Cambridge, Cambridge University Press).

Pyatt, G. & I.J. Round (1977): 'Social Accounting Matrices for Development Planning', *The Review of Income and Wealth*, 23, 4 (December), 339-363.

Pyatt, G. & E. Thorbecke (1976): *Planning Techniques for a Better Future* (Geneva, ILO).

Ward, M. (1981): 'Limitations of the Social Accounting Matrix for Development Policy and Distribution Analysis' (Paper written for the 7th Conference of the International Association for Research in Income and Wealth; Gouvieux, France, 16-23 August; mimeographed).

Appendix

In this Appendix we present in rather more detail the meaning of the data stored in the various segments of the SAM. We do so by referring to the respective rows and columns number (1) to (6) in Table 1, and by discussing a number of intersections made by them.

Row 1 Related to the income received by the various factors of production. Thus, at the intersection of row 1 with column 4 we have the distribution of income between factors. Depending on the disaggregation of factors adopted, this will show the income of labour (of different kinds), i.e. wages, profits as a return on capital, and rental incomes of natural resources (such as land and mineral rights); and, at the intersection with column 4, its dependence of the various kinds of production activities. The intersection with column 7 shows the factor incomes received from abroad.

Col. 1 Shows how factor incomes are paid out to providers of the factors of production, i.e. institutions. For example, agricultural wages go to rural households, industrial wages go to urban households, and rental incomes to those institutions that own natural resources, etc. (intersection with row 2).

Row 2 The primary source of income for institutions is from factor services. There are also transfers between them: taxes paid to government; profits distributed by companies to shareholders (households); subsidies paid by government (intersection with column 2).

Aggregating all sources of income in the row we get the total income of each institution, and in particular the personal income distribution between different types of household.

Col. 2 Institutions pay out some of their incomes as transfers. For the rest they either save their income, or spend it on consumer commodities which can be either domestically-produced or imported (intersections with rows 3 and 5). Savings represent a transfer to their capital account.

Row 3 Institutions acquire capital funds in the first instance from their own savings. Beyond this there are transfers between them through savings institutions and capital markets (intersection with column 3). The total of funds available to the economy as a whole is increased by capital receipts from the rest of the world (intersection with column 7).

Col. 3 The funds acquired by each institution are in part transferred to other institutions as described above. Beyond this they are spent on capital goods supplied either by domestic production activities or by imports (intersection with row 5).

Row 4 Production activities receive money from the supply of different kinds of commodities, like consumer goods, capital goods and exports. They also receive revenue from the supply of intermediate commodities to other production activities. Together, these revenues make up the total sales or gross output of each of the production activities.

Col. 4 The sales revenue of each production activity is taken up in part by purchases of raw materials which may be either domestically produced or imported (intersection with row 5). The remainder of production costs takes the form of value added which is paid out to factors of production in the form of wages to different types of labour, rents on land and other natural resources, and profits as the reward of capital (intersection with row 1).

Row 5 The various types of commodities that are supplied are purchased and used by the different kinds of domestic institutions, as well as by the rest of the world. The values involved can be found in the intersections with columns 2, 3, 4 and 7).

Col. 5 The supply of the various types of commodities comes from domestic and from foreign resources. The domestic sources are the different production activities distinguished (intersection with row 4), the foreign sources are the rest of the world, which might also be further sub-divided (intersection with row 7).

Row 7 As indicated above, imports in the economy are allocated on the different commodity types distinguished.

Col. 7 Shows the various kinds of receipts from the rest of the world, e.g. factor incomes and non-factor incomes, capital flows, and receipts and commodity exports (intersections with rows 1, 2, 3 and 5).

From the above it can be concluded that a SAM may provide statistical information on the following aspects of the economic process:

- the link between various types of activities and different factors of production inasfar as the generation and distribution of the value added is concerned;
- the total factor income earned by the different factors of production;
- the distribution of factor incomes over the various types of institutions, including the different kinds of households distinguished;

- the redistribution of income among institutions;
- the relationship between expenditures on different types of commodities and the various kinds of institutions;
- the relationship between the use of different types of intermediate commodities and outputs of various productive activities;
- the relationships between the different types of commodities supplied and the different sources of supply, i.e. the kinds of domestic productive activities, and imports from abroad;
- the savings patterns of, and capital transfers between, institutions.

This list can be considered as relating to a number of data sets that are essential ingredients for the construction of numerical models whose aim is to portray simultaneously and coherently in monetary terms the productive, distributive and re-distributive dimensions of the economic process, as a system as a whole, and as a set of interrelated sub-systems.

PART TWO

SOCIAL PLANNING AND DEVELOPMENT

INTRODUCTION

I As we have observed earlier, social indicators were first developed to provide information for the planning of social services. Correa's contribution is a straightforward example of this line of thought. He provides an economist's methodology with which to reduce a great variety of information in such a way that decision makers can make a choice. He also provides support for Koskiaho's statement in Chapter 10 that social indicator research must sometimes twist available data to suit the purpose at hand. Koskiaho says this in the framework of a discussion of the usefulness of social indicators for the interpretation of reality. She has an important point here, and Correa is aware of it. But whereas Koskiaho tends towards the conclusion that as long as problems of interpretation remain one should refrain from using them, Correa inclines in another direction.

Correa's paper could be seen as a courageous attempt to find a way out of a dilemma that bothers all planners. All decision makers require a certain amount of information in order to function properly and they want the available quantitative and qualitative data to be presented in such a way that they can respond to the problems they are expected to solve. Within the framework of the dominant paradigm on the role of the state and the functioning of the bureaucracy, the planner's role is to provide the reduction in information variety that is required by the decision maker. Planners, in turn, have to cope with a shortage of data; more often than not, they are also aware of the lack of necessary insight into reality which would provide the principles on which to bring cohesion and order to the information available. As it is, if planners do not perform at all, decision makers can only provide correct choices by chance; on the other hand, if they do perform, they will certainly cause decision makers to make mistakes. Thus, whatever choice the *planner* makes, the result is unlikely to be satisfactory.

This dilemma appears in various of the following papers, but the authors seem to ignore the question of whether decisions taken with the aid of planners are worse than those made without them and without a certain degree of quantification. Correa is clearly of the opinion that decision making with planners and a certain amount of quantification would be less faulty than without. Wolfe, in Chapter 8, has a different opinion. In his view, the Latin American data base is so untrustworthy that, in general, the use of quantitative information would cause serious misinterpretation of reality. However, he does assign a role to planners. If we read him correctly, he considers that they should provide qualitative analysis and policy options based on such analysis. His own paper is an example of what will result if this is done.

II Sovani, similar to Wolfe and Correa, departs from the same paradigm on the role of the state. To them, planning for social development is basically a matter in the hands of the state and decisions on issues related to it should be made by the government. To Van Nieuwenhuijze and Koskiaho this is not altogether obvious, apparently due to the circumstance that their analyses move on another plane. They raise the more basic issue of development as such and of social development as part of it. Whereas for the first three this is beyond dispute, the other two, by bringing out explicitly the objectives of development, can take the role of the state as a variable. But whereas Van Nieuwenhuijze, given his point of departure, concludes that development must be socioculturally relevant, Koskiaho, who speaks from her position as a Scandinavian, goes a good deal further. Van Nieuwenhuijze, whose concern is with development in the First, Second and Third Worlds, starts from the influence that the First World has had on the others. Koskiaho takes her investigation from the question of why certain values in the West could become so predominant: the work ethic, the stress on the individual's welfare, and so on. Both, however, seem to question the heavy emphasis on the material aspects of welfare in Western values and both focus their investigation on social development. For Koskiaho this confronts us in the first instance with the idea that the logic of the state is no longer coherent with that of individuals, and secondly, with the contradiction that whereas the state provides public goods, individuals want more participation in a society's political, economic and social resources. This contrasts sharply with Sovani's view that the masses of the poor in developing countries are so uneducated and backward that they have motivations and values which are not conducive to social development. Casteism and other disintegrative aspects of society are so strong that public participation remains little more than a dream of social planners. For Sovani, a sense of despair would be more apt than the optimism that Correa is able to show.

III Sovani is of the opinion that UN thinking on social development has strongly influenced social planning concerns in developing countries. For Koskiaho, this thinking contains elements from Eastern and Western philosophy, but she seems to pass over the points made by Sovani and Van Nieuwenhuijze on the relevance of certain external influences to a Third World country's development. Whereas Van Nieuwenhuijze criticizes economism, Sovani questions the relevance of social planning understood as social services planning, considering that the emphasis ought to be on social development as change in social structures and institutions, and attitudes and motivations. To Sovani, with his Indian background, the stress on social services planning is in imitation of developed market economies; in his words it 'amounts to nothing more than a slightly better distribution of poverty and shortages which has hardly any regenerative effect'. It is not clear, however, what distresses Sovani most: the fact that a Western example is so easily introduced; the fact that so many people are so uneducated that they don't know what is good for them, or the fact that the bureaucracy which should execute the social services plans is unable to function properly.

Behind Sovani's stinging criticism of social planning and social planners, there seems to lurk a more important question. If present-day India does not have the social institutions and structures nor the attitudes and motivations on which social planning should concentrate, and if the Western model is not to be imitated, whither should India move?

To Wolfe also, the question of development alternatives is basic. In his view, however, the beholder of Latin American reality should not make the choice, but should judge the feasibility and effectiveness of such alternatives. He sees two alternatives concerning societies that are basically Western, and thus the points raised by Sovani and Van Nieuwenhuijze do not pose themselves in any obvious manner. The choices that Wolfe speaks of are within the existing set of values of the West and concern two strategies: a first that implies that, through solidarity, the poor should reach for a new social order; and a second that places responsibility for solving the problems of the poor on those who support the existing social order.

The point made by Sovani on the uneducated masses also appears in Koskiaho's paper when she speaks about the relevance of quality of life indicators. Thus, she says that, 'the less educated the people considered, the more concise is their degree of consciousness'. Leaving aside the obvious conclusion that more education would seem to be called for, a differentiation seems to be implied. The reference to 'less educated' seems to point to the existence of 'more educated' and therefore of elites, if not with political then at least with other power. The conclusion that this leads her to will be taken up below, but at this point it is perhaps interesting to note that later in her paper she in fact distinguishes not one but two elites: those who lead society on to new values and new life styles, and those who want to maintain the existing situation. The latter provides the logic of government bureaucracies, whereas the former make it increasingly irrelevant. This distinction also seems to be implied in Wolfe's two groupings of development alternatives, as put forward by various researchers in Latin America.

IV Wolfe's argument against the use of quantitative information is of a practical nature and does not touch the principle. Koskiaho's questioning of its usefulness is of a more basic nature. With regard to social indicators, her position is that their use is acceptable in periods of societal construction, when the logic of societal measures is congruent with the logic of people's lives. The relevance of quality of life indicators is much reduced, in her opinion, since answers to questions on people's opinions, assessments and attitudes are not independent of one another, of current ideas, or of the people's degree of education. The results are superficial. On the basis of this argument Ellis's contribution would fall into this category. Instead, social indicators should be measured in association with interpretive qualitative studies of a population's life.

This, as well as other critical observations by Koskiaho and other authors in this volume, seems to be besides the point. Social indicators as such were introduced first and foremost as tools for planners. Only in the second instance did they become part of the information needed by social scientists for epistomological purposes. Not only did their limitations for such purposes become apparent, but also the misnomer that the expression 'social indicator' really is. These latter views are not contested here. What *is* contested is that the proponents of social indicator research would have proposed even more than they did, namely, that social indicators are meant as a basically simple reduction of information on social services by which decision-making on these services can be improved. If more meaning than this is attached to them, this would seem to be erroneous; if less value is attached to them, it would seem to be forgotten that their introduction in planning organizations around the world has contributed significantly to the provision of social services to those who previously had had to go without them, and to those who had come to depend on them.

6 AN OPERATIONAL MODEL FOR THE OPTIMUM ALLOCATION OF RESOURCES TO SOCIAL EXPENDITURES

Hector Correa

I Introduction

This paper deals with the use of social indicators for social planning. More precisely, a model for the optimal allocation of social expenditures, closely related to that presented by Drewnowski (1974), is developed and applied to a sample of about twenty countries.

For the development of the model, a social welfare function must first be specified. This means that a system of weights evaluating the impact of the chracteristics of the social processes on wellbeing must be determined. Drewnowski (1974) suggests that these weights should be established by the planners themselves, according to their preferences. The methodology needed to obtain them from observations of actual behaviour is presented below and applied to the sample of countries.

Next, the constraints to the optimization of the social wellfare function are specified. Drewnowski (1974) considers as constraints the interdependence of social factors among themselves, of economic factors among themselves, and finally, among social and economic factors. In the presentation below, only the interdependence among social factors and the limitation imposed by the scarcity of financial resources are considered. The method used for this can easily be applied to the analysis of the other types of interdependence; however, this would have extended this paper beyond reasonable limits.

II Specification of the Models

To specify this model, it is necessary: (1) to define social expenditures; and (b) to specify the social welfare function and the constraints to the maximization of this function to be used. These problems are solved below.

No attempt will be made here to define precisely the term 'social expenditures', since this definition is not required either for the presentation or for the application of the method to be described. The intuitive idea conveyed by the fact that the total of individual plus government expenditures on goods and services used to improve the nutritional, health, educational, etc. status of a population can be considered typical social expenditures is sufficient for the purposes of this paper. Drewnowski (1966, 1974), Drewnowski & Scott (1966) and Higgins (1971), among other authors, also include nutrition, health and education among the social factors that influence social wellbeing.

The well-known problems of aggregation of individual preferences will also be assumed away. In the analysis below, a social welfare function will be used. This is unacceptable from the point of view of pure logic. However, keeping in mind that there is always a gap between thought and reality, estimates of social welfare and of its dependency on the states that determine it are likely to be useful for actual planning and policy analysis.

More specifically, it will be assumed that an index of the wellbeing in a community can be derived from the wellbeing of a representative individual. To study the wellbeing of an individual, its utility function, as studied in the theory of consumer behaviour, can be used. For the operational model, it will be assumed that this utility function can be written as:

$$U = P_i^n X_i^{a_i} \quad (1)$$

where:

U denotes utility

P denotes product

X_i i = 1,..., n are indices of status that elicit wellbeing, and

a_i constant elasticities of U with respect to X_i.

In the numerical example below, only three determinants of wellbeing will be considered: X_1 will denote nutritional intake measured in calories per capita, X_2 health status measured with life expectancy at birth, and X_3 educational status measured with years of education completed.

It should be observed that the arguments of the utility function 1 are indices of states that elicit wellbeing and not, as in the usual case, quantities of goods and services consumed. This approach is also used by Fox (1974) and Lancaster (1971). It seems to have more intuitive appeal. It seems clear that a person's wellbeing does not depend on the amount of health services he or she buys, but on the health status that he or she enjoys. Similar examples can be presented for the other arguments of the function in 1.

On the other hand, the resources available limit directly the amount of goods and services consumed, and only through them, the states that elicit wellbeing. As a consequence, to relate status and resources it is necessary, first, to relate status with goods and services consumed. Three approaches can be used for this.

First, one may use a relationship of the form:

$$X_i = b_i V_i \quad i = 1,\ldots, n \tag{2}$$

where:
b_i denotes parameters; and
V_i denotes amounts of goods or services 'type' i used, i.e. for the model used here:
V_1 amount of food intake
V_2 amount of health services used, and
V_3 years of education acquired.

Second, a relationship of the form:

$$X_i = S_j b_{ij} V_{ij} \quad i = 1,\ldots, n \tag{3}$$

where:
S denotes sum, and the
b_{ij} are parameters

perhaps has more intuitive appeal than equation 1 because it reflects the interdependence among the determinants of wellbeing. In this case it is assumed that, say, health status depends not only on health expenditures, as in equation 1, but also on expenditures on the goods and services that contribute to nutrition, education, etc. However, some reflection shows that the health status of an individual is likely to be influenced directly by his/her nutritional and educational status, but not by expenditures on food and education. This means that a more acceptable presentation of the interdependence between states that determine wellbeing and expenditures is the following:

$$X_i = S_{h \neq i} d_{ih} X_h + d_{ii} p_i V_i \; . \tag{4}$$

where
d_{ij} i. j = 1,..., n, denote parameters, and
p_i denotes price of goods and services type i.

The relationships in 2 and in 4 will be used below. It will be assumed that the relationships in 2 are those used in actual practice when no well-identified and explicit efforts are made to consider the interdependences among the determinants of wellbeing reflected in 4. If this point of view is applied to the level of one individual, it means that individuals do not act with perfect information and complete rationality, and this is reasonable for a practical application. It also seems acceptable to apply the assumption above to government allocations of resources to social expenditures.

In a complete analysis of the relationship between the goods and services V_i and resources used to produce them, both real and financial resources should be considered. For instance, human work, capital goods and financial resources are used to produce education. In this presentation, only the relationship of the V_i with financial resources will be considered. More specifically, the constraint to be used is

$$S_i p_i V_i = I \tag{5}$$

where I denotes financial resources available for social expenditures.

The equations above make it possible to give three alternative forms to the problem of optimal allocation of social expenditures.

The first form is the optimization of the utility function in 1 subject to the constraints in 2 and in 5. As already mentioned, it is assumed here that this approach is used by individuals and governments unless they make explicit efforts to consider the interdependence of the wellbeing-producing states, as in 4.

With the method of Lagrange multipliers, it can easily be shown that, according to the first order conditions for the maximization,

$$X_i = a_i b_i I / p_i \, . \tag{6}$$

From equation 6 it follows that

$$a_i = p_i V_i / I \, , \tag{7}$$

i.e. the parameters a_i of the utility function in 1 are equal to the proportion of expenditures on goods and services of type i with respect to total expenditures. This result will be used later.

It should be observed at this point that the decision rule in equation 6 specifies the condition for the maximization of wellbeing subject to the implicit constraints of the existing distribution of income and of the level of monopoly or competition that exists in the political and economic environments in which the decisions are made.

In the second form of the problem of optimal allocations of social expenditures, the utility function in 1 is maximized subject to the constraints in 4 and 5. This means that the two forms of the problem differ in the first constraint used in them.

The process of obtaining the mathematical solution of this problem is simplified with the following approach. First, the constraint 4 is written as

$$p_i V_i = X_i/d_{ii} - S_{h \neq i} d_{ih} X_h/d_{ii} \ . \tag{8}$$

Next, adding over i the equations in 8, one obtains

$$S_i c_i X_i = I \tag{9}$$

where

$$c_i = 1/d_{ii} - S_{h \neq i} d_{hi}/d_{hh} \tag{10}$$

With the transformations above, the optimization of 1 subject to 4 and 5 reduces to that of maximizing 1 subject to 9. The use of Lagrange multipliers shows that the optimal values of the X_i are obtained with the equation

$$X_i = a_i I/c_i \ . \tag{11}$$

Once the values of the X_i are obtained with equation 11, those of the social expenditures can be obtained with equations 8.

These two approaches, i.e. those that lead to the decision rules in equations 6 and 11, solve, at least at a theoretical level, and without much novelty, the problem of optimal allocation of resources to social expenditures. It remains now to consider the application of these results in actual planning and policy-making problems. This topic will be discussed below.

III Application of the Models in Section II to Actual Planning and Policy Making Problems

III.1 Selection of the Model to be Applied

The first question to be considered when dealing with the application of the models in Section II to actual planning and decision-making problems refers to the choice between the decision rules presented in equations 6 and 11.

From an intuitive point of view, it seems that the conditions that lead to the decision rule in 11 are more appropriate to planning and policy-making. The reason for this is that it is derived taking into consideration the interdependence among the determinants of wellbeing.

The main reason for the attention paid to the constraints in 2 which lead to the decision rule in equation 6 is that they seem to be those currently taken into implicit or explicit consideration in most countries of the world. As a consequence, equation 7 can be used to estimate the parameters a_i of the utility function in 1. With this, the problem of applying the decision rule in equation 11 is greatly simplified. More specifically, combining equations 7 and 11, one obtains

$$X_i = p_i V_i / c_i \ , \tag{12}$$

and the values of p_i, V_i and c_i can easily be obtained from actual data. Once the optimal values of X_i are computed with 12, the optimal values of expenditures, when the interdependences of the determinants of wellbeing are considered, can be evaluated with equations 8. With this, only the problems of collection and analysis of data remain to be solved.

III.2 Method to Estimate the Parameters of the Model

In order to use the model for actual planning or policy-making, it is necessary to estimate the values of the parameters in its equations. The solution given to this problem will be presented in this Section. More specifically, the approach used to estimate the parameters in the system formed by equations 1 and 4 will be described below. The estimation of the parameters in equations 2 and 3 is not considered because they are not used in this analysis. The estimation problem does not affect equation 5 because it does not include any parameters to be evaluated from statistical data, since it is an accounting identity.

The first possibility that should be considered is the simultaneous estimation of the parameters in 1 and 4. However, standard econometric methods do not seem to be appropriate in this case, since an index of the endogenous variable U is not available. For this reason, the parameters in equation 1 and those in equation 4 will be evaluated separately.

Correa & Kim (1974) have suggested the use of the method of principal components analysis to estimate the parameters of a utility function like the one in 1. However, unpublished studies based on montecarlo methods have shown that the approach does not produce acceptable results.

Two alternative approaches are based on equation 7. The first is simply to use as estimates of the parameters a_i in equation 1, in a specific country, region or income level, the observed proportions of expenditures associated with state i to total expenditures. As observed, these estimates are based on the assumption that the constraints in equation 4 are not considered while allocating resources for social expenditures, but depend on the level of competition that influences the decision-making units and the characteristics of the existing distribution of income. It is also assumed in this case that the observed values of the proportion of expenditures do not include any sampling errors.

In the second method, this assumption is eliminated. In this case, the estimates of a_i are obtained by minimizing with respect to the a_i the sums

$$S_i S_j (f_{ij} - a_i)^2$$

where

f_{ij} denotes the proportion of expenditures i observed in sampling unit j, subject to the constraint

$$S_i a_i = 1 \ .$$

The first method mentioned will be used below. For this reason, no additional analysis of the second method will be made here.

It is useful to observe that the approach suggested above to estimate the parameters of a utility function is conceptually identical to that used in references by Correa (1963, 1970), Denison (1962), Solow (1957), Tinbergen (1959) and others to estimate the parameters of a production function in order to evaluate the contribution of changes in productivity to increments of production.

The system of equations in 4 includes n equations and 2n variables, the n, X_i and the n, V_i. This means that the system by itself is not completely specified. For this, n of the variables should be considered exogenous. It also happens that this condition, i.e. that n of the variables are considered exogenous, is needed to obtain identifiability for the estimation of the parameters of the equations. It will be assumed below that the V_i are exogenous variables. It can easily be verified that, with this, the order condition for exact identifiability is satisfied. As a consequence, it is acceptable to use ordinary least squares to estimate the parameters in equations 4. This method will be applied below.

III.3 Data Used

Countries were selected as units of analysis for application of the models in Section II. The main reason for this is that data for such units are systematically collected by the U.N. and other international organizations. It should be observed, however, that other units such as income groups, could also be used as units, and that at least in some cases, data are available for them.

It was possible to find all the information needed for only the following twenty-two countries: Australia, Austria, Finland, Ghana, Greece, Honduras, India, Israel, Italy, Japan, Korea, Norway, Panama, Sierra Leone, Spain, Sri Lanka, Sudan, Sweden, Thailand, Togo, UK, and USA. Using information published by the World Bank, they were divided into four groups, namely, low income, low middle income, high middle income, and industrialized countries.

The model in Section II, and the method presented in Section III.2 to estimate the parameters in its equations, can be applied to the study of the allocations of resources among any number of determinants of wellbeing. Due to limitations on the availability of data, the analysis below is limited to only the three determinants mentioned above, namely, nutritional status measured with calorie intake, health status measured with life expectancy at birth, and educational status measured with years of education achieved by the population of 25 years of age and over. In addition to these data, information on the corresponding expenditures, i.e. on food, health and education, was collected. The main sources of data were the UN *Compendium of Social Statistics* and the UN *Yearbook of National Accounts Statistics*.

A first limitation of the data can be mentioned here. The health and education indices measure stocks, while the nutritional index, and all of the information on expenditures, measure flows. The mismatch becomes clear when it is considered that only by stretching one's imagination can it be said that expenditures on health and education made during one year influence the life expectancy at birth of a population or the average number of years of education completed. No attempt will be made here to solve the problems generated by this mismatch. All that can be said is that additional thought is needed about them.

The lack of comparability of the data results in a second type of problem. The different qualities of the years of education completed constitute an example of this. The differences in the type of services that can be purchased with a given amount of expenditure constitute a second example. Clearly, expressing expenditures in a common monetary unit such as dollars is only a very rough preliminary correction. Unfortunately, very little additional information that could be used to improve comparability is available.

Since preliminary analysis showed that the price differences seemed to introduce important distortions in the results, an attempt was made to use UN cost of living indices in different cities of the world as guidelines to make otherwise arbitrary corrections of the expenditure data.

III.4 Results

Two sets of results are presented in this Section. The estimates of the parameters in equations 8 and 9 are presented in Table 1, while the estimated optimal values of the determinants of wellbeing and of the amounts of financial resources that should be spent on the goods and services associated with them are presented in Table 2. These two tables are analyzed below.

Table 1: Estimates of the Parameters of Equations in 8 and 9

Dependent Expenditures on	Nutrition	Explanatory Health	Education
	Low Income Countries (N = 5)		
Food	.072345		-.319206
Health	-.001214	.082072	
Education	-.002074		18.241518
Total	.069057	.082072	17.922312
	Low-Middle Income Countries (N = 4)		
Food	.106823		
Health		.323535	-10.706667
Education	-.004117	-.117233	28.759577
Total	.102706	.206302	18.052910
	High-Middle Income Countries (N = 4)		
Food	.313928		
Health		1.372150	-13.125362
Education		-.400230	37.711592
Total	.313928	.971920	24.586230
	Industrialized Countries (N = 9)		
Food	.431724		
Health		5.022100	-3.975013
Education		-.292782	63.811714
Total	.431724	4.729318	60.714701

To interpret the results in Table 1, it should be observed that it does not include the regression estimates of the coefficients of equations 4; instead, the results have been obtained giving to these equations the form in 8. In this form of the equations, expenditures appear as the explained variable.

For further analysis, let us consider as an example the first equation in Table 1. According to this equation, the expenditures on food will increase with caloric intake, and decrease with increases in the number of years of education. This simply indicates that education has a positive effect on nutritional status.

From the interpretation just given to the positive and negative coefficients in Table 1, it follows that nutritional status is an important determinant of the conditions of health and education in the low income countries. This role disappears at higher levels of development, in which a clear interaction between health and education becomes evident.

At this point it should be emphasized that the results in Table 1 have a very limited reliability, due to the size of the groups used to obtain them and the arbitrary corrections made on the data. Despite the restricted confiability of the results, however, it should be observed that they seem quite reasonable from an intuitive point of view.

The results obtained for levels of the determinants of wellbeing and resources that should be used in them for each of the four groups of countries considered in the analysis, are presented in Table 2.

Information about the levels of caloric intake, health and education appears in the first three columns of Table 2, while that dealing with expenditures appears in the last three columns. Actual data appear in columns (A) and (D), while the results computed with formula 12 appear in column (B) and those obtained with the information in column (B) and in Table 1 appear in column (E). Comparisons of actual and computed values appear in columns (C) and (F). Finally, in the row corresponding to the totals of the right-hand side, it can be verified that the results simply suggest a redistribution of resources among the different expenditures.

The results for the low income and the low middle income countries suggest a shift of resources towards food, even with some detriment to health and education in the first group, and only to education in the second group. The improvement of health conditions in the low-middle-income countries could simply be the result of a level of education that is more in balance with their conditions.

The results suggest different policies for the high-middle-income and the industrialized countries. In these two groups of countries, some of the resources used for health should be shifted toward education, with the result that the levels of both health and education will tend to improve, as a consequence of the interaction among them.

Table 2: Averages of Data and Results for Four Groups of Countries

	Levels			Expenditures (Dollars Per Capita)		
	Actual Values (A)	Computed Values (B)	100*B/A (C)	Actual Values (D)	Computed Values (E)	100*E/D (F)
Low Income Countries						
Calories	2070.50000	2166.46760	104.63500	149.60975	156.60885	104.67824
Life Expectancy	53.00000	49.95918	94.26261	4.10025	1.47016	35.85534
Years Education	1.68100	0.38922	23.15417	6.97575	2.60674	37.36357
Total				160.68575	160.68575	100.00000
Low Middle Income Countries						
Calories	2354.50000	2243.41810	95.28215	230.41250	239.64865	104.00853
Life Expectancy	57.25000	66.05123	115.37332	13.62650	8.36575	61.39323
Years Education	2.39550	1.21459	50.70267	21.92675	17.95135	81.86061
Total				265.96575	265.96575	100.00000
High Middle Income Countries						
Calories	2987.00000	2808.56920	94.02642	881.68851	881.68851	100.00000
Life Expectancy	72.00000	89.68022	124.55586	87.16200	54.27428	62.26829
Years Education	4.58025	5.24027	114.41014	128.83850	161.72624	125.52633
Total				1097.68900	1097.68900	100.00000
Industrialized Countries						
Calories	3311.88890	2918.94620	88.13539	1260.17910	1260.17910	100.00000
Life Expectancy	73.44444	63.60255	86.59953	300.79667	290.94386	96.72443
Years Education	6.04600	7.16337	118.48115	434.92189	438.48526	100.81931
Total				1995.89770	1989.60820	99.68488

Table 3: Data and Results for Selected Countries

Countries		Levels			Expenditures (Dollars Per Capita)		
		Actual Values (A)	Computed Values (B)	100*B/A (C)	Actual Values (D)	Computed Values (E)	100*E/D (F)
Sudan	Calories	2067.00000	2353.46160	113.85881	162.52300	170.09191	104.65713
	Life Expectancy	46.00000	63.85856	138.82296	5.24100	2.38390	45.48555
	Years Education	0.37500	0.53029	141.41033	2067.00000	2353.46160	113.85881
	Total				177.26800	177.26800	100.00000
Ghana	Calories	2302.00000	2529.97880	109.90351	259.84400	270.25993	104.00853
	Life Expectancy	48.00000	63.69303	132.69382	13.14000	4.35202	33.12037
	Years Education	0.56700	1.51820	267.76084	2302.00000	2529.97880	109.90351
	Total				300.39200	300.39200	100.00000
Spain	Calories	3187.00000	3698.05500	116.03561	1160.92300	1160.92300	100.00000
	Life Expectancy	73.00000	125.15536	171.44570	121.64100	90.09398	74.06547
	Years Education	3.78300	6.21986	164.41617	3187.00000	3698.05500	116.03561
	Total				1435.48700	1435.48700	100.00000
Australia	Calories	3339.00000	3793.50920	113.61214	1637.74900	1637.74900	100.00000
	Life Expectancy	72.00000	87.15591	121.04987	412.18800	401.43098	97.39026
	Years Education	6.96600	9.12568	131.00317	3339.00000	3793.50920	113.61214
	Total				2604.00000	2604.00000	100.00000
Sweden	Calories	3033.00000	3955.49010	130.41510	1707.68000	1707.68000	100.00000
	Life Expectancy	75.00000	113.32903	151.10537	535.96900	524.74934	97.90666
	Years Education	6.60600	11.16986	169.08666	3033.00000	3955.49010	130.41510
	Total				2921.82400	2921.82400	100.00000

Table 3 includes information about a selected group of countries. They deserve special attention because the results obtained for them show that, within the limits imposed by current expenditures, it is possible to redistribute the expenditures so that levels of nutrition, health and education increase simultaneously. This result is a direct and actual consequence of the interdependence among the determinants of wellbeing. As a consequence of this interdependence, a transfer of resources from, say, health to nutrition may improve the nutritional status and, through it, the health status.

IV Conclusions

This paper suggests a method by which to obtain rather precise results on the optimal allocation of resources for balanced social development. The method itself and its application serve to show, on the one hand, that some promising results have been obtained, and on the other, that critical areas need additional exploration. This is particularly true with respect to the characteristics of the data used.

References

Correa, H. (1963): *The Economics of Human Resources* (Amsterdam, North Holland).

Correa, H. & S.B. Kim (1974): 'Statistical Estimation of Utilities', *De Economist*, 122, 5, 399-409.

— (1970): 'Sources of Economic Growth in Latin America', *The Southern Economic Journal*, 37, 1 (July).

Denison, E.F. (1962): *The Sources of Economic Growth in the United States and the Alternatives Before Us* (New York, Committee for Economic Development).

Drewnowski, J. (1966): *Social and Economic Factors in Development* (Geneva, United Nations Research Institute for Social Development).

— (1972): 'Social Indicators and Welfare Measurement: Remarks on Methodology', *Journal of Development Studies*, 8, 801-821.

— (1974): *On Measuring and Planning the Quality of Life* (The Hague, Mouton, for the Institute of Social Studies).

Drewnowski, J. & W. Scott (1966): *The Level of Living Index* (Geneva, United Nations Research Institute for Social Development).

Fox, K.A. (1974): *Social Indicators and Social Theory: Elements of an Operational System* (New York, Wiley).

Higgins, B. (1971): 'Planning Allocations for Social Development', *UN International Social Development Review*, 3, 47-55.

Lancaster, K. (1971): *Consumer Demand: A New Approach* (New York, Columbia University Press).

Solow, R.M. (1957): 'Technical Change and the Aggregate Production Function', *The Review of Economics and Statistics*, 39, 3 (August).

Tinbergen, J. (1959): 'On the Theory of Trend Movements', in L.H. Klaassen, L.M. Koyck & H.J. Witteveen (eds): *Selected Papers* (Amsterdam, North Holland).

7 SOCIAL PLANNING FOR UNDERDEVELOPED COUNTRIES

N.V. Sovani

Social planning, as contrasted to economic planning, has been fashionable for quite some time among the developed and developing countries of the world. The United Nations has played a significant part in making it so fashionable worldwide and has spawned most of the writing and cogitation in respect of it. Despite this, however, even today social planning remains as amorphous as when it was first sponsored and emphasized in the context of the UN development decades. The main reason for this seems to me to be the steady refusal of social planners to face and define the problems of social planning, and to see them as problems differing in orientation and texture from land to land and time to time, and thus not capable of being tackled by a universal method or technique. This refusal is embedded in the old methodology of social analysis which is now found wanting. I shall illustrate my arguments mainly from experience in India but also from the experiences of other countries.

The difficulty with social planning begins with its scope and definition. The following is culled from several UN documents.

> It seems appropriate to raise here the question of the definition, or lack thereof, of the term 'social' as used in relation to planning and development. For the purposes of the International Survey of Programmes for Social Development (E/CN=5/501/Rev 1, U.N. Sales No. 55 I.B.8, March 1955) it was claimed that 'it would be futile to engage in elaborate distinctions between 'social' and 'economic' on the avowed notions of national policy makers. The measures here treated are those regarded as 'social' by the United Nations and the specialized agencies; in general they are measures that are directly related to human welfare. In furtherance of this concept of 'social' as directly related to human welfare, the fields of social action have come to be identified in terms of the components of the level of living (UN 1970: para 5).

This is further clarified in Background Paper No. 1 entitled 'Role of Social Factors in Development' to this conference as follows:

> These components [of the level of living] are not social facts in isolation but are closely related to the country's societal and cultural setting. Hence it becomes necessary to widen the meaning of social to encompass social structure, institutions, attitudes and motivations where direct relationship to human welfare is less

obvious. We therefore broaden our interest from social services to social development which we would define as 'the greater capacity of the social system' (social structure, institutions, services, policy) to utilize resources to generate favourable changes in levels of living, interpreted in the broad sense as related to accepted social values, and a better distribution of income, wealth and opportunities (para 6).

The Stockholm meeting of Experts on Social Policy and Planning also concluded that

It is most necessary to view the development process as a complex whole, comprising economic elements, *sensu stricto*, but also other social as well as political and administrative elements. Any design for development strategy, national or international, has to cover all the above mentioned fields if it is to be meaningful, internally consistent and capable of effective implementation.

But although in theory and spirit the field of social planning is thus widened from social services to social development, the social planning that is talked about and discussed in international bodies is mainly confined to social services. This is the type of social planning that the developed market economies of the world practice and know about. As they dominate the international bodies that spawn social planning, their view shaped by their own experience prevails and is imitated by the developing economies.[1] There is certainly some justification for such social planning in the developed free market countries where poverty is marginal or peripheral if it exists at all, and the social structure, institutions, attitudes and motivations are not a hindrance but a help to development, being well-attuned to it. An extension and intensification (improvement) of social services in such an environment can promote welfare and that is what is expected of social planning. So what has been said about economic planning in these countries is

still on the margin of economic life in the sense that decisions of most economic agents are not taken with reference to the plan, although they are affected by the broad trends foreseen and by the general orientation of government policies. Even in countries where the plans are also designed to bring about structural changes, there is no intention to exercise detailed influence on all the various sectors or branches of the economy and the instruments of plan implementation are not radically different from the traditional instruments of government policy (UN 1965: 4).

Substitute 'soical' for 'economic' in this and everything is said about the nature of social planning in the developed countries.

Now this kind of social planning is mostly irrelevant to the poverty-stricken underdeveloped countries: their underdevelopment is not only economic but also social, political, organizational, valuational, etc. Underdevelopment is a multi-dimensional complex and needs to be tackled much more comprehensively than is visualized or practised in development planning today. To confine social planning to social services in such societies amounts to nothing more than a slightly better distribution of poverty and shortages, which has hardly any regenerative effect. To parody a Keynesian observation: 'social services as a bubble on a steady stream of economic development is alright, but when development becomes a bubble on a flood of social services it is disastrous.' Yet in the underdeveloped countries, social planning is mainly conceived and practised in terms of social services on the pattern of the developed countries, partly because it suits the vested interests to maintain the *status quo*, and partly in imitation of the developed countries in order to gain political and economic prestige.

One can readily concede that social welfare is not a rich man's luxury from which a poor nation should abstain:

> The urgency of social welfare activities is much greater in a poorer country ... by and large, the more underdeveloped a country, the higher ought to be the fraction of total consumption allocated to social consumption. This is so because the gaps that social welfare expenditure has to fill in a poor country are much more than gaps in a rich country. Inequality of income may deprive the lower income brackets of comforts and luxuries in a rich economy but in a poor community it robs them even of basic necessities of life (Sen & Naqvi 1963).

The important point in this connection is that care must be taken to see that the large portion of consumption that is allocated to the welfare of the poor is not at the cost of the long-term task of economic development which, after all, is the only source of increasing welfare for the poor in the long run. More often than not this aspect does not receive much attention, and the plea for more welfare expenditure is defended on the grounds that such expenditure by itself is productive of economic growth. Social planners have put this argument in a felicitous phrase: 'the welfare effect of economic growth and the productivity effect of social welfare', but this has so far remained unsubstantiated. Myrdal has claimed that increased consumption by the poor and the deprived, contrary to the belief of Western economics, is productive in the economic sense because it increases the capacity of the poor to work harder and thus is capable of increasing production (Myrdal 1970: 28; see also Myrdal 1968: Appendix 2, Section 21). This seems plausible at first sight but closer examination shows two flaws. The first is that all this derives basically from certain arbitrary nutritional norms that are supposed to determine the capacity of human beings for physical labour, based mostly on European data. Recent researches have exposed the fallacy of such norms and the arguments derived from them. The argument is not as soundly based as it was at one time thought (cf. Sukhatme 1965, 1977).

Even more important is the second flaw, i.e. that granted the increased capacity of the poor to work harder with better nutrition, what would they work harder at in a poor country where production capacity and resources are limited or even scarce? What else is poverty? For example, supposing that welfare schemes enable the landless agricultural labourers in India to consume more food than at present and render them capable of more work than before, what would they work hard at if the total employment available to them is not increased at the same time, which depends on increased investment in agricultural production? If they work harder than before because of increased nutrition, they will be able to complete the total employment-work available in terms of man-days in less time than before (i.e. in a smaller number of man-days) and thus increase their own underemployment. In underdeveloped countries where acute underemployment has been the fact of life for decades, the tendency of workers to spin-out available work over a longer time than is ordinarily necessary is not only a well-established custom but also a fine art. Over-staffing even in industrial factories is chronic and historical in underdeveloped countries, to say nothing of over-staffing in bureaucratic and other tertiary employment. It may relevantly be pointed out in this connection that the aim of increasing employment laterally, which is one of the important tenets of welfare and social policy, is broadly in conflict with the whole argument. This does not mean, however, that nutrition should not be improved or that it is wrong to do so. What is questioned is the alleged automatic productivity effect of such increased nutrition, which does not seem to be much in evidence. Let it be done for its own sake and not for any alleged productivity effects.

The multi-dimensional character of poverty in underdeveloped countries is almost always ignored in planning because the basic assumption of any plan, whether economic, social or political, is that the sectors other than that for which planning is being made are alright (i.e. not underdeveloped), and that they are sufficiently developed to plan for the other sectors: they know what needs to be done and are capable of doing it efficiently. This is totally unrealistic and unwarranted because all facets of an underdeveloped country are underdeveloped. They all suffer equally from their respective and collective underdevelopment. The experience of planning in many underdeveloped countries shows all too easily how this leads to defective planning and poor implementation of plans.

It is wellknown that planning is first and last a political process in which political considerations override economic as well as social ones, a fact which, partially at least, is accepted by social planners. The Stockholm meeting of Experts on Social Planning observed: 'Training of planners in techniques of introducing social concern into planning decisions and for allocation of resources to social sectors and further development of these techniques deserve high priority. Yet these techniques do not offer an escape from politics. Thus an understanding of the political process leading to planning decisions, and the political and social factors and forces behind such decisions are of vital importance for our understanding of social planning.' Having recognized this, however, there is a tendency to believe that political initiatives can achieve almost anything in this field. This is exemplified by the observations of another group of social planners, mostly from the ESCAPE region: 'The view was also advanced that social planners in the region are prone to overreach themselves by setting objectives such as the transformation of the social system that are beyond practical attainment with the relatively primitive social planning techniques at present available to them.' It was further observed that the validity of this criticism depended upon how one defined 'social planning'. 'If the term is interpreted in a strictly technical sense, it is no doubt true that the scope for action is limited, but if on the other hand the concept is extended to include deliberate acts of policy initiated from the political level, then there is no limit to the scope of planning. The grounds for misunderstanding here, it was felt, lay in the common tendency to confuse the function of planners with those of political authorities.'

It is not necessary to go at length into the confusion that social planners seem to betray in this statement. It is sufficient to raise only two points. First, whether the naïve belief that they express regarding the potential power of political initiatives in the underdeveloped countries is true; and second, whether the political set-up in these countries, which is also characterized by underdevelopment, is capable of taking such initiatives, even granting that it is capable of seeing them through in action. From the information available, the answers to both questions can only be negative. In regard to the first, one can begin by noting the array of vested interests in the underdeveloped countries which dominate the political scene and are interested in, and capable of maintaining the *status quo*. Even more decisive in this connection is the fact that the general population, the masses, are not only inarticulate and deprived of political power but are uneducated and backward; as such, they have, if anything, motivations and values that are not very conducive to the kinds of social policies and plans that the social planners generally have in mind. For example, the masses are not convinced about the need for family planning or birth control and have been known to resist it. In India they have not displayed sympathy or response to the extension of social, political or economic equality to the downtrodden or deprived groups. They have displayed strong casteism, parochialism and regionalism, the elimination of which is a prominent target of social planners and planning. Because of this, the social planners' other tenet is also in jeopardy, that of public participation. Public participation on an increased scale could be expected to sway the planning act and process away from the path that the social planners have in view. The almost religious belief that the native instinct of the masses is in the general direction of social upliftment of the poor, resulting in growing social, economic and political equality, is illusory as far as the masses of people in underdeveloped countries are concerned.

To go on to the second question, granting that unrealistic assumptions regarding the first are non-existent, we have to consider whether the political system in the underdeveloped countries is capable of executing such policies? The political machinery in these countries is also underdeveloped and its efficiency in carrying out policies that run against the grain of the people is very low. Myrdal has characterized the polities in Asia as 'soft states' that are incapable of enforcing any discipline on the masses. Moreover, these polities are characterized by what has come to be known as 'mass politics' or 'populist politics' where political action, inefficient as it is, is directed to things that rightly or wrongly are popular with the masses. As remarked above, such popular things frequently run contrary to what social planners regard as essential to progressive social planning. For example, birth or fertility control is not very popular with the Indian masses. In the 1977 elections, family planning measures enforced by the government in previous years was made a political issue and became quite a significant factor in defeating the party then in power. Family planning programmes have since slackened-off considerably and even though the old party was returned to power in 1980 by the same voters, the once-bitten twice-shy government is going about the family planning programme as though walking on eggshells.

The belief in the unlimited possibilities of political initiatives in regard to social planning in underdeveloped countries is hardly tenable for the simple reason that the polities of such countries are equally underdeveloped. And because this is so, planning, whether economic or social or whatever, is misdirected into wrong channels purely to suit the immediate and short-term needs of the polity. This can be illustrated by the experience of community development projects in India during recent years.

The Community Development Project was launched in 1952 with the express purpose of: 'to set free the creative energies of the people so that they may build up through their own effort and through their own institutions a richer and improving social life' (Government of India 1955: 51). The inspiration for this programme came from what was then known as the Etawah Experiment in a district of Uttar Pradesh, conceived and carried out by Albert Mayer and associates. Realizing the necessity to encourage the initiative and to improve the education of the rural masses, Mayer introduced a development experiment in ninety-seven villages in the Etawah district; extension workers lived in those villages, fostering through help, example and education the productive instincts of the villagers by gradually modifying their old mores and habits. The experiment was successful and agricultural productivity and social conditions in the experimental villages improved markedly over a period of four to five years. The scheme received well-deserved publicity and the political effect was naturally to generate the demand that community projects on the Etawah model should be started elsewhere in the country, but Mayer's experiment, being based on careful tending and gradual modification of the attitudes of the people, was not suitable for conventional expansion at the hands of the government machinery (see Mayer 1958).

Under pressure, however, the real causes of the success of the Etawah Experiment were ignored by the political authorities; in order to extend it all over India it was transformed into an administrative programme. The results were to be expected. Later appraisals of the Community Development Programme, both official and unofficial, indicate clearly that the objective of the programme was not realized; that there had been more concentration on welfare aspects than on productivity aspects; that the programme had settled into a dead administrative routine that smothered the growth of local leadership and initiative.[2]

When the Community Development Programme faltered in this way, attempts were made to improve it by another political device that was equally harmful:

> Based on the recommendations of the Balvantray Mahta Committee in 1958, people's backing to the Community Development Programme was sought to be institutionalised through a three-tier Panchayati Raj system. Though in some of the states like Maharashtra, Gujaraṭ and Tamil Nadu, Panchayati Raj institutions have become the main instruments of people's participation, by and large, these are merely agents of the state governments and are becoming integral parts of the state administration machinery (Chandhay 1975: 304).

This is not an isolated instance but is almost typical of the overwhelming political pressure that distorts the planning process in India. Many other instances and developments of a similar nature can be quoted or adduced.[3]

Social planning as conceived and practised today does not seem to bother about such problems because, as we have remarked earlier, it has been conceived and practised for a set of social, political and economic conditions of the developed free economies which are totally different to conditions in underdeveloped countries such as India. The problems of social planning in underdeveloped countries are primarily in the region of 'social structures, institutions, attitudes and motivations' which social planners include in the wider definition of 'social'. And in this region, the field of social planning is unexplored, almost without experience, and therefore quite inarticulate. In fact it can legitimately be doubted whether planning with the known techniques at the hands of government is possible. The experiences of developed countries are of little help in this context. The planning of population or fertility control by deliberate government effort or direction in underdeveloped countries, for example, cannot draw on the experience of developed countries: that which happened there more or less spontaneously at the initiative of the people provides no clue as to how to bring it about in a planned way at the hands of government. Or take the question of national integration. Many developing countries are not nations in the proper sense of the word, but still have to attain nationhood and all that it means. This happened naturally and over a long period in European countries, and is therefore hardly a guide to developing countries which want to take planned action at the hands of government to bring it about. And lastly, how can the governments of underdeveloped countries, which themselves suffer from underdevelopment, be regarded as capable of bringing about such things, even supposing that clear guidance and direction were available?

The long and short of it is that social planning as conceived today is of little use if not totally irrelevant to the developing countries, while the social planning that they so desperately need is non-existent.

Notes

1. This is similar to the situation with regard to economic planning. The recognized or implied objectives of development planning everywhere are acceleration of economic growth and structural change, but in practice the emphasis on the second aim differs from one group of countries to another. In the socialized economies of Eastern Europe structural change is regarded as a prerequisite for a

high level of growth, and the main instrument for structural change is high investment in basic industries. In most developing countries the idea is firmly held that development planning can be effective only if it includes basic institutional reforms. But in actual practice, vested interests in these countries see to it that nothing very much happens to change the *status quo*. On the other hand, in the planning of some of the developed countries with market economies 'the amount of institutional change is so small that the line between development planning and anti-cyclical planning becomes tenuous' (Waterston 1965: 17-19).

2. Among several reports and books testifying to this may be mentioned a very perspicacious analysis by Carl Taylor (1959).

3. This has been recognized, though in spirit only, at the international level as, for example, in the UN Report on Planning for Economic Development:

> Not only the aims of planning but also the means selected for implementation of plans are closely bound up with political and social purposes; likewise, the methodology of plan formulation is greatly influenced by the aim of planning and the means of implementation.... Prevailing political and social circumstances, as well as the level of development, not only determine the general aims and purposes of planning; they also delineate the boundaries within which choices between policy instruments can be made (1963: 2-3).

References

Chandhay, D.P. (1975): 'Community Development Comes of Age', in S.D. Gokhale (ed.): *Social Welfare: Legend and Legacy* (Bombay, Popular Prakashan).

Government of India (1955): *Evaluation Report on the Second Year's Working of Community Projects* (Delhi, Programmes Evaluation Organisation).

Mayer, A., & Associates (1958): *Pilot Project, India (The Story of Rural Development in Etawah, Uttar Pradesh)* (Berkeley, University of California Press).

Myrdal, G. (1968): *Asian Drama* (London, Allen Lane).

— (1970): *The Challenge of World Poverty* (Harmondsworth, Penguin).

Sen, A.K. & K.A. Naqvi (1963): 'Social Welfare in Relation to Economic Development', *Report of a Seminar on Social Welfare in a Developing Economy* (New Delhi, Planning Commission).

Sukhatme, P.V. (1965): *Feeding India's Growing Millions* (Bombay, Asia Publishing House).

— (1977): 'Measurement of Poverty Based on Nutritional Needs', *Bulletin of the International Statistical Institute*, XLVII, IV, 553-56.

Taylor, C. (1959): 'Two Major Evils', *Kurukshetra*, 26 January.

United Nations (1955): *International Survey of Programmes for Social Development* (New York, UN, E/CN.5/501/Rev.1).

— (1963): *Report on Planning for Economic Development* (New York, UN, A/5333/Rev. 1).

— (1965): *Economic Survey of Europe in 1962* (Geneva, UN).

— (1970): *United Nations Approach to Social Planning* (New York, UN, SD/EGSD/BP-1).

— (1970): 'Role of Social Factors in Development' (Background paper to UN Conference on the Approach to Social Planning; New York, UN; October).

Waterston, A. (1965): *Development Planning: Lessons of Experience* (Baltimore, Johns Hopkins).

8 POVERTY IN LATIN AMERICA: DIAGNOSES AND PRESCRIPTION

Marshall Wolfe

Alternative Identifications

Since the 1950s a series of theoretical and ideological explanations for the failure of large parts of the Latin American population to share appreciably in the fruits of economic growth and social modernization have waxed and waned in influence, the waning due at least in part to their protracted confrontation with recalcitrant realities (Portes & Ferguson 1975). A parallel series of policy prescriptions for making the underdogs more 'productive' or helping them to 'participate' have flourished for long enough to demonstrate their incapacity to achieve more than localized and precarious gains, at costs precluding their application on a national scale. A very few serious attempts to apply 'structural' prescriptions have foundered on their incompatibility with national and international power structures, or on the factionalism, voluntarism or tactical weaknesses of their proponents.

Social scientists, ideologists and political leaders have advanced several alternative identifications or labels for the underdogs, projecting on them the hopes and fears of educated elites, conservative, reformist and revolutionary. These sectors of opinion have cast the same actors in roles as 'proletarians and sub-proletarians' seeking to overthrow and replace the existing dependent capitalist order, 'oppressed' seeking spiritual as well as political liberation, 'people' seeking majority rule and curbs on exploiters, 'marginals' seeking social integration, 'unemployed' seeking jobs, an 'informal sector' seeking state recognition and facilitation for their sources of livelihood, or 'critically poor' seeking material benefits and guidance from the state in order to achieve a tolerable level of living.[1]

Two main instrumental-ethical orientations can be distinguished behind these alternative identifications.

According to one orientation the main purpose is to help the underdogs become conscious of their own situation and their own interests so that they can acquire realistic strategies for transforming this situation and thus transforming the social order as a whole. Different versions lead to quite different strategies, but they agree that the group must free itself through solidarity informed by its own vision of the existing social order and the kind of future social order that will meet its needs.

According to the other orientation, the main purpose of the identification is to make *other* elements in the national society and the international order aware that the situation of the 'target group' is unacceptable in terms of their own professed values and incompatible with perpetuation of their own preferred life styles. Different versions of this orientation also lead to differing strategies, but these are strategies for the state, for the international order made up of states, for the wealthy and powerful, or for all educated men of good will, only secondarily for the underdogs themselves. The orientation assumes that their deficiencies can be overcome only if guidance, policy-oriented research and material support are forthcoming. Such an orientation must be basically more congenial than the first to external identifiers of the disadvantaged, since it enables them to address their natural educated audiences and gives them legitimate leading roles in the strategy to be adopted. In recent times, this orientation has been associated particularly with diagnoses focussing on 'critical poverty'.

The Quest for Quantification

Interest in statistical indicators of the numbers and characteristics of the disadvantaged has naturally been associated with identifications responding to the second orientation. In very simplified terms, one can find an upswing during the 1950s and early 1960s associated with efforts to add a social dimension to the optimistic economic developmentalism then current. This culminated in the social targets of the Alliance for Progress and the setting-up of elaborate regional machinery for assessment of progress and justification of external financing. During the 1960s, as the Alliance lost its reforming and planning impetus and dwindled into fragmentary aid programmes, interest in social indicators waned to some extent, to revive during the 1970s with a more pronounced emphasis on basic needs and poverty, for reasons that will be suggested below.

The United Nations Economic Commission for Latin America (ECLA) had been the main source of the ideas on economic development that seemed to become a new orthodoxy at the beginning of the 1960s. With two collaborating institutions set up at that time – the Latin American Institute for Economic and Social Planning (ILPES) and the Latin American Demographic Centre (CELADE) – it became the main focus for efforts to give a quantitative basis to aspirations for planned economic *and* social development.

It soon became evident that basic statistical information for practically all Latin American countries was hopelessly inadequate to meet the demands being made on it. The casual observer could see that most people in Latin America were badly off and without access to the public services taken for granted in the 'rich' countries, and this lent plausibility to the quantifications that were in circulation, but the sources of the latter did not bear close scrutiny. Assessments of progress or international comparisons based on them could hardly be better than guesswork decked out with figures.

The persons grappling with these problems reacted in quite different ways that coincided to a large extent with their academic specializations. Demographic statistics were the least inadequate, and the demographers embarked on a slow and patient labour of testing them, calculating margins and sources of error, disseminating sampling methodologies, and improving the national sources of data through training and technical advice. Educational planners and health planners could also gradually improve their basic information. Sociologists at first embarked with enthusiasm on local investigations using quantitative survey techniques borrowed from the United States, and thus built up a body of information on urban low-income groups which did not lend itself to the kinds of national indicators that were most in demand, but provided a valuable corrective to generalizations. Soon, however, the majority of Latin American sociologists rejected theories of United States origin and the research methodologies associated with them, and turned to questions of power, dependency and class potentialities for revolutionary transformation which left them relatively indifferent to social statistics.

Information on incomes, consumption levels and employment was particularly fragmentary and indirect, and these areas were taken in charge mainly by economists who needed quantifications to insert into models and 'comprehensive' development plans. The economists and planners were chronically frustrated by the reluctance of the demographers to let their statistics, projections in particular, be used in ways unjustified by their margin of reliability; and by the inability of the sociologists to provide any kind of national aggregates suitable for planning. The economists did what they could to improve the statistics they were using, but at the same time they dared to concoct quantifications of income levels and distribution, and of underemployment or 'unemployment equivalent' through techniques comparable to the work of paleontologists constructing dinosaurs from a few fragments of bones; as, in fact, they had done during the 1950s in their construction of national accounts for the Latin American countries.

During the late 1960s and early 1970s a number of household surveys collected information on income distribution, and ECLA, in cooperation with the World Bank, was able to renew its income distribution studies under more favourable conditions. However, a 1975 paper on methodological problems by the director of this project documents frankly the continuing weaknesses of the informational bases for quantifications:

> Social scientists ... must choose between carrying out their analyses on some empirical basis or keeping to the level of relatively general abstractions. The commonest solution to this conflict consists in making use of the most accessible information that can cite an honorable source at the foot of the table, relegating doubts on the reliability of these data to the subconscious. This work has tried to bring back the problem of reliability to the level of the conscious.... The fact that it has been necessary to resort for this purpose to heuristic rules depending more on common sense than on statistical precision is imposed by the situation predominating in Latin American statistics (Altimir 1975).[2]

The probable biases are most pronounced in data referring to the high income groups and the low income groups, and different sub-groups within these two extremes are affected by different kinds and degrees of bias.

ECLA economists have distilled from the data estimates, often quoted without the original cautions, to the effect that in 1960 the richest five per cent of the Latin American population received thirty-three per cent of personal income, and in 1970 thirty per cent, while the poorest twenty per cent received 3.1 per cent and 2.5 per cent in the same years. The figures are certainly plausible, but whether they and their national equivalents constitute 'indicators' serving as a basis for policies and a means of assessing their results is another question.

During the 1970s work on distributional and other social indicators faced quite different conditions. Economic growth in the majority of countries of the region had proceeded as rapidly as development theorists could have hoped. Structural changes in production and employment had been profound. However, the 'comprehensive development plans', indicators and targets of the 1960s seemed almost irrelevant to what had happened. It had become evident that the forces controlling most governments had no intention of applying the reformist socially-oriented planning they had endorsed at regional conferences. The few governments that wanted to do so found the techniques the planners offered them of very limited applicability. They found themselves continually improvising distributional measures in order to hold together enough support to remain in power, and the planners could not show them how to make these unavoidable manoeuvres less wasteful and contradictory (see Mattos 1979).

At the same time, it was evident that 'trickledown' expectations from economic development were not being realized, and even the governments most wedded to economic liberalism protected from its enemies by military repression could not altogether ignore this. Reformist technocrats and planners, finding themselves marginalized, needed to come up with demonstrations of need and remedies likely to be acceptable within existing structures, without altogether abandoning their previous hopes for planned structural change.

They had at hand the argument, repeated in numerous ECLA reports, that Latin America's rising levels of production and per capita incomes, making the more dynamic countries of the region a kind of international middle class between the rich central countries and the very poor countries of Africa and Asia, permit the elimination of critical poverty through reallocation of a part of future income increments, if only the power holders are convinced that this can be done, with only a moderate compression of the consumption of the well-to-do and without preventing adequate capital accumulation. They could link themselves to world campaigns on poverty and basic needs stimulated by the World Bank and the International Labour Organization. They could count on a good deal of information accumulated by the ECLA-World Bank income distribution project, the ILO's Regional Employment Programme (PREALC), and other regional and national initiatives.

Thus, in 1975, ECLA, with financing from the United Nations Development Programme, embarked on a research project on 'Critical Poverty in Latin America'. This project grappled once again with the venerable problems of definition and measurement; in particular, the fixing of cut-off lines for 'poverty' and 'critical poverty'. It eventually adopted an 'absolute concept of poverty according to which families spending all their incomes on food yet failing to satisfy their nutritional needs are considered to be indigent; and families which, given their income and the percentage they spend on food, fail to satisfy those needs are considered to be poor' (Molina & Piñera 1979).[3] On the basis of income distribution data the project concluded that around 1970 nineteen per cent of the population of Latin America lived in indigence and forty per cent in poverty. The project also defined an 'absolute poverty gap' 'equal to the resources that would have to be transferred on a permanent basis to the poorer groups if they are to emerge from their situation of poverty.' It estimated this gap to amount to about six per cent of disposable personal income in 1970, or twelve per cent of the disposable income of the richest ten per cent, making the eradication of poverty appear to be a 'feasible task'. The 'poverty gap', however, also amounted to about twenty-two per cent of 1970 public expenditure, which suggested that 'the State will have great difficulty in carrying it out.'

One might be tempted to elaborate indefinitely on the incognita behind such percentages and the difficulties in the way of their use in policy-making, and in fact the documents of the project do so. The definition's concentration on capacity of income to satisfy food requirements obviously responds to the greater measurability of these two variables rather than to any integrated theory on the nature and causes of poverty. In fact, the data basis for estimates of food consumption in Latin America is just as shaky as in the case of income levels and distribution, and the problem of determining minimum food requirements is more complicated than it seems at first sight. When the project documents arrive at policy recommendations it is evident that the exercises in quantification have served only to demonstrate that the eradication of poverty is feasible. The recommendations are eclectic and partly descriptive of policies that have been attempted here and there, covering most of the conventional sectors of state economic and social action, constrained by awareness of the wide differences between countries and political regimes, striving for acceptability under existing conditions. There is no suggestion that anti-poverty policies should be incorporated in comprehensive plans or governed by quantitative indicators and targets.

Peripheral Capitalism and Poverty

While the 'critical poverty' project was unfolding Dr Raul Prebisch, the main originator of the ECLA propositions and development and planning, was pursuing a line of thinking that seemed likely to demolish the arguments for anti-poverty policies to be carried out by the power-holders within the bounds of enlightened self-interest and within the constraints of the existing style of development. In two essays in the *CEPAL Review*[4] he argued that:

1. The distribution of wealth and incomes in peripheral societies such as those of Latin America derives from the previous distribution of power. Peripheral capitalist development, however dynamic, enables the powerful few to continue to concentrate the lion's share of its fruits in their own hands.

2. The distribution of power also determines the distribution of opportunities to acquire the formal qualifications of 'training' for entering into the managerial, technical and bureaucratic positions required

by the style of development. Once the rate of expansion of the resulting 'intermediate strata' exceeds the expansion of real demand for their services, the share of power that determined the acquisition of formal qualifications also requires the 'spurious absorption' of the possessors into favoured areas of employment. At lower levels of skills and incomes within the activities generated by the prevailing style of development similar processes are at work. The distribution of power and the sluggish labour-absorptive capacity of these activities guarantee that the initially poor and weak will remain excluded.

3. The distribution of power and of incomes generates the 'consumer society' in its present concentrated, wasteful and imitative form. It also influences the patterns of introduction of technologies and the failure to generate technologies better suited to the relative scarcities of capital and labour in the peripheral countries.

4. The consumer society for stratified minorities is incompatible with the achievement of a sufficient rate of accumulation to permit eventual absorption of the marginalized masses into productive well-paid employment.

5. While peripheral capitalist development permits broadening of the minorities able to participate in the consumer society and indeed requires this for its own functioning, it cannot do so beyond a certain point owing to insufficient dynamism and the insatiable appetites of the groups already participating. To the extent that the excluded groups, now condemned to 'infra-consumption', gain in ability to use organization and democratic political processes to force an entry, either inflation accelerates, or the power-holders replace formal democracy by open reliance on force, or both.

If this diagnosis is valid, the prevailing style of development can support either a highly concentrated 'elitist' distribution of incomes or a broader 'mesocratic' distribution (see Graciarena 1976), and may support somewhat more material assistance to the critically poor than it has done heretofore, but it cannot afford to let them participate on equal terms as producers, consumers and citizens.

Research on poverty lines and poverty gaps will undoubtedly continue, and so will the manufacture of prescriptions for the alleviation or eradication of poverty, in which terminological innovations can always give an appearance of novelty to policies that have been current for many years. However, one might well ask whether the poor are not now going out of fashion, or becoming less visible, because of the repetitiousness of the descriptions of their plight; because of the meagre results of the prescriptions; because the disadvantaged have shown so little inclination or ability to undertake the revolutionary role that has been used as an argument to alarm the powerful into paying attention to them; and, above all, because of a presentiment that mutations in the prevailing style of development are going to strain the 'crisis management' capacity of the dominant forces even without the diversion of significant resources to the parts of the population least able to make themselves heard. Persistent poverty is neither the greatest immediate threat to these dominant forces nor the most promising rallying-point against them of the counter-elites. Recent political shifts in the United States are naturally of considerable importance for the Latin American elites' perception of poverty, both in relieving direct pressure to do something about it and in providing a respectable model for rejection of redistributionist policies.

The Prebisch diagnosis implies that the critically poor are on the whole superfluous and inconvenient to the peripheral capitalist style of development, although what Dr Prebisch labels their 'regressive absorption' insures the abundant supply at very low cost of services and artisanal goods that are valued by the well-to-do. The diagnosis implicitly rejects the hypothesis that the poor are necessary to peripheral capitalism as an industrial reserve army and a source of 'super-exploited' labour power. Latin American Marxists have devoted a good deal of polemical zeal to efforts to relate the under-employed and 'marginalized' strata to Marx's categories. It is probable that some of them have been too prone to advance from demonstrations that some of the poor are highly advantageous to the prevailing patterns of industrial and agricultural growth and that others are convenient to the beneficiaries of the consumer society, to theoretical conclusions that all are necessary and that it is necessary to the style of development that all the poor should be kept at the margins of subsistence.

The more dynamic industrial development processes of the region do in fact seem to have made use of a labour force recruited in part from the critically poor and only marginally better off in their 'modern' jobs: with harsh working conditions, a degraded urban environment, and lack of public services resulting in a short working life, but with docile replacements guaranteed by the flow of migrants from an even more impoverished hinterland (see Kowarick 1981). Such conditions, resembling those of the early stages of the industrial revolution in Europe, have been made possible by suppression (as in Brazil) or co-optation (as in Mexico) of the trade union power that Dr Prebisch emphasizes as the main means for the regularly employed workers to separate their lot from that of the groups consigned to 'regressive absorption' or precarious survival strategies. In such cases, it is arguable that this separation is bound to be re-established through some combination of rising skill requirements in industry, a resurgence of trade union power, and shifts in government policy, as may now be happening in Brazil, considerably reducing the advantages to the dominant forces of an industrial reserve army of such overwhelming size and dubious physical, educational and motivational qualifications for industrial work, at a time when international and national economic conjunctures seem to preclude recovery of the past high rates of industrial growth. Under such conditions, the judgment that at least a high proportion of the critically poor are superfluous and burdensome if not dangerous to the functioning of the style of development would seem more plausible.

Policy Alternatives for the Dominant Forces

If this is the case, and if no convincing alternative to the prevailing style of 'peripheral' or 'transnationalized' capitalist development is in sight, what future can one foresee for the poor of Latin America and for official policies aimed at them? A Brazilian political scientist has given the harshest answer:

> There are many indications that the huge marginal tertiary which is being rapidly formed in the semistagnating cities of the third world, formed by the migrants of a fully stagnating subsistence agriculture, is flooding those cities and ruining their precarious public services and feeding facilities. The provincial administrations of the near future will probably be led to establish internal controls for population movement, obliging the rural population to remain in the countryside, and thereby create a sort of reserve of natives, whose admission to the modern sectors of their countries will be contingent upon the real increase in the demand for labor in the cities. Malnutrition and the lack of appropriate sanitary conditions and medical care will gradually reduce these populations (Jaguaribe 1973).

Something like this might come to pass for a time in countries with authoritarian regimes powerful and ruthless enough to control population movements and, in particular, forcibly prevent the 'superfluous' migrant poor from improvising their own shelter and sources of livelihood in the cities as they have done up to the present. Or some of the larger urban agglomerations might become so unlivable and opportunities for a minimum subsistence so precarious that most of the poor would remain 'voluntarily' in the hinterland and relatively invisible to the groups in a position to influence policy. However, it seems unlikely that tendencies in the style of development will progress to a logical conclusion generalizing either of these 'solutions'.

For the immediate future, in the absence of revolutionary changes in the distribution of power or an improbable change of heart among the power-holders, one can expect the continuation, in shifting combinations, of several policy approaches that have been on the stage for some time. The overall orientations governing the combinations of more specific measures may continue to swing between a populist pole featuring inflationary redistribution, mainly to the better-organized 'relatively poor' and to clientèles; and an elitist pole, featuring the suppression of trade union power, the dismantling of social services accessible mainly to the 'relatively poor', and the offering of token aid to the 'critically poor'.

The approaches accessible to either orientation include population policy, employment expansion, social assistance, social control or repression, and aided self-help.

'Population policy' in the restricted sense of intensive promotion of family planning so as to reduce the fertility of low-income families, and thus eventually the numbers of the poor, is likely to retain a secondary role. Publicly-financed family planning programmes directed to the poor will undoubtedly continue to expand, responding to very real demands from urban women, but the claims of a few years ago of their decisive importance were never convincing to the power-holders in Latin America, with a few temporary exceptions. For one thing, it is now generally conceded that the survival strategies of the rural poor, and in a more qualified way of the urban poor, make children assets rather than liabilities. Promotional campaigns are unlikely to overcome the families' perception of this and the state, however repressive, is in no position to do so by force. For another thing, the results of fertility control would at best be too long-term to receive a very high priority from regimes concerned by the immediate political and resource allocation problems presented by the poor. Thus, quite different sectors of opinion readily accept the argument that raising the levels of living of the critically poor must precede or accompany rather than follow upon major changes in their fertility rates.

It has often been pointed out that international migration, of very great importance in relieving pressures from the poor during the capitalist economic growth of 19th century Europe, and also in providing a cheap labour force for economic growth elsewhere, is not an accessible option for most of the so-called 'developing' countries today. Nevertheless, Latin America has become a region of significant net out-migration and the poor, although not necessarily the most critically poor, account for the greater part of this migration.

The main current has been from Mexico and some of the Caribbean countries to the United States, and it seems probable that this population movement will increase in scale and involve additional countries as sources of migrants, in spite of efforts by United States authorities to bar them out; unless, of course, the U.S. economy falls into a deep protracted depression. Presumably the migrant population and its descendants, after an initial period as a cheap and docile increment to the labour force, will assimilate itself in part to the domestic working class and in part to the sub-proletariat dependent on and trapped by the welfare system. The governments of the countries of origin will not usually be in a position to subject the outflow to controls or agreements with the host country, but will turn a blind eye, torn between approval of its functions as a safety valve and a source of foreign exchange, and disquiet at the resulting international complications, including the permanent threat of massive expulsions from the host country. Quantitatively, such migration will be more important for the future composition of the labour force and of poverty in the United States than in Latin America. At most, it is unlikely to do more than slow the growth in numbers of the critically poor in the latter region.

Policies aimed at employment expansion can take quite different forms. The main form accessible to Latin American governments has notoriously been the expansion of bureaucratic employment, and this has naturally helped the 'relatively poor' striving to escape from manual labour more than the 'critically poor'. The state has been unable, and generally has made no effort, to counteract the externally-generated trends of capital-intensive technological innovation in agriculture and industry which have restricted their capacity to offer jobs. Indeed, the main thrust of public policy, in relation to credits and imports, has supported this trend. Publicly-supported vocational training programmes supposed to make the poor more employable, have been practically irrelevant, both in their scale and in their divorce from the demands of industry.

In a good many countries, also, bureaucratized social security, minimum wage, and labour protective measures, emerging from a combination of populist political tactics and copying of international standards, have raised the cost of labour to private employers and presumably motivated them to restrict employment. It does not follow that the elimination of such hindrances to labour mobility, in which the technocrats of authoritarian regimes have invested high hopes, will overcome such hindrances to a significant degree.

Public works employment at subsistence wages has been a recurrent means of relieving the plight of some of the critically poor, especially during times of high visible urban unemployment – that is, when an economic slump has rendered the mechanisms of the 'informal sector' conspicuously unable to absorb workers displaced from the 'formal sector'. This policy approach is closer to the assistentialism next to be discussed than to employment expansion envisaged as part of a strategy reconciling development with alleviation of poverty.

To the extent that a government can mobilize resources or obtain them from external sources, it is easier for it to distribute free or subsidized food and possibly housing and to offer elementary educational and health services to the poor than to change the structure of employment and land tenure to the extent needed to enable the groups most in need to achieve an adequate livelihood. The valid argument that better nutrition, health, family relationships, etc. are prerequisites for advances toward the broader objective helps to justify assistentialism. Assistential social service programmes have other practical advantages for political leaders which contradict the overt purposes: they provide considerable numbers of jobs for the educated middle strata, thus relieving one of the most insistent pressures on the state. They provide opportunities for profits to suppliers and builders, and through them to politicians and administrators. In their early stages, they have been able to attract external aid meeting a major part of the costs, particularly in the case of food distribution programmes. They can win political support in the form of votes from the 'critically poor' themselves, or at least reduce the incidence of rioting and crimes against property, while meeting less opposition from other strata of the population than would alternative measures.

Assistential and social service programmes aimed at the 'critically poor' have emerged in practically all Latin American countries, at least in token form. In principle they might achieve major importance in some of the larger countries in which (a) the per capita national income has climbed to a level well above the Third World average and the state is able to capture an important part of it; (b) the 'critically poor' in the sense of inability to meet a socially-determined minimum subsistence, constitute a relatively small part of the national population; (c) a significant part of the 'critically poor' is concentrated in cities and has some political importance, if only as potential counterweight to the better organized and more radicalized 'relatively poor'.

Under the above conditions, the more extreme consumption deficiencies of the critically poor – or at least the *urban* critically poor – might conceivably be alleviated and their access to basic educational and health services improved, at burdensome but manageable cost to the state, without any significant impact on their access to productive employment or their place at the bottom of the income ladder; in other words, accentuating their superfluity to the style of development.

The urban bias of such an assistential policy and probably the impact on agricultural production incentives and labour demand of subsidized food imports and price-controlled distribution would further stimulate the movement of the critically poor from the countryside to the cities associated with the present trends of capitalist agricultural modernization. At the same time, the agricultural surpluses that motivated the United States in the past to offer aid in the form of food may not recur, and this by itself might preclude a major expansion of assistential programmes involving food distribution. On the contrary, Latin American governments are likely to have to give more serious attention to incentives for domestic food production that will use more labour and be less demanding of energy and industrial inputs, thus benefiting the rural poor at the expense of the urban.

Information on coverage of assistential programmes in Latin America up to the present is as fragmentary as the programmes themselves. In a good many countries they seem to have reached a rather high proportion of the urban poor but to have reached them too thinly and intermittently – depending on availability of food aid from abroad or on populist electoral tactics – to have made a significant contribution to their consumption.

In national settings in which the critically poor are numerous, doles and subsidized services (including public employment designed mainly to provide minimum incomes for the otherwise unemployed) must either be confined to certain clientèles or must be spread very thin. As awareness of the possibility of assistance spreads, demands are bound to rise faster than benefits and to become increasingly organized, though usually remaining localized.

Therefore, as long as the state is unable to move beyond assistential measures and non-productive job creation, the very expansion of these measures forces it to develop mechanisms of control and repression in order to keep the demands from getting out of hand. These mechanisms become all the more necessary when the state moves, as periodically happens, to curtail assistance because of changing priorities, financial crisis, or simply the drying-up of external earmarked aid. In the milder forms of control, it may be exercized through bureaucratic agencies or through an official political party able to identify and placate dangerous grievances, give or withhold aid, co-opt and reward local intermediaries among the poor. To the extent that the dominant forces perceive serious unrest and a need to demobilize popular movements, such mechanisms can be made more openly repressive, through the deliberate recruitment of some of the poor into police-managed systems of informing, intimidation and removal of potential leaders. Moreover, while the assistential programmes offer paid employment mainly to the educated non-poor or relatively poor, the repressive mechanisms can become an important source of jobs for the lowest strata of the society, in the police and armed forces.

Policy approaches incorporating aided self-help are diverse both in content and in terminology, and are by no means aimed exclusively at the critically poor. In the view of many of their proponents, however, they represent a means by which the poor can raise their levels of living without burdening the system with the high costs of assistentialism-cum-repression, and also without requiring an egalitarian revolution – judged unattainable or unacceptable – in social and economic relationships.

The state, with the assistance of voluntary agencies, is to raise the employability of the poor through training and guidance; help them produce enough to meet their basic needs as cultivators or artisans; and help them organize cooperatively to exchange goods and services among themselves, provide their own housing and community services, and obtain fair returns in their dealings with the rest of the society.

If there is no immediate prospect that the economic system can absorb even the more employable among the poor into 'modern' or 'formal sector' productive activities, as seems to be the case in most of Latin America, the aided self-help approach must fall back on a kind of parallel economy of the poor, insulated from the dominant 'modern' economy and subjected to controls and incentives different from those applied to 'modern' enterprises. The poor would then, arguably, achieve levels of productivity and consumption above their present precarious subsistence, but the question of their full incorporation into the more dynamic sectors of the economy could be postponed to the relatively distant future. Meanwhile, the latter sectors could advance more vigorously, freed of the greater part of the costs and dangers now associated with critical poverty and its concentration in the cities.

Small-scale initiatives of this kind have proliferated over the years within community development and cooperative programmes, and are now being promoted as means to economic independence for women of the poorer strata. Generally they offer their target groups supplementary incomes for handicraft production in the home, chicken raising, etc. The public programmes have typically been weak on the marketing side, sometimes leaving the producers with no return for the output that has been called forth until the marketing function is turned over to private middlemen who can find outlets and enforce quality controls in exchange for a major share in the returns. Indeed, in a number of countries such middlemen have organized their own systems of home piecework, particularly in handicrafts for the tourist market and in garment manufacture, making the poor more productive and evading the costs imposed by social security and labour protection laws, without notably raising the levels of living of their suppliers.

The more ambitious schemes for parallel economies seem to have tempted some public authorities but have not been applied on a significant scale. Such schemes suppose a governmental capacity to isolate the target group from the remainder of national societies in the throes of uneven modernization that does not exist – at least as yet. The required willingness to accept modest improvements in living conditions in exchange for unremitting toil with primitive tools, and to provide out of their poverty basic services that the state provides for the better-off strata in the society, would be likely to break down precisely when and if initial progress had generated hope and organizational capacity.

The propensity to over-generalize about the potential of aided self-help and to assume that localized achievements can be duplicated on an ever-larger scale, irrespective of the constraints of the wider social and economic order, has been particularly evident in the changing fashions of diagnosis and policy prescriptions for urban shantytowns. The earlier observers looked on these as sinks of abject poverty peopled by unemployable rural migrants who would be better off if persuaded or compelled to go back where they came from. As the above quotation from Helio Jaguaribe indicates, this general attitude continues to shape a good many observations on poverty in Latin America and other parts of the Third World.

Since the early 1960s, however, studies of some unregulated occupant-built settlements in some cities have been used to support equally sweeping generalizations to the effect that such settlements are constituted by 'dynamic and creative people' who are able to solve their own problems with a little of the right kind of aid from the outside. Such a conclusion is repugnant to traditional city planners and to the construction industries that dominate public housing programmes, but attract authorities by their promise of cheap and politically viable solutions. In fact, the dynamism and creativity are much more evident in some settlements than in others and in some political and economic conjunctures than in others. At best, they cannot enable the families concerned to extricate themselves from the costs of urban sprawl and the polluted urban environment to which the settlements contribute, nor to compete on equitable terms in the job market and the educational system that helps determine access to jobs.

Policy Alternatives for the Poor

At the beginning of this paper, two alternative instrumental-ethical orientations were distinguished behind the various identifications of disadvantaged target groups and the prescriptions associated with these identifications. The policy approaches discussed above correspond to the second orientation and to identification of the target group as the 'critically poor'.

What can be said about the first orientation and the guidelines it implies for disadvantaged or excluded groups trying to cope with a world they never made? In one way or another, this orientation implies the 'conscientization' of the disadvantaged to the incongruities between their real needs and the prevailing social, economic and political order. It implies participatory roles and techniques for social research, quite different from the calculation of national aggregates and the construction of indicators to meet the needs of planners. But once the disadvantaged become conscious, whether spontaneously or aided by the interpretations of external researchers, mobilizers and ideologists, what are they to do? The alternatives can be summed up as follows, in rising order of participation in the national society.

1. Withdrawal, non-cooperation, denial of information to agents of the state. An important part of the Latin American population resorts to this tactic for lack of any visible alternatives. Its consistent use, however, requires that the family or local group command its own sources of subsistence, so that it can survive with a minimum of contact with the wider society. Ability to do this has practically disappeared, even among *minifundio* cultivators and tribal peoples in the forests, so that the tactic now manifests itself as a persistent but subordinate component in the dealings of disadvantaged groups with agents of the state as well as local power-holders.

2. Escape from intractable local problems through migration to the frontier, to the larger cities or abroad. At the frontier, the migrants usually find that the powerful are able to exploit or exclude them with even fewer inhibitions than elsewhere. In the cities, they at least have more ability to try the tactics listed below, and sociological inquiries continue to find that most migrants perceive gains from the move, in spite of their precarious lot.

3. Reliance on personal, paternalistic ties with individuals higher in the national or local power structure, at the price of submission and reciprocal favours. As the assistential-repressive activities of the state become more prominent, this quest for protection shifts from the local

magnate to the state itself, in the person of the highest official to whom the local group or individual can gain access. In regimes with open political competition the proffering of votes in exchange for aid partially replaces the previous offers of personal services or produce. Elsewhere, as mentioned above, some individuals achieve gains by entering into the control mechanisms of the state.

4. Mass demonstrations, land seizures and destruction of property (particularly public transport equipment) may be resorted to in order to prod the state into favourable action and obtain a higher priority for the needs of the group engaging in the violent action. Such tactics appear when consciousness of the possibility of influencing the authorities has penetrated, but local interest-group organizations and intermediaries between the state and the local group remain rudimentary or ineffective. As urbanization proceeds, this tactic becomes increasingly formidable, although by its nature and semi-spontaneous manifestations participants can never be sure how far they can safely go. Various studies have pointed out that 'representational violence' of the urban poor, when not crushed by force, has had the main result of gaining them some limited benefits, including a sense of accomplishment, and has been followed by a decline in politicization. The same thing seems to be true of successful peasant movements.[5]

5. Strengthening and adaptation to new purposes of pre-existing community, tribal or religious institutions. The availability of this tactic, of course, depends on the pre-existence of forms of local solidarity and participation in which the disadvantaged groups have had or felt a stake. For most of Latin America such institutions are lacking or weaker than in Africa and Asia. Linguistically and culturally distinct Indian peoples in the Andean countries, Mexico and Guatemala have clung to community organization as a means of self-defence, but their functioning for this purpose is either disintegrating in the face of agricultural modernization, deteriorating land resources and increasing spatial population mobility, or evolving into new forms of peasant organization.

6. Organization of co-operative systems of production, credit, marketing, construction and maintenance of housing and local public works. Use of this approach depends on some combination of co-operative traditions, a consciousness of common interests overriding local class and other divisions, a minimum level of education, and a certain amount of legal, technical and material support (unaccompanied by bureaucratic domination) from the state. The tactic has been discussed above from the state's point of view. If Dr Prebisch's diagnosis of the functioning of the style of development is correct, it would be ingenuous to expect either the state or the disadvantaged groups acting auto-

nomously to modify it significantly in this way. Moreover, if successful group solidarity in economic activities and self-provision of services did result in a reasoned rejection of dependence on the state and large-scale withdrawals from the market system as suppliers of labour and consumers, this might prove harder for the state to tolerate than occasional violence in pursuit of assistance or price controls. It is unlikely that the state could bring into being a 'parallel economy' if it wanted to, but it could certainly stifle such an economy if it did emerge.

7. Interest group organization for collective bargaining backed by the threat of strikes or boycotts. This tactic has been temporarily effective for a good many workers in the 'modern' sector, and in fewer cases for peasants confronting landlords, but the gains have generally been dissipated by inflation, suppression of trade union power, or co-optation of the union leadership by the forces controlling the state. For the most disadvantaged strata the main visible target for demands has not been an employer, landlord or other private exploiter, since these strata are either self-employed or employed in small enterprises that can survive only by paying low wages and evading taxes and labour regulations, but the state itself as the source of services and consumption subsidies. In dealing with this interlocutor, it is natural to perceive clientèlism, to resort to political intermediaries or disruptive protest as more promising than permanent organization.

8. Participation in national electoral politics; choice between movements and candidates based on assessment of their programmes and their ability to carry out these programmes. This requires (a) a reasonable degree of capacity in the disadvantaged groups to aggregate their aspirations and act collectively rather than as localized competitors for political favours; (b) a reasonable degree of openness and competitiveness in the national political system, so that different political movements can offer real alternatives and have real incentives to broaden their electorates to include the poor; (c) a reasonable degree of ideological coherence and realistic appreciation of national capabilities in the political movements; (d) a reasonable degree of shared confidence in the possibility of deciding questions of resource allocation by democratic procedures; (e) voting mechanisms reasonably free of manipulation by local or national power-holders. Under typical conditions of peripheral capitalist economic growth and penetration of the illusions of the consumer society, it is hard for any political movement relying on mass support to avoid falling into the populist trap: an escalation of social promises combined with evasion of the realities of power and administrative capacity that rule out easy fulfillment of even modest promises. As Dr Prebisch has indicated, political democratization through the escalation of promises breaks down at the point when the

larger disadvantaged strata begin to enter the game. The dominant forces in the style of development then slam the gate of the consumerist paradise shut in their faces, and commonly expel many of the better-organized 'relatively poor' as well.

9. Participation in national politics for the purpose of revolutionary transformation of the society. In principle, the underdogs might become so convinced of the radical incompatibility between their aspirations and their place in the society that they would collectively envisage revolutionary action leading to the construction of a new society as the only realistic alternative. This expectation was present explicitly or implicitly in the conscientization movements that flourished in Latin America during the 1960s and early 1970s. Such a choice, however, can only under exceptional circumstances be clearcut and lasting, and the circumstances depend very little on the most disadvantaged groups. These groups, as many studies have pointed out, even in urban settings are normally more concerned with local power relationships and survival strategies than with the national scene. To the extent that revolutionary leadership brings about satisfaction of their immediate demands, a revolutionary posture tends to fade into a defensive one. If, as is more often the case, it brings about brutal repression, the group is likely to withdraw into apparent apathy, the fate of various urban as well as rural settlements originating in land seizures and for a time constituting egalitarian 'new societies'.

Moreover, the competing political movements that aspire to mobilize the underdogs make it very hard for them to grasp the content and implications of 'revolution'. In a given national setting, most of the competing movements may claim to be revolutionary; revolution may be advanced as a populist slogan, or as an attribute of an official development policy, or as a tactic for the seizure of power, or as a comprehensive strategy for rapid and thorough-going societal transformation. The different categories of disadvantaged – proletarians, sub-proletarians, peasants, etc. – confront (or would confront if they paid any attention) interminable disputes among the ideologists of the political movements concerning their roles as protagonists or more or less unreliable allies of the revolution.

Information and Action

The preceding pages suggest that quantitative information on the underdogs of Latin America remains far from complete or trustworthy, although gains have been made since the 1950s, and the continuing ideological debate has at least subjected the earlier generalizations to questioning of the supposed empirical evidence. Researchers aspiring to guide policy are still tempted to feats of statistical witchcraft in order to produce aggregates bearing on the distribution of incomes and consumption: the main weaknesses are on the side of demand for rather than supply of information. Planners, by and large, have retreated from the advocacy of comprehensive long-term plans harmonizing multiple objectives of social and economic development, requiring elaborate indicators of progress. A good many governments in the region have pinned their hopes on economic liberal policies calling for a minimum of state interference in welfare; others are concentrating on a few policy areas that the political leaders consider strategic; still others are improvising from day to day in the face of crises. Under such conditions, governments are satisfied with relatively crude statistical indicators, preferably indicators that will demonstrate the success of their policies and conceal problems they are not prepared to tackle.

Economists, sociologists and demographers, dissatisfied with national aggregates, continue to urge the introduction of methods of information-gathering and analysis capable of throwing more light on the real patterns and meaning of livelihood and consumption in specific settings, but these are expensive and time-consuming, confronting questions of costs and benefits and of linkages between information and action.

If the information that enters into national policy-making consists of separate quantifications of deficiencies in food consumption, housing, sanitation, schooling etc., aggregated at the national level or by major territorial sub-divisions, it is probable that the response will be both assistential and compartmentalized in separate programmes. If, on the other hand, certain proposals for localized and integrated monitoring of living conditions were to be applied, and the policy-making organs were to confront exhaustive information on the conditions of each impoverished hamlet and shantytown, each marginal occupational group and each type of family in the national territory, it is inconceivable that they would be able to digest the information and reconcile it with the kinds of standardized action that the state can in practice carry out.

One might hope for the emergence of information-gathering methods that would convert the 'critically poor' from statistical abstractions into groups of people with diverse reasons for under-consumption, exposed to diverse forms of exploitation and discrimination, with diverse potentialities for emerging from poverty. Ideally, such information should not only be accessible to the disadvantaged groups but should emerge from their own felt needs to understand their own situation and decide on tactics feasible within the wider social, economic and political order. A good many sociologists and anthropologists in Latin America have identified themselves with initiatives of this kind, but they are necessarily scattered and localized, informed by differing ideological preconceptions, and vulnerable to shifts in the degree of repressiveness, tolerance or co-optation in the tactics of the state. Generalization on their prospects would be premature.[6]

Notes

1. These identifications are discussed in detail in Wolfe (forthcoming).
2. For a more general study emphasizing the limitations of income distribution statistics see McGranahan 1979.
3. This document summarizes a considerable number of studies produced in the course of the project. Altimir (1981) examines the same problems from a somewhat different point of view.
4. Prebisch 1976 and 1978. In a third essay (Prebisch 1980) he rejects socialism as a remedy, mainly because of the excessive power it vests in the state, but calls for 'socialization of the surplus' and its planned use for structural transformation, implying a reinvigoration of the reformist planning of the 1960s.
5. A recent study has argued that such disruptive protest is the only really effective tactic open to the poor in a capitalist society such as the USA, and that only in precariously favourable conjunctures. The supposedly sounder tactic of permanent interest-group organization leads mainly to the domestication of protest and co-optation of leaders into the establishment. In Latin America, while the tactic has had temporary successes, the dangers to the participants are much greater and the state's capacity to buy off protest less (Scott Piven & Cloward 1979).
6. The United Nations Research Institute for Social Development is now undertaking, within its Inquiry into Participation, a study of these initiatives in Latin America which will include debates on theory and methodology among their practitioners.

References

Altimir, O. (1975): 'Estimaciones de la distribución del ingreso en América Latina por medio de encuestas de hogares y censos de población: Una evaluación de confiabilidad' (Comisión Económica para América Latina – Banco Internacional de Fomento y Desarrollo; Santiago; August).

— (1981): 'Poverty in Latin America. An Examination of Concepts and Data', *CEPAL Review* (April).

Graciarena, J. (1976): 'Types of Income Concentration and Political Styles in Latin America', *CEPAL Review*, 2 (Second Semester).

Jaguaribe, H. (1973): *Political Development: A General Theory and a Latin American Case Study* (New York, Harper & Row).

Kowarick, L. (1981): 'El precio del progreso: Crecimiento económico, expoliación urbana y la cuestión del medio ambiente', in O. Sunkel & N. Gligo (eds): *Estilos de Desarrollo y Medio Ambiente en la América Latina* (Mexico, Fondo de Cultura Económica).

Mattos, C.A. de (1979): 'Plans versus Planning in the Latin American Experience', *CEPAL Review*, 8 (August).
McGranahan, D. (1979): *International Comparability of Statistics on Income Distribution* (Geneva, UNRISD).
Molina, S., S. & S. Pinera (1979): 'Poverty in Latin America: Situation, Evolution and Policy Guidelines' (E/CEPAL/PROY.L/1, 20 June).
Portes, A. & D.F. Ferguson (1975): 'Comparative Ideologies of Poverty: Latin America and the United States' (Los Angeles, University of California, School of Architecture and Urban Planning).
Prebisch, R. (1976): 'A Critique of Peripheral Capitalism', *CEPAL Review*, 1 (First Semester).
— (1978): 'Socio-Economic Structure and Crisis of the System', *CEPAL Review*, 6 (Second Semester).
— (1980): 'Towards a Theory of the Transformation', *CEPAL Review*, 10 (April).
Scott Piven, F. & R.A. Cloward (1979): *Poor People's Movements: Why They Succeed, How They Fail* (New York, Vintage Books).
Wolfe, M. (forthcoming): 'La probeza como fenómeno social y como problema central de la política de desarrollo', in R. Franco (ed.): *Pobreza, Necesidades Básicas y Desarrollo en América Latina* (Santiago de Chile, ILPES-UNICEF).

9 IS THERE A 'NON-ECONOMIC' DEVELOPMENT?

C.A.O. van Nieuwenhuijze

In just over three decades, 'development' has gone through a sequence of metamorphoses. An unknown notion at first, it seems bound to end up as a problematic one. In between there has been an interval of prominence in apparent lucidity and credibility. This paper offers an analysis of the present quandary, designed to help envisage a way out. It must inevitably begin with a brief retrospect, designed in its turn to help identify the inherent problematic core which, in becoming manifest, is spoiling the game.

Retrospect

In the not too distant future it will be in order to find out what has caused the rapid curve of upsurge and decline. There is all the more need for this because it is typically complicated by numerous epiphenomena of the same kind, namely, the fashions that in their coming and going have incessantly destabilized professional work in development. Here, we only have space for some scattered observations.

Constitutionally, colonial domination-*cum*-dependence and equal sovereign status are worlds apart. Practically, the main effect of the transfer of sovereignty has been the diffusion of the advanced-developing relationship which previously tied metropolitan countries to their colonies on to a wider circle of newly-independent countries. Labelled 'underdeveloped', these were deemed – and reciprocally declared themselves – to stand in need of aid. This was provided as a matter of course by the developed countries: *noblesse oblige*. 'Development' became the catchword, and 'aid' its practice.

To some extent this absolved those in the West who gained control over the notion and the effort attached, along with their adepts in the rest of the world, from having to attribute a distinct significance to this freshly minted (or was it reissued?) term. They fell back, almost naturally and no doubt tacitly, on the notion of transfers: of goods, of money, and of that other commodity deemed readily available, namely 'know-how'. In this way, discontinuity seemed to blend tearlessly and fruitfully into continuity.

Indeed, the promotive effort of enlightened colonialism and that of development aid are hard to tell apart. Was this aid a post-colonial or a neo-colonial phenomenon? Beauty, and also ugliness, are in the eye of the beholder. Had decolonization been achieved, or had nothing more been gained yet than a first step in its general direction?

In raising these questions I am being unfair to those concerned. To them other issues were at stake. In working their way through a host of theoretical and practical questions, they managed to build something like a part-tacit, part-explicit consensus. In gradually becoming established notwithstanding recognized fuzziness at the seams, a development paradigm seemed to obviate the need for acute definitional quibbles. A complex of dubious consistency, retrospectively speaking, it was made up of an economic preoccupation inadequately matched by various and varying 'non-economic' concerns. It was congenial to the economically-inclined politicians and bureaucrats, and did not greatly upset the others. Academic theory-builders and field researchers readily played their reinforcing part, supported reciprocally by abundant funding. Problems did occasionally emerge, of course, and disputes to match, but these were rarely seen to refer to basics. Preferred issues were matters such as levels of commitment and availability of resources. Altogether, the consensus about the need for development and the way in which to meet it, although never perfect, seemed adequate and workable. To many, in fact, it still seems so today.

Among the issues that were intermittently raised and debated, however, there were some which seem in retrospect to have gone deeper than most. One example out of several is the critique launched against Western development professionals during the first half of the 1970s. (A rather striking instance of this occurred in Abidjan in 1974, at a meeting of directors of development studies centres.) Their preoccupation with the ailments of the Third World and with possible prescriptions for their cure, it was then alleged, made them ignore the real interrelations between the West and the Third World. The then prevailing conception of vital interrelations is now obsolete. It was supposed to be a direct cause-and-effect linkage in which the West, having first manoeuvred the Third World into the unenviable position in which it finds itself, makes sure of keeping it there. Propagandists of various feathers have eagerly availed themselves of this theme in subsequent years. When it was still fresh it was responded to by the so-called 'adjustment policies', never successful and now in turn obsolete. Still, the claim that developed and developing parts of the world together form one nexus has paved the way for more recent and better insight.

There is now an emerging realization that, to be grasped properly, the interrelations between developed and developing countries must be envisaged not on and by themselves but in context. They are instances of interaction-in-interdependence world-wide. The demand voiced in the later 1970s for a new international order is an as yet inadequate rendering of this budding insight. Unfortunately, the inadvertent addition of the epithet 'economic', a glaring and far from innocent anachronism in the connection, has worked as a stumbling block.

Meanwhile, these and other concerns have had the effect of eroding the consensus about the established development paradigm, both in the West where it originated and in the Third World into which it has spread (cf. Seitz 1981). The symptoms are unmistakable. UNRISD has published a booklet ventilating some of the pertinent concerns, in terms fit to make a U.N. diplomat blush (UNRISD 1980).[1] The Rector of the United Nations University, Soedjatmoko, used his inaugural address to announce a reorientation of his organization, away from the overriding concern with Third World development (Soedjatmoko 1980). Still, more economically-oriented agencies such as the World Bank and the profession of development economists appear to be hesitant in picking up and interpreting these distress signals. Some indeed, convinced that offensive is the best defence, claim new certainties.

Circumstances Unfavourable to Maintaining Consensus

A number of factors, none of them brand-new, have gradually gained cumulative effect to the detriment of the credibility of the established development paradigm. They challenge the very construct of a conceptual-operational nexus consisting of two categories of countries, the one developed and the other developing. The brunt of this challenge is directed at the relationship as such. Upon closer inspection, it is the cumulative effect of challenges addressed to each side of the nexus separately and to both simultaneously.

The relationship as such is under scrutiny. A significant number of people on both sides believe that the way it functions tacitly presupposes categorical and therefore unalterable inequality. The West features as superior for the very purpose of defining its relationship to the non-West. It necessarily and self-evidently stands as model. It necessarily and self-evidently provides aid. The historical backdrop to these phenomena and their essentially coincidental nature are ignored.

This is where decolonization finds its proper focus. One does not have to be a non-Westerner or a deviant to want to pursue it.

But all this is the aggregate conclusion from what is happening on each side and what is affecting both.

As regards the West, ongoing change is the undoing of any claim that it is the invariant element of the complex. The modern lifestyle, of which the development paradigm is an umistakable exponent, is on the way to being replaced by a successor pattern of as yet unclear characteristics. Expansivism and economism, along with so many other features of modernity, have residual meaning at best, pending redefinition, realignment or whatever else is in store for them.

As regards the Third World, revitalization is necessarily at odds with both a categorical role as model and a categorical function as donor being reserved for the evicted masters of yesterday. A profoundly and acutely ambiguous posture in their regard seems inevitable.

Taken together, these pressures on each side amount to a direct challenge to the established development paradigm and, consequently, to the developmental nexus as a pattern of global ordering to replace the colonial one.

A curious side effect, worth more attention than it is receiving, is that categorical notions such as Third World or 'developing countries' stand exposed as intrinsically meaningless. Unless the West is the effective centre of the earth, there is no basis for categorical definition of the entire rest of the world in residual terms of contradistinction.

More important are the responses to this resurgent need to redraw the world map, the common pressures on both sides, as just mentioned.

The West, in searching for a new identity – or rather, a configuration of identities – to replace the modern one, is at the same time groping for a new place and role in the world. What seems to many to be lingering expansivism is, to a duly updated viewpoint, interaction-in-interdependence according to rules of the game that are as yet hazy.[2] Those who decry as neo-colonial what is in fact post-colonial are the ones who block progress.

The Third World, a fictitious entity of limited politico-economic use for the time being, is, in its diverse components, struggling with basically the same issues. Self-reliance, far from amounting to effective self-insulation, is the equivalent counterpart to what appears on the part of the West as involvement. The apparent difference is a matter of coefficient, so to say. This in turn is a historical coincidence, nothing more.

The intrinsic sameness of the Western and 'non-Western' experiences is obfuscated by particularistic labelling. In the West, the talk is about a comprehensive culture crisis, and the art of futuribles is at a premium.

In the Third World, socio-cultural revitalization puts terms such as 'culture crisis' under taboo. It is this revitalization urge that has been the prime mover of nationalistic independence movements. It has been obscured temporarily by developmentalism, with its narrowly economic overtones and its strident political accompaniment. It has resurfaced more recently in diverse appearances. One is fundamentalism, of various imprints; the other is self-reliance. Under the lingering impact of modern-Western developmentalism it is still too often misrepresented as economistic and political.

To argue that the process of cultural transition is global and therefore common, *mutatis mutandis*, to both the West and the Third World, is correct to a limited extent only. An implication of this argument is that, rather than 'the West' and 'the Third World', the true settings of the manifestation of this process are, on the one hand, the globe as a whole and, on the other, specific culture areas, however defined. In this perspective 'the West' and 'the Third World' stand exposed as being, in the last resort, conceptual-analytical rubrics rather than live entities. Their reification made sense as long as the developmental nexus worked, through the practice of the established development paradigm, as an effective global order. This has become less and less the case. With the reality, its construction proves outdated.

The next question to arise is what will then hold the world together. The existential fear that marked the morning after the transfer of sovereignty, the morning of 'blossoms in the dust' (Nair 1962), namely, that 'things fall apart' (Achebe 1959), returns. In breaking-up, the developmental nexus as a global pattern risks throwing mankind on the mercy of that insatiable man-eater, the sovereign state. The only recourse from it is to 'spaceship earth' (Ward 1966): a mere notion that remains by and large to be operationalized. The obvious first step towards its operationalization is the domestication of ethnocentrism which is now given a free institutional rein under the sanctifying label of sovereignty.

In this perspective it stands to reason that decolonization, rather than continuing to be seen as the never-met restitution demand of some, should being to feature as the accomplishment of all. No doubt an imperfect accomplishment: but the perfection that remains to be achieved requires a different, prospective rather than retrospective, approach.

Is The Established Development Paradigm Vitiated?

From discerning the prospect of One World of interaction-in-interdependence, not as a utopia but as the necessary condition for the survival of mankind and a daunting one to boot, we must now return to the problem of today, the quandary of the established development paradigm and its corollary, the developmental nexus as a global pattern.

What can be overtaken so readily cannot have been very solid. On the other hand, the development paradigm, even as a case of imperfect consensus, is not the product of fools. Nor is there evidence to support the allegation, voiced in certain quarters, that these were fiendish minds. What then was wrong or went wrong?

I submit that the problem here is a matter of limitations inherent in the human condition and ignored on this account. This submission has been anticipated by extending the previous argument to the point where the problematic of ethnocentrism, typical instance of such limitation, was identified.

In necessarily living 'here and now', people will first mistake the specificity of their 'here and now' for universality. To them it is what water is to the fish. Secondly, they do not normally have to bother to render explicit what makes for this specificity-deemed-universality, the things that 'make it tick'. Their own *philosophie vécue* is their least concern. It is only when conditions change drastically, whether due to internal or external causes, that they become alerted to these matters. And it is an arduous road from shock to articulate awareness.

The argument in this section will be based on the conclusion of the previous one, namely that the West, and not the West alone, is currently going through the kind of shock just evoked. The quandary of the development syndrome is one of its symptoms. A line of reasoning will be adopted which sets out from the anticipation of a concluded effort at self-explicitness. For this reason it is somewhat hypothetical. Still, it appears probable enough. The first matter to be addressed is that which informs the development syndrome: the core of the modern-Western lifestyle or *philosophie vécue*. Next will come its relativization, and the consequences thereof. This sequence is not self-evident. Things do not become explicit without relativization. The obverse is also true. I have therefore chosen to begin at what seems a convenient starting point.

It is increasingly recognized, and has been alluded to repeatedly earlier, that the development syndrome – paradigm-*cum*-nexus – is a typical exponent or product of the modern-Western lifestyle. 'Modern' in this connection can be defined roughly as the period from the beginning of the Industrial Revolution until World War II. What needs to be made explicit, then, are the salient features of modernity as one phase of Western civilization.

This matter is currently subject to vigorous and still mounting debate.[3] This paper offers no scope for an attempt to present it, however summarily. And inasmuch as it remains inconclusive for the time being, there is also no occasion for a statement which might seem to pretend to be the final word. What can be offered is a tentative profile that appears plausible.

In one word, modern-Western civilization has been economistic. Post-modernity is at once the agony of economism and the search for an imprint to replace it.

The premise of Western modernity is that man, in conceptual primacy, relates to (Berger and Luckmann [1966] would say constructs) his *Umwelt* or context, i.e. his relevant surroundings both human and 'natural', in the capacity of subject. Concomitantly this *Umwelt* will feature as object. In further consequence, the nature of the relation is action on the part of subject with regard to object, rather than interaction between the two. This action in turn is geared towards drawing maximal rather than merely optimal returns from effort made. Cognitive mastery entails effective domination. 'Knowledge is power'. A comprehensive philosophy goes hand-in-hand with a pattern of action.

The ramifications of this basic construct are multi-dimensional and pervasive. For present purposes it will suffice to mention four features by way of illustration.

The nexus of cognition and action is nowhere clearer than in the link-up between science and technology. Science is there to be applied. Whenever modern Western man faces a constraint to his self-realization as self-assertion, he interprets it as a challenge. Challenges exist in order to be met, obstacles in order to be overcome. Technology is the choice means to make this possible. It literally moves mountains. Science, in being applied, thrives on the feedback elicited from its applicaton: a self-maintaining and self-reinforcing proposition. Scientific man is Promethean man, in virtual control of life, of reality. Still, the control is virtual. A moment may arrive, indeed is bound to arrive, when the Promethean stance will be exposed as *hybris*, an arrogant lack of sense of proportion. This moment is upon us. But I am anticipating.

Considered in a perspective of metaphysical concerns, modernity is profoundly secularist, with a hedonistic penchant. Religion is not dead, but countervailing orientations have the upper hand. Were the pendulum to swing back, modernity would be in trouble.

Next, as regards the reflection on collective human existence in line with the premise of modernity. This is the domain of the humanities and the social sciences, and in a way of public affairs. The symptom to be noted here is the preponderance of the economics discipline as the privileged intellectual instrument of modernity. The economics profession is riding the crest of an incoming wave: lucky as long as luck endures. It is because economics features as the main intellectual exponent of modernity that it seems appropriate to coin the term 'economism' to denote this life-style in its entirety.

In its turn, the practice of collective existence is marked by relentless expansive urge. This is neither new in human history nor specific to modernity. Its relentless efficacy is another matter. Modern expansiveness has changed the shape of the world. In so doing, it has provided what could only be read as proof of the true and effective universality of modernity. No room was left for the pedantic consideration that after all the efficacy of Western domination in the world was no more than a matter of historical coincidence. On the contrary, the development syndrome has come to the fore as the concluding part of the expansion process.

Now for the relativization. Relativization has come in the wake of over-extension. This over-extension has not been a matter of countervailing forces encountered but of countervailing forces engendered. This is specific to Western modernity as compared with other cases of dramatic expansiveness in human history. Where interaction, as a matter of principle, has given way to one-sided action as the dominant pattern, no built-in contraints are at work. Instead, the self-sustained impetus runs on until adverse feed-back and fall-out come to the fore, when it is too late to control them.

Resources proved not to be inexhaustible. Side-effects and after-effects, unintended and undesirable, have gradually but inexorably thrown modernity off course. Within the West and also in its relation to the non-West questions arose as to fellow man's worth. Indispensable to man, yet his object for domination and exploitation, fellow man is sooner or later bound to pose the question of mutuality. To make things worse, once this becomes a conscious act, retaliation is likely to take precedence over mutuality. The true alternative to one-sided action, namely interaction, risks becoming obscured. Trade unionism and national liberation movements in colonies address the same philosophical issue, both in a manner that fails to remedy what is basically wrong. As the pendulum swings in their favour, modernity becomes prone to withdrawal phenomena.

This is not the occasion to pursue this line of reasoning to the point of asking why such movements of antithesis fail to address the issue in a constructive manner after having thrown their spanners into the works. In seeking redress, they remain tied within the very pattern that worked to their disadvantage: not so much because it singled them out as persons or groups with pre-existent characteristics, but simply because the price had to be paid.

On the order now is the question of what was the Achilles heel of modernity which eventually became its undoing. I submit that in the last resort there are two features of success, necessarily related, which have turned into root causes of erosion.

One is that human control over reality – intellectual and then operational – hinges on the effectuation of the analytical bent of mind, to the point of dealing with a segmented world. Consider the relation between man and fellow man. Abstract categorical man, in identifying as the subject, takes primacy in all the universe: Promethean man. Equally abstract, equally categorical man, in being relegated to the status of object, is left with no more than residual, instrumental value. Personal uniqueness of incalculable value as against a commodity, replaceable at any time, and of calculable economic value. Had this been a matter of cultural schizophrenia, as some now pretend, it could not have worked. Mutuality of perspectives was operationalized as interchangeability of roles, a workable proposition except at the very top and bottom of the ensuing social stratification. It was in fact the built-in tension that lent modernity its tremendous force and resilience.

Consider also the relation between the distinct segments into which human existence has been broken up: religious, cultural, social, economic, political, and so forth. In being elevated to a status of primacy, the economic segment is implicitly made to feature as a *pars pro toto*: come to terms with the economics of the problem, and its other aspects will follow suit. In fact, the other aspects are relegated to marginality. That this is inherently and necessarily problematic will become clear, belatedly. For the development of the present argument, this point is of eminent importance.[4]

The other crucial matter is that this vision-and-life-style is not merely imagined to be universal, in the normal ethnocentric fashion that seems common to all mankind. It is workable only as an effective, or at least potential or virtual, universal. As mentioned, it is not this which is specific to Western Modernity. Nor is it that a relentless effort is required to effectuate this universality claim, implicitly questioning its validity as a world view. Rather it is that obstacles encountered are in this case products of the expansiveness itself.

This is new, which is why the outcome is likely to differ from that of earlier instances of the rise and fall of civilizations or civilizational phases.

At this point the ambiguity of post-colonial versus neo-colonial announces itself once more, as a symptom of the interim phase of post-modernity and its echoes world-wide. The development syndrome, whilst an outstanding corollary to Western modernity in its inspiration, is a neat case of cultural lag in its timing. It represents what Sartre has called *indépassabilité*: the paradigm may be recognizedly obsolete, but for lack of an adequate successor we remain caught within it as our perhaps inconvenient yet seemingly natural frame of reference (Sartre 1960). As the uneasiness mounts, the outcry for 'rethinking development' becomes louder, but its effectuation not necessarily more convincing.[5]

Rethinking Development

Some people persist in saying that the trouble with development work is precisely the urge to rethink. To them this is far from new, indeed it is something close to a *vitium originis*, a basic flaw. They certainly have a point. But if the present demand proves in fact to be new, for instance by being of a different order, they may yet turn out to be wrong.

The hazy complexity of the established development paradigm, with its rapid turnover of fads and foibles, is not all that elusive. It is alike a constellation. The various and forever varying 'non-economic' concerns (tell-tale label this) are so many moons orbiting around the steady planet of economics. The role of the gravitational pull goes to the *philosophie vécue* of economism. It is in this configuration that 'non-economic' concerns acquire their puzzling appearance: marginal without being derivative, and forever problematic. A fresh challenge would be truly new if, instead of contributing to the turnover of subsidiary concerns (increasingly presented as all-absorbing panics), it were to challenge the configuration as such.

Prior to pursuing this thought, some illustration of what has just been said may be helpful. In selecting the social aspect or dimension of development for this purpose, I am also anticipating what will become the focus of the argument as it develops further.

Concern with the social aspect or dimension of development – some have simply spoken of social development – has played a role from the early days. Repeatedly left in abeyance, it was equally often resuscitated. This was not primarily a matter of certain academic disciplines vying with economics for a place under the sun. It has mostly been the bureaucrats, especially in international agencies, who have returned to the issue, not without reliance on expert help. In reviewing the record of pertinent discourse, one is struck by a merry-go-round of poorly-argued and largely inconsequential postulates. Two are recurrent: one postulates 'economic means toward social goals', or for that matter the obverse; the other counsels a 'balance between social and economic'. The hidden agenda beneath such theoretical fireworks is invariably diplomatic. This can explain but not excuse the fact that attempts to define 'social' mostly abort into inventories of fields and sub-fields of bureaucratic competence (van Nieuwenhuijze 1979a).

The dichotomy of 'social' and 'economic' in the developmental perspective unmistakably echoes that prevailing in the modern West. The ceaseless effort there to come to terms with it has resulted in the welfare state, now a problematic issue in its own right (van Nieuwenhuijze 1979b).

The parallelism between replica and original is limited: what interferes is the structure of colonial society. The institutional effectuation of the model of one-sided action as self-reinforcing domination precludes an accommodation of mutuality as a corrective, except belatedly. This is the tragedy of enlightened colonialism. In the modern West, 'social' has become the categorical and flexible label under which anything can be assembled that relates to adverse fall-out from economic pursuits. In the colonies, the slowly accumulating adverse fall-out was not readily identifiable as resulting from economic pursuits only. In a somewhat different manner, this also applies to subsequent developmentalism. Its economic features were no doubt more outstanding, but they were also more clearly at loggerheads with the political ones. Hence a negative label such as 'non-economic'. Basically it is not more inadequate than is 'social' in the West, but it is more embarrassing.

This may prove an advantage in the longer term. Indeed, its unsatisfactory nature should have an alerting effect.

The exercise in comparison between post-modernity in the West and developmentalism in the Third World leads to some far-reaching conclusions.

The post-modern interim in the West is the process-*cum*-effort to grope one's way from a lifestyle of one-sided action rendered workable by subsidiary concessions to mutuality, towards what appears provisionally as a prospect of interaction. A philosophical anthropology to match will be in order. The same applies to the Western posture and role in the world. The prospect is for a return to the Common Human Pattern (Romein 1957), from which modernity had deviated to its temporary advantage. This common pattern is undoubtedly no longer the same, amongst other things because of the Western deviation in the past and its impending and ineluctable reinsertion. A new self-image, perhaps not so much of the West as of each of its components, is the needed corollary.

Economism as the main feature of this lifestyle is on the wane, and there is only a hazy prospect of the imprint that will succeed it. Meanwhile, demarginalization and the ensuing deproblematization of the other aspects of reality – and beyond these, reconsideration of the extent to which and the ways in which its segmentation is workable – seem to be on the agenda.

In all this the need is to move beyond a mere reversal of roles and optiques, lest the *indépassabilité* of the obsolete paradigm be worsened. The blockages are many. To sum them up, one may paraphrase Fromm's notion of 'fear of freedom' and speak of 'fear of destabilization' (Fromm 1942).

The same, *mutatis mutandis*, goes for the Third World so far as it is affected by developmentalism. This is the case to a limited extent only. Besides, it is really a matter of the past. Both as an orientation and as a practice, developmentalism is open to challenge. Its presuppositions – modernity in vigour in the West coupled to Western domination in the world – have evaporated.

Under these conditions, the components of the figment that is named 'Third World' are thrown back upon themselves in what inevitably amounts to an identity crisis, a struggle for the public mind. The circumstance that sovereign states everywhere claim to have or be the answer can only deepen it.

In this context decolonization is primarily a conceptual problem. Post-colonialism turns out to be neo-colonialism only to the extent that it is a state of mind. If there is a relatively quick answer to this quandary, it may well have to be adumbrated by rethinking development (or should one say, thinking beyond development?) for the simple reason that, for the time being, it is the notion with the highest salience, the widest scope and the worst elusiveness. The elusiveness may help in that any rethinking may be announced as clarification. Still the need is for a deep probe. The virtual demise of both the aid nexus and economism have to be accounted for.

The burden of this rethinking, in the sense of thinking beyond development, as an effort at decolonization, undoubtedly falls upon those of the Third World. This need not exclude that some from the West would offer a contribution. Self-reliance is not achieved by self-entrenchment. The rest of this paper represents an effort to make such a contribution, motivated by the simultaneous exercise of rethinking the Western stance.

Unveiling 'Non-Economic' Development

Those interested in the 'non-economic' side of development have tended over the years to use such terms as 'social' and, more recently, 'cultural'. In its turn, religion is no longer unmentionable. In choosing such notions, they follow what Western modernity did in adopting 'social' when in similar straits. The question is whether, in following the terminological lead they will next also fall into the same conceptual trap, namely, of introducing in an afterthought a corrective of merely cosmetic effect.

Having argued the specifically cultural aspect of this matter elsewhere (van Nieuwenhuijze 1983), I propose here to reopen the discussion of social development. This cannot be done in disregard of culture, but the focus will be social.

A new round of debate on social development presupposes a fresh approach; a clear departure from the standing approach, or at least from its crucial elements, is required. This departure is indicated by the virtual demise of economism as the conditioning frame of reference. At the same time it is rendered hazardous to say the least by the circumstance that the successor frame of reference is still far from clear.

It seems beyond doubt that a reconceptualized social sector (or aspect?) will have to be a demarginalized one. Demarginalized, it need not be inherently problematic.

Perhaps one can reason up to a point on the strength of the assumption that economism is effectively, not just virtually out. But this is a precarious perch, all the more so if beyond conceptualization we consider operationalization, as would seem to be in order. (At the present juncture it seems too far-fetched to dismiss the conceptual-operational nexus as if it were another achievement of modernity fit only for the scrap heap. It deserves more careful reconsideration than that.) On the other hand, the assumption of discontinuity, with regard to economism in this case, is a helpful one. Prognosis in the manner of extrapolation of ongoing trends is hardly the proper means under conditions of obvious change. Awareness of discontinuity and of the problems it causes is a much better trigger for creative anticipation.

'Social' Development?

The argument hitherto leads to a double realization with an element of inner contradiction built in. The meaning of 'development' needs to be redesigned in such a way that its sociocultural dimension is given its due, no doubt together with other 'non-economic' dimensions or aspects. At the same time, the relevant effort is hampered by the hold that economism exerts upon the mind, even in its dying hour.

Under the circumstances, careful stocktaking is necessary to prevent one moving around in circles. Analysis of ongoing debate in the West and here and there in the Third World, is one means by which to avoid the most obvious traps; the exercise in conceptual clarification is another. Both have been given their due above, but a summary may be useful at this point.

The debates in the West and in the Third World show significant differences. In the West there are in fact two separate circuits. The one, 'post-modern', addresses in more or less random fashion the symptoms of what some call a culture crisis. Their clarity of vision is hampered by the current fascination with the quandary of the welfare state. The other, 'post-colonial', refers to allegedly social issues that block the efficacy of economic development aid. There is little evidence of awareness that each circuit is trying to come to terms with a set of symptoms of what is basically a deeper order of problems unwittingly confronted by both.

In the Third World there are again two circuits of debate, perhaps less drastically apart but in turn failing to coalesce. One is a weak replica of the Western circuit just mentioned; the other is the self-reliance issue debated mostly in the wrong, i.e. economic-political terms, for the wrong reasons (namely, the wish to continue to receive aid without having to recognize it for what it is).

The 'post-modern' Western debate evinces all the ambiguity that might be expected when the established paradigm (in a somewhat broader sense than that of Kuhn [1962]) is no longer satisfactory and its successor not yet operational. The debate about the 'culture crisis' is fragmented into uncounted issues, each deemed a matter of the survival of mankind. Prophets of doom have a field day,[6] albeit not without meeting some competition, more recently on the part of bringers of good tidings.[7] These things should be contemplated with more detachment than the media, with their distortive ways, will allow their consumers.

Une civilisation peut faire preuve de dynamisme tout en étant pessimiste. C'est notre cas. Ce fut aussi celui de nos ancêtres, au début de la modernité européenne (Delumeau 1983: 110).

Moreover, one should realize that any post-modern Western debate about anything concerning culture is handicapped by the marginal sense of culture according to modern thinking. Hence the near-inevitability of mistaking symptoms for core issues. Hence again, the difficulty of coming to terms with such symptoms in a non-regressive manner. The quandary of the welfare state is painfully illustrative in this regard. Too readily it will be assumed that the proper response is to ask how the economy can be made to resume support of the welfare paradise.

Nevertheless, here and there there are budding discussions that may conceivably lead out of such vicious circles. For example, in the face of the overheated conservatism of trade unions and their politicians, questions are beginning to be raised about the significance of labour as a phenomenon specific to Western modernity rather than as the natural and universal means to provide a person's livelihood. Properly pursued, these could help anticipate the shape of things to come (Van Nieuwenhuijze 1984).

So much is beyond doubt that the sense of 'social' which has become enshrined in the welfare syndrome is being challenged, even where the discussion seems to avoid probing into it. Much will depend on the outcome of these efforts, at once timid and inevitable.

Separately, the Western debate on 'rethinking development' seems to drag along without leading to new openings. Faddism and professional vested interests, *bien étonnés de se trouver ensemble*, seem to cause a mood of tiredness for which even the most frantic preaching of good causes or, for that matter, the most indignant denunciation of evil schemes provides no cure.

The more recent fads have included the attempt to refocus attention upon the social concomitants or preconditions to (always 'economic') development. Where even the sociologists involved think economistically in the last resort, this is doomed to be of little avail. The elusiveness of things categorically conceived as social has been remedied, serendipitously, by the somewhat lurid accent placed upon 'culture' by agents whose conceptual apparatus favours less antiseptic terms, such as 'religion'. This has not facilitated the matter except in one not insignificant respect: it has obviated derailment of the debate into issues of 'national culture', of World War II notoriety.

The Third World replica of the latter Western debate is weak in that those eligible to conduct it are loath to do so: their very role and status hinge upon the vigour of the standing development syndrome. By questioning it, they can but undermine their own position. This need not be true in the long term, of course, but for the one who does not survive in the short term there can be no long term.

It is also weak in that the connotations of the division between 'economic' and 'social' or 'socio-cultural' tend to differ from those in the modern and post-modern West. Where the 'modern' Western-trained intelligentsia, in their relatively new role as the élite and political leadership, are identified perhaps unwittingly with the economics of the matter (whatever the matter: in fact, with economism), the common man, by contradistinction, may end up wearing the label 'socio-cultural'. This is very different from the Western situation, except that here, too, 'socio-cultural' is inherently problematic, all the more so since it has been proven potentially amenable to revolutionary (or 'counter-revolutionary'?) impulses. The net effect is that to those in control 'social' tends to acquire ominous overtones: hardly the best inducement to an exercise in conceptual and practical clarification which nonetheless appears to be acutely in order. The prospect of a power struggle between exponents of the economic and socio-cultural sides of public affairs is nightmarish, yet real.

Finally, the 'self-reliance' debate in the Third World is a remarkable affair. At least two strands intermingle in it, to the point of being inextricable. First, the renewed self-assertion engendered by high-colonial involvement of 'natives' in the colonial enterprise, and unintentionally fostered by late colonialism, is clearly a primarily socio-cultural urge. Its cultural aspect, however, is soon hidden beneath the surface. To be effective, self-assertion has had to adopt an appearance that is sufficiently contradistinctive to enable it to establish a working relationship, however potentially antagonistic, to its counterpart, colonial power. It does so by becoming political, thus exposing the true nature, under the new circumstances, of the economico-administrative operational pattern of colonialism. Much the same goes for its social component, the yearning for social justice which has been another motive force prompting the liberation urge. Its net effect, as in most socio-political revolutions, has been the substitution of a new autochthonous élite for the departing colonizers. The main part of the revindication was transferred to the development syndrome. There it stays, as an unpaid bill.

Another strand in the self-reliance debate is the curious way in which the substitution of the development syndrome for late colonialism has shifted attention away from the constitutional ground where political liberation had landed it, back to the economic-administrative mode of high colonialism. This is in fact where the ambiguity of post-colonialism and neo-colonialism most poignantly comes to the fore. Hidden beneath it is what is nowadays called, dramatically yet inadequately, an identity crisis.

For all practical purposes the self-reliance debate appears to have been distracted from addressing this issue of collective identity and collective purpose in One World, to concerns that are constitutional and largely economistic. The reason is that the latter appear to be more acute. The question is whether acuteness is the proper measure of importance.

What remains to be underscored is the common element in these disparate circuits of discourse. In each, one can notice something like a tragic misconception at play. The minds are engrossed in apparently vital issues of immediate importance and, what is worse, of maddening intractability. What causes all the preoccupation and frustration is that there is something inherently elusive about the issues identified and addressed. In the conceptual-terminological game of hide-and-seek which seems to result, the suspicion arises of a rift between economic, political, organizational-managerial, and such-like concerns on the one hand and, on the other, socio-cultural and other considerations in the realm of what is warily termed 'values'. Is it a matter of the more manageable versus the more sensitive, indeed thorny, side of public affairs? Is it the longer versus the short term? Is it the more basic versus the more superficial layer of real problems faced? Or, on the other hand, is it the division as such which is the cause of so much embarrassment? By busying oneself with the former one fails to account for the latter, to one's detriment; and vice versa.

Perhaps it can be summed up by identifying a need to come to terms with what, for all practical purposes, has long remained the dark side of the moon. I refer to that part or aspect of reality which, whether named 'non-economic' or 'socio-cultural', has been either elusive or problematic by necessity or indeed by definition, for no better reason than that, in the view of modernistic economism, it had to be marginal as a matter of principle.

Envisaging a Prospect

The argument has reached the point where the question has been raised and its validity and timeliness argued. What of 'social' or 'socio-cultural' development as a concept-*cum*-practice to countervail or perhaps correct 'economic' development?

To propose or prescribe an answer at the present juncture would be idle pretense. If it were possible, things would not be as difficult as they are.

The nature of the feasible exercise is limited. It is anticipation without benefit of either extrapolation or expansive-ethnocentric transmogrification. It is in problems identified and as yet unresolved that one may hope to find clues. At the same time there are some obvious caveats to heed and temptations to avoid.

One of these is to postulate a social or socio-cultural segment or aspect of reality in such a way as to ascribe to it the same primacy and comprehensive-expansive vigour as economism ascribes to the economy. To do this would amount to proclaiming a virtual replica of the modern world view, with one element changed. True, it is the most salient element. But once it would have been replaced, the encompassing world view would prove at least as important as its most salient element. Indeed, this kind of substitution could hardly provide the answer to the quandary of modernity as the *philosophie vécue* of a particular civilization during a particular period. There must be better ways to demarginalize 'social' as a precondition to redefining it.

In the post-modern West reconsideration and eventual redefinition of 'social' requires anticipation of the demise of economism as the dominant world view, and ensuing latitude for fresh constructive thought. It is a matter of groping one's way rather than a free exercise in blueprinting.

This also applies to the parallel effort in respect of 'Third World development'. But important additional considerations come into play here. To the Third World, economism has initially been a matter of effective Western expansiveness, indeed imposition. Currently it remains a matter of availability for adoption. This, however, is no longer a clear proposition inasmuch as the obsolescence of economism will increasingly demand attention. Thus, it is not merely a question of socio-cultural relevancy of the imported-adopted model. Over and above it, there is the question of the proper frame of reference, presupposing a socio-cultural identity that is effectively in force. Decolonization is not a simple and straightforward proposition.

Nor are these the only hurdles on the path that remains to be traversed.

In the realm of public affairs, the language and mode of operations of government constitute a case of cultural lag in their own right. They are bound to prove at odds with any conceptual-terminological framework and concomitant action pattern which deviate from the established economic-political one. In particular, the implicit refusal to abstain from rocking the boat in respect of such matters as social structure is downright frightening.

In view of these difficulties, academia could appear to have a calling. The expectation is that it will pave the way for updating and adaptation by divulging new insights. This challenge is hard to meet, however, due to internal obstacles. These are in part a matter of professional vested interests as reflected, for instance, in the pecking order of the social science disciplines. More importantly, it is once more the lack of a new paradigm (now more strictly in Kuhn's sense) which, in ensuring the belated sway of modernity and its standard bearer, economism, puts an ineluctable hold on creativity. This is the more embarrassing as, with modernity, the pretense that scholarship moulds reality is going by the board. The current ambiguity of critical versus reinforcing social science illustrates this stalemate, whilst pointing up the need to overcome it by constructive interpretation of ongoing developments.

On the other hand, by not speaking the language of government and not keeping up with the academic Joneses, is one in an unenviable position? Were government in excellent shape and achieving development without fuss and were development economics a fail-safe prescription, it would be foolish to go out on a limb in the way this argument is doing. But there is general concern that not all governments achieve what they set out to achieve, and there are economists who talk about a crisis in economics.[8]

Under such circumstances, not speaking the language of government may have a positive rather than negative meaning. It may eventually help to break through some vicious circles. Indeed, it may help to liberate governments from the counterdevelopmental fall-out that increasingly seems to ensue from their established patterns of operation. Only the government that insists upon seeing its power as a goal in itself rather than as a means to some further purpose, is beyond the salvaging effect of this vision.

One question remains. If rethinking development is in order, why not simply rethink 'economic development', as many intentionally or unwittingly appear to advocate? Why opt for an alternative label, and one that is far from self-explanatory?

The answer is that it is proper to mark a new stage by an appropriate signal. The signal chosen is primarily negative. It does away with 'economic' as the symptom of pervasive economism. It thus accepts the challenge posed by the obsolescence of economism, as well as that ensuing from the realization of its cultural specificity. It is also positive in that 'social', or rather 'socio-cultural', begs the question in two strategic regards, namely, demarginalization,[9] and relevancy to socio-culturally specific conditions.

To avoid any misunderstanding, let it be said that this paper has not been inspired by the wish to cut the economists down to size, let alone to chase them away from development work. What trouble there is is not with the discipline of economics as such. Rather it is with this discipline as the conscious or unwitting exponent of a world view which, for one thing, is on the way out, and for another, has never had more than dubious relevance when and where imposed outside its native lands. No discipline currently faces graver difficulty in consequence of cultural transition than economics. This refers to its standing among the social sciences, and even more to its stature and potential as a vision of reality. All this is beyond the scope of this paper. What does deserve mention here is that the array of disciplines at work on public affairs (whether labelled 'development' or otherwise) stands to be reshuffled as each of them struggles to overcome the constraints and liabilities of economism. In this connection, reconsideration of the old and forgotten ideal of interdisciplinarity may well prove indispensable.

Notes

1. This has been followed more recently by another UNRISD publication (Wolfe 1981).
2. No longer expansive, the West remains necessarily involved in the world at large. The distinction eludes many in the Third World: a difficulty caused by cultural lag. Another factor of misunderstanding is that, contrary to the prevailing Third World perception, the West is not one. Precisely in regard of expansiveness, the 'East wing' lags behind the 'West wing'. To this writer's awareness, modernity appears to be waning much faster in the latter than in the former. The present argument is, in this respect, by and large restricted to the West wing.
3. See, for example, Reiss 1982.
4. This observation may lack credibility coming from a sociologist. Professional jealousy could seem to be the motive. It is therefore in order to note that the same argument can be heard from economists. See, for example, Attali & Guillaume (1974). Guillaume has recently summarized his views in an interview in *Le Monde*, 22-23 April 1984, p.V. Compare also de Radkowski 1980.
5. The periodical of the Dag Hammarskjöld Foundation, *Development Dialogue*, published a special issue in 1980 entitled *Another Development, Perspective for the 'Eighties*.
6. The series of publications by the Club of Rome, especially the opening volume, offers fair illustration. Fairly recently, the late chairman, Aurelio Peccei, has struck a particularly ominous note (Peccei 1981). See also Ehrenfeld 1978.

7. Examples include Toffler 1980, Servan-Schreiber 1980, Capra 1982. A slightly different and in some ways more curious work representing the same mood is Ferguson 1980.

8. As a recent work (Bell and Kristall 1981) proves, economists do not avoid the term 'crisis' in referring to their discipline. But do they dig deep enough in analyzing it, or do they fall for the temptation to seek shelter in more or less apologetic stocktaking?

9. The repeated accentuation of the need to demarginalize offers an implicit response to the somewhat supercilious challenge thrown at the 'non-economists' by someone like van Dam (1982) who does not hesitate to write off the interest pursued here (and elsewhere by others) as a 'flight into the margin'.

References

Achebe, Chinua (1959): *Things Fall Apart* (Greenwich, Conn, Fawcett).

Attali, J. & M. Guillaume (1974): *L'anti-économique* (Paris, PUF).

Bell, Daniel, & Irving Kristall (eds) (1981): *The Crisis in Economic Theory* (New York, Basic Books).

Berger, Peter, & Thomas Luckmann (1966): *The Social Construction of Reality, A Treatise in the Sociology of Knowledge* (Garden City, N.Y., Doubleday).

Capra, Fritjof (1982): *The Turning Point: Science, Society, and the Rising Culture* (London, Wildwood House).

Van Dam, F. (1982): 'Vlucht in de marge', *Economisch-Statistische Berichten*, 67, 3374, 29 September.

Delumeau, Jean (1983): *Le péché et la peur, La culpabilisation en Occident (XIIIe-XVIIIe siècles)* (Paris, Fayard).

Ehrenfeld, David (1978): *The Arrogance of Humanism* (London, Oxford University Press).

Ferguson, Margaret (1980): *The Aquarian Conspiracy, Personal and Social Transformation in the 1980s* (New York, St Martins Press, distributor).

Fromm, Erich (1942): *The Fear of Freedom* (London, Kegal Paul, Trench, Trubner).

Kuhn, Thomas (1962): *The Structure of Scientific Revolutions* (Chicago, University Press).

Nair, Kusum (1962): *Blossoms in the Dust, The Human Factor in Indian Development* (New York, Praeger).

van Nieuwenhuijze, C.A.O. (1979a): *Social Development, Supplement or Corrective to Economic Development?* (The Hague, Institute of Social Studies, Occasional Paper 69).

— (1979b): *Social Development: The Social Welfare Approach* (The Hague, Institute of Social Studies, Occasional Paper 76).

— (1982): *Development Begins at Home* (Oxford, Pergamon).

— (1983): *Culture and Development, The Prospects of an Afterthought* (The Hague, Institute of Social Studies, Occasional Paper 97; to appear in *Civilisations*).

— (1984): 'The Prospect of "Work"' (The Hague, Institute of Social Studies, mimeo).

Peccei, Aurelio (1981): 'Auf dem Weg in die Katastrophe', *Der Spiegel*, 18 May, 81-104.

de Radkowski, Georges-Hubert (1980): *Les jeux du désir* (Paris, PUF, Croisées).

Romein, J.M. (1957): 'The Common Human Pattern', *Journal of World History* IV/1, 449-63.

Reiss, Timothy (1982): *The Discourse of Modernism* (Ithaca, Cornell University Press).

Sartre, Jean-Paul (1960): *Critique de la raison dialectique* (Paris, Gallimard, NRF).
Seitz, K. (1981): 'Die Krise der Entwicklung in der Dritten Welt', *Europa Archiv*, 36/14, 417-27.
Servan-Schreiber, Jean-Jacques (1980): *Le défi mondial* (Paris, Fayard).
Soedjatmoko (1980): 'The United Nations University's Next Stage' (Statement Before the Sixteenth Session of the Council of the UN University, 1 December; Tokio, UNU, mimeo).
Toffler, Alvin (1980): *The Third Wave* (New York, Marrow).
UNRISD (1980): *The Quest for a Unified Approach to Development* (Geneva, UNRISD, Report 80.3).
Ward, Barbara (1966): *Spaceship Earth* (New York, Columbia University Press).
Wolfe, Marshall (1981): *Elusive Development* (Geneva, UNRISD).

10 SOCIAL INDICATORS AS APPLIED IN PLANNING: NOTIONS, CRITERIA AND METHODS

Briitta Koskiaho

Changes of Paradigm and Social Indicators

A paradigm is a general perspective, or a way of breaking-down the complexity of the real world. It is related to the socialization of researchers and planners at the moment, and narrates what is important and what is legitimate and reasonable. Thus, a paradigm is also normative. While a strong commitment to a paradigm exists, no consideration or deliberation is needed concerning the problems of existence and epistemology (Patton 1978).

Research methods are more sophisticated when consensus exists in the scientific community regarding the approaches to be used. Such a situation was dominant in Western social sciences in the 1950s and 1960s when the development of social indicators relied on the positivistic conception of science.

What kind of paradigm dominates social indicator thinking? The tradition of liberalism which prevailed in Western industrial countries, enriched with the ideas of the protestant reformation and with the philosophy of enlightenment, is behind the generation of social indicators. This is reflected, for instance, in the following facts. Emphasis is placed on the importance of the individual, while society and state are regarded as faceless background figures. This has contributed to the fact that the development of social indicators has often been rather atomistic. Indicators do not form a theoretically sound system which can be outlined and understood as a whole. When a problem occurs that is considered to be important, it is simply added to the indicator repertoir without further discussion.

What is 'good for people' is the utmost ideal in the development of social indicators. According to the liberalistic tradition the 'good' is an individualistic one: every person is regarded as being the best judge of his or her own good.

A contradiction arises, however, when social indicators are applied in transmitting information for the use of planning – a contradiction that is caused by the fact that planning, even in Western countries, is understood as a rather centralized activity requiring information that is essential from the point of view of the totality. The problem of combining what is good for the individual with what is good for society is complicated. Moreover, when thoughts according to which the 'good for society' cannot conceptually be derived from 'good for the individual' are transformed into the idea that the societal good as such cannot exist but only the 'good for the individual', then the theoretical basis of social indicators becomes lost.

Under the philosophy of enlightenment, society was a coalition of sovereign individuals. Society was regarded as important because, through it, individuals could guarantee the realization of their existence and of their welfare. Society was understood only from the point of view of individual interests, and it remained an abstraction. This kind of thinking, although criticized by Hegel and his followers, has continued up to the present day, stronger in some countries and weaker in others. An understanding of the nature and functions of social indicators obviously depends on this kind of comprehension, reflected in present-day society through different notions of state. It is necessary to examine the relations between the services of society, i.e. public consumption, on the one hand, and private consumption on the other; or the nature of the relationship between human self-actualization and society.

Apart from understanding the role of the state, another primary conception is the understanding of economies. The protestant reformers emphasized new ethical values and the importance of continuous exertion. The work ethic was created. But it was not until the 1750s, while the change from mercantilism to physiocratism was taking place, that these patterns of thought were reflected in economic theories. This change anticipated the emphasis on economic growth which has since become so important. In the doctrine of the physiocrats the static notion of economies was replaced by a dynamic one; it was said that the total stock of wealth could now increase whereas before only the preservation of wealth had been understood. The notion of growth and the dynamics of economic agents generated the basis for the rise of industry and for the fact that economic growth later became the leading idea of industrialization. As liberalism gradually superseded the doctrine of the physiocrats, the importance of work as an essential element for economic growth came to be established. Work is productive when its results can become part of what is referred to as the economy.

During the 19th century classical liberalism, which emphasized merely the importance of the individual, met with some criticism. It was transformed into social-liberalism, which recognizes, in addition to economic activities, the state as a regulator, and which proved meaningful for the later appearance of social indicators. The influence of Millian liberalism is clearly noticeable, for instance, in the Scandinavian notion of economies. As the process of work has become ever more restricted through industrial development, unrestricted human self-actualization in work is no longer possible. Leisure time has become the substituting arena: people actualize themselves during their leisure time.

The lists of social indicators that have been developed show that they concentrate on that sector of human activity which takes place for the greater part outside working time. True, employment and working conditions are also represented on these lists, but this is quite modest inasfar as the totality is concerned. The Millian notion is reflected in the extensive inclusion of public consumption, and in the appearance of public services as a producer of 'good for the people' together with private consumption.

This pattern of thought is associated with the Keynesian economic policies which later gained predominance. Keynesian economic theory awarded labour the role of essential factor of production, and the forestalling of unemployment became a principal objective of government control. In fact, unemployment is represented among social indicators.

The Friedmanian thinking of economic policy, which has lately evolved into a new and rather significant school of liberalism, gives major attention to other aspects of the economy than the role of labour, in particular to monetary and financial policies. This means that the role of government as an independent agent of change has fallen into the background and that the sphere of economics has been pushed into the forefront. This is well-suited to the latest developments in social indicator research in which the focus is no longer on 'good for people' actualized through public consumption, particularly through various kinds of services, but is instead on the analysis of people's attitudes and assessments: a shift from the analysis of publicly-produced services to the study of the thoughts of individuals as members of society is now taking place. Actually, it would be quite contradictory to measure the good produced by public services at the same time that their substantial reduction is made a target of economic policy.

The golden era of social indicators occurred when Western industrial nations enjoyed the strong post-Second World War expansion. The striving for economic growth also induced researchers to unite in analyzing development. Later it was realized that to start research merely from the viewpoint of economic growth considerably narrows the possibility of perceiving all dimensions of development: social and economic aspects should be considered together. Recognition thus grew that the social sphere cannot be studied through the economic one, that the social sphere is important in itself, and that there is a social goal of development.

That the independence of the economic and social spheres should be emphasized was understandable while the economic sphere dominated the other, but the distinction was to become detrimental to the social sphere. Since social development was expected to prove its capability of competing with economic development, social progress also had to be measured. Measurements were developed by imitating economic indicators, and no attempts were made to study the social sphere by more adequate means. The social sphere remained subordinated to the economic one regardless of its endeavours to become independent. This was due partly to the fact that economists and statisticians were the first to give any attention to the measurement of social development, and that they developed the initial idea of social indicators.[1] They fulfilled this task within the framework of their own educational background and way of thinking, causing rules of measurement of the economic sphere to be transferred to the social sphere.

This was necessary in the 1950s and 1960s, however, when social scientists were unable to liberate themselves and to achieve independent thought and study of the social sphere under different paradigms. Their thinking was associated with the positivistic conception of science, and it was thus easy for them to understand the social indicator measurement introduced by economists and statisticians. Measuring united them under a common paradigm. If the qualitative paradigm, characterized by a phenomenological, inductive, holistic, subjective, process-oriented and social anthropological approach would have had any effect on the social sciences, comprehension of the social sphere would have been broadened and deepened. On the other hand, it is unthinkable that the quantitative paradigm of economic research could have suited the qualitative paradigm of the social sciences, qualitative being understood as a hermeneutic concept: a conceptual language would have been missing. And so the social sphere was understood to be measurable.

In view of the predominantly quantitative notion of planning, it was unthinkable that any other kind of information but measurable data concerning the social sphere would have been accepted. Also, planning is associated with the dominant paradigm of science.

The Need for Measurable Information Associated with the Social Order*

The philosophy of social indicators has seldom been submitted to thorough analysis. Obviously, their development is associated with ideas concerning the measurability of social reality and human behaviour which gained ground within the social sciences after World War II. This notion of measurability, for its part, was associated with the positivistic concept of science.

Primarily hard data are utilized in positivistic research. In the search for different kinds of invariances, a point has been reached at which a definite demand for the measurability of information concerning society and people is expressed. Measurable quantities can be understood as comparable when moving in time and from one place to another. Cultural barriers are not considered as insurmountable; in fact, comparative studies formed one of the mainstreams of social research during the 1960s.

The request for measurable data was also connected with the need of social planning to have varied and comprehensive information about society. The social order, i.e. the request for useful societal information, presupposes the production and further presentation of readily comprehendible information. Measurable information is easier to disclose than qualitative information, which is more versatile and may have various meanings. To a positivistic researcher, the difference between quantitative and qualitative becomes meaningful in relation to the subject matter or, more accurately, in relation to measurement. In interpretative sociology, which is based on the phenomenological interest of knowledge, qualitative means comprehension (*Verstehen*) (Laitinen 1981).

The approach taken by the person who measures is based on three fundamental ideas: on the axiom of the mathematical structure of reality that originated with Copernicus; on the theory of primary and secondary qualities created by Galileo; and on the concept of causality which forms part of Newtonian mechanics. Thus, theories of measurement seek their support from the paradigm that has a natural science orientation, and from the classical notion of measurement that has been applied in a variety of ways and from which different kinds of transformations have been derived.

In the classical notion of measurement the empirical appears as a

---

* The term 'social order' refers here to the continuously existing request for useful societal information.

numerical structure, and scaling of this is endeavoured. The process of measurement in the primary meaning of the term is displayed in Figure 1 (Randolph 1979). In applied measurement, observation taking place through the senses is replaced by measurement; this is what we call the epistemological (*erkenntnistheoretische*) interpretation (see Figure 2).

Figure 1.

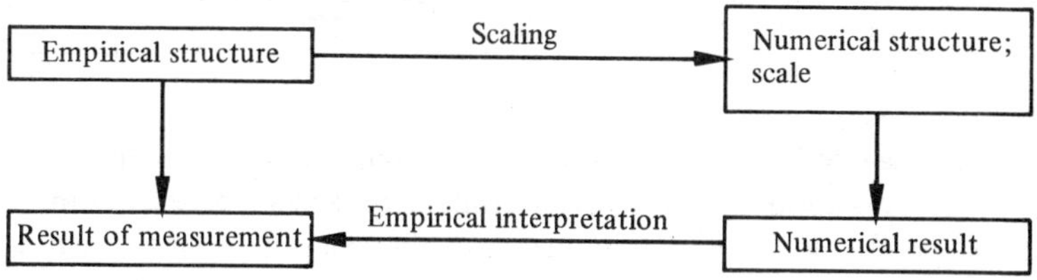

Figure 2.

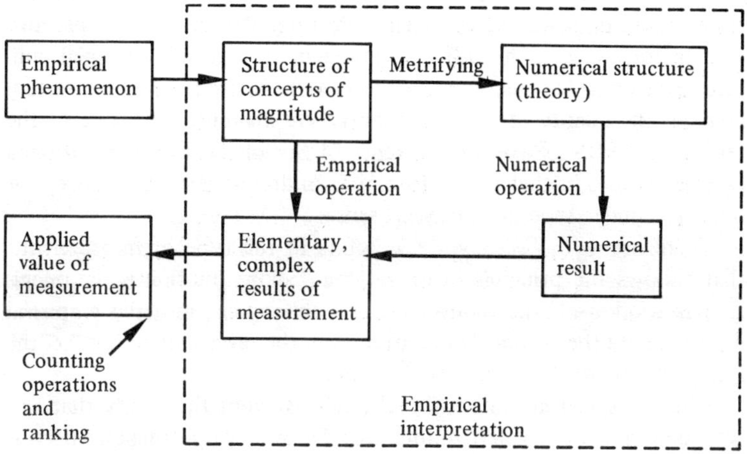

In social indicators research, measurement is usually indirect. It is not sufficient to carry out the applied measurement only, but operationalization is also necessary. Indeed, it has often been recognized that one of the most crucial problems of research on social indicators is the successfulness of the operationalization. The virtual measurement is connected with the primary measurement, as shown in Figure 3.

In the measurement procedure illustrated, the measurable concepts are derived from the theoretical construction through operationaliza-

Figure 3.

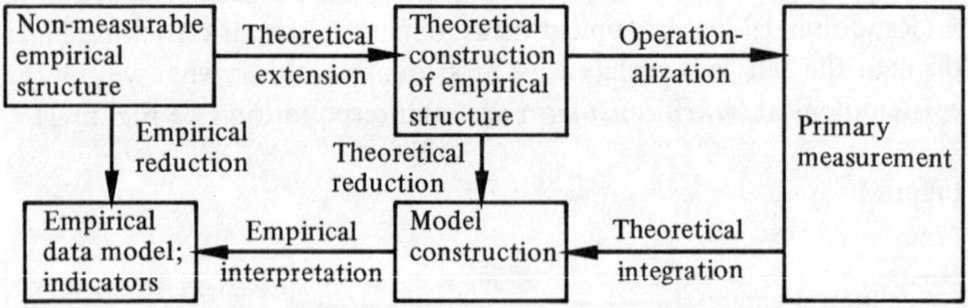

tion, using the law of correspondence as a supportive principle. Theoretical terms are linked to the empirical. Here, an idea arises according to which that which is measurable has to be measured, and that which cannot directly be measured must be converted into measurable form. Thus, it frequently happens that the researcher of social indicators forcibly twists matters that are not in measurable form in the Galileo-Newtonian sense. This has become particularly obvious during the later period of research on social indicators. Measurable and quantifiable factors formed the original approach for research on social indicators, after which qualitative matters were arrived at. The measurement of the quality of life in a quantitative manner, the theme of the report of the 1978 World Conference of Sociology, can be mentioned as an example. In that report (Szalai & Andrews 1980) the concept of quality is understood in a positivist sense.

There are two basically weak points in the type of measurement that follows the principle of operationalization: the first is the operationalization itself, i.e. converting the theoretical into the empirical construction; the second is the attempt in the reverse direction, i.e. the interpretation of the information obtained.

What do social indicators actually tell us about the reality that surrounds us and what is left untouched? This way of putting questions is especially important because indicators have often been developed for use as means of planning, i.e. their function is to produce information in support of decision-making. Thus, research into social indicators as research for decision-making becomes pragmatic, and is associated with the problem of valuation. Valuation does not occur according to the researcher's own interests, but he or she is required to produce relevant information for the interest of decision-making. This brings us to the question of what kind of information is acceptable to the decision-makers.

This can be illustrated with an example. The results of children's day-care systems are in the interest of decision-making. Based on this interest, researchers have been asked to develop suitable indicators that may be used in measuring the effectiveness of day-care systems from the point of view of child care, the promotion of children's development, and the solution of parents' problems related to day care. Additional information is required concerning the amount of inputs used in producing the outputs. The decision-maker expects those people who are the supposed objects of day-care services to behave in a rational manner, i.e. they are expected to use the services for those purposes and in those forms which have been determined by the decision-maker.

The results of this investigation will show that utilization of the service has been very small. People have not resorted to this form of care in the way that had been expected. The inputs are great but the output is small. Why? With the help of social indicators we can show that outputs do not correspond to inputs, but substantially the social indicators express nothing about the basis of the problem. This is illustrated in Figure 4 (Randolph 1979).

Figure 4.

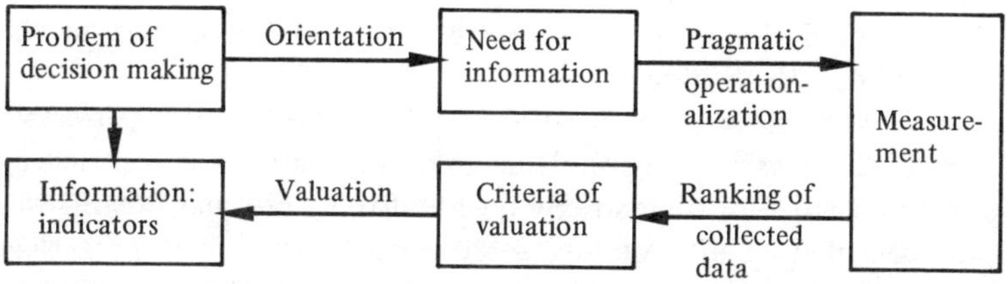

Our example concerning day care shows that information received through measurement is insufficient to solve the information problem of decision-making, and it is necessary to resort to another kind of information gathering. The information of 'hard' facts is based on given norms. In anticipation, day care had been expected to yield results that would correspond with those norms. This concept of information is an absolute one; it is thought to be applicable universally in different places and at different times.

The use of 'soft' facts is based on the phenomenological and hermeneutic interest of knowledge. How can it be understood why day care does not yield the expected results? What is the unique cultural milieu that produces a certain kind of thinking? What historical process is going on in the community that is being researched? Analysis of these problems might make us think that there is little sense in organizing a universal day-care system based on general norms when people's own perception of their life with their children and at home is completely different to that of the social services system.

In the example dealt with above, the way of life of the families was traditional. In some families the grandparents still cared for the children. Moreover, mothers were willing to retire from work while their children were small. The logic of the social services and the logic of the family life had different approaches. It was as though two parallel cultures existed: the official and the unofficial.

The first had its origins in industrialized society with the forms of behaviour produced by that society. The indicators used therefore measured the situation according to this notion of culture.[2] This also concerns the dynamics of social change: who sets the objectives for the change and what are these objectives? The establishment of large societal machineries that produce standardized systems has left no scope for this way of putting the questions before the problems become so critical that they start to destroy the system from within. New viewpoints now have to be considered in the pragmatic argumentation.

This is the problematic of social indicators: while the indicators in general take a position as automatic monitoring systems of the problematics of decision-making, they are not capable of uncovering the truth beneath those systems.

This problem was given partial recognition when fumbling attempts were made towards achieving something qualitative while criticizing social indicators for their strictly quantitative nature, and when it was proposed that quality of life, degree-wise, is something more than quantifiable and objectively-observable information. Then the approach became something like the following: people must be approached directly with questions concerning their opinions, attitudes and assessments.

The following problem the arises: people are products of their own society, and their cognition rests on the information produced by that society. The less educated the people, the more concise is their degree of consciousness. What do these civic opinions as such demonstrate? In general, they reflect trends of the present society: signs of dissatisfaction are vaguely expressed, or persons who seemed content may show clear symptoms of illness originating in psychic stress, or those symptoms may be manifested as aggressive and even criminal behaviour or as escapism.

Such studies of satisfaction seem to bring rather superficial results. To a certain extent this research belongs to the same category of studies as those to which their criticism is directed. They take a stand on behalf of the dominating pragmatic interest of knowledge. As far as the deepening of knowledge is concerned nothing has changed, especially since the explicit aim of studies on the quality of life is to reduce information concerning attitudes and assessments into measurable form. The social order (i.e. the request for useful societal information) remains unchanged. The approach of such studies falls into the realm of the positivistic interest of knowledge and not of interpretative sociology. The simultaneous application of social indicators measurement and of the interpretative qualitative study of the life of a population would help to discover the truth far better than quality of life research.

The UNRISD Programme on Social Indicators

The UNRISD programme on social indicators is based on quantification of the level of living/standard of living carried out by the United Nations in the 1950s and 1960s. In the background was the economic notion of welfare, although empirical measuring attempts no longer have much in common with welfare economics: the common elements are associated rather with the empirical approach of national accounting. The measuring of social development, in conjunction with economic growth and economic development, became one of the research objectives of UNRISD which was founded in the 1960s.

As we have seen, the social indicators that have been developed in Western industrial countries are atomistic. UNRISD's propositions are different and comprehensive information has been aimed at. In the background, the conscious or unconscious influence of developments of the theory on welfare in the socialist countries can be traced. The concept of welfare is differentiated by degrees from a theoretical-conceptual level to a practical one, arriving at the production of information that will be supportive to government social planning.[3] The level of living and welfare developments of UNRISD are related to corresponding developments in the socialist countries.

The aims of UNRISD have been to apply welfare theory in a practical manner in a global context, so that measurements could be carried out within the various industrial countries and comparisons between these could be made. Principal attention, however, has been given to the measuring of social development in developing countries and to comparison of these countries.[4]

The concept of level of living refers to the flow of needs satisfaction generated basically through public and private consumption. Services and goods used for satisfaction of the needs of the population constitute the latter's level of living. The level of living index measures this flow of satisfaction of needs from the point of view of the population (Drewnowski 1966; Drewnowski & Scott 1966). This concept is collectivistic: the viewpoint is that of the whole society, although welfare is considered in regard to the satisfaction of the needs of the population. The share of public consumption is pronounced in the defined notion of the level of living because the components used for operationalizing the concept of the level of living, and the indicators applied in the measurement of those components, implicitly emphasize public consumption. In the 1950s and 1960s the measurement of welfare in socialist countries was based largely on measurement of the efficiency of public consumption.

The concept of level of living brings us to the notion of welfare, i.e. a concept with a situational nature referring to the actual conditions of the population at a given moment. The level of living is a flow-concept; welfare is a stock-concept. It is difficult to measure welfare as such: the ability of labour is the concept used as criterion. Whether or not the flow of welfare directed from society to the population is appropriate can be seen in the condition and ability of labour. This final criterion of welfare originates in economics and not in the social sciences. Moreover, it resembles the pattern of thought that was applied in the measurement of welfare in the socialist countries during the 1950s and 1960s. On the other hand, the ability of labour as the highest criterion of welfare is associated with the social-liberalist way of thinking. The formation of welfare in the West differs from that in socialist countries in that moral and ethical questions have not been put up as criteria: in socialist countries, moral rights and obligations in the construction of a better society are the highest criteria.

The developments achieved by UNRISD are thus more vigorous, more logical, more theoretical and more comprehensive than most attempts at social indicator analysis that were developed in the Western industrial countries during the 1960s. In the 1970s, more theoretical activity began to appear in the western countries, for instance in Scandinavia. UNRISD's social indicators are associated with the theory according to which the welfare of society (versus the welfare of individuals) is essential. While the purpose was to develop measurements to be used as planning tools in the analysis of social development, the same problems of measuring were encountered as in positivist and quantitative research.

The activities of UNRISD have also been of the nature of basic theoretical research. Finnish researchers of levels of living in particular have been inspired by UNRISD's work.[5] This, in retrospect, has been associated with the development of a logical chain of concepts and with the understanding of welfare as a process. In addition, Finland has a mixed economy in which the role of the public sector, i.e. the share of the state and local authorities, is great and the share of public consumption is considerable. The government is an important actor and regulator, as is pre-supposed by the ideas of social-liberalism.

UNRISD's understanding of the role of measurements, of the services of society and of the realization of people's welfare, approximated that of the Finnish researchers of the 1960s. Another country where, to my knowledge, the developments of UNRISD in measuring welfare have been comprehensively studied and analyzed, is Poland.[6]

The measurement of welfare as a theoretical problem developed through UNRISD's research activities was subjected to revision; at the same time, the quantitative nature of social indicators was criticized and the development of qualitative criteria was requested. This discussion took place within the limits of the positivist conception of science characterized earlier in this article. Professor Jan Drewnowski revised the concepts of welfare early in the 1970s, and thus participated in the discussion on the quality of life that was then taking place. The title of the publication that this brought forth was no longer 'level of living' or 'welfare' but 'quality of life' (Drewnowski 1974).

While it was demanded that factors other than the services and goods acquired through public and private consumption should be included in the notion of people's quality of life, Drewnowski extended his list of the components of welfare to include environmental factors, for example. The quantification of factors that are ambiguous as far as their measurement is concerned proved a new problem: research on the quality of life has its limitations in capturing reality. The problem of these limitations arose as demands for the same explicitness and differentiation which had characterized research on the level of living, were extended to the new notion of quality of life. The reality that is associated with our social environment, however, can only partly be measured.

Research into the quality of life has gained little footing in Scandinavia, least of all among Finnish social scientists. This is due to the ambiguity of this line of research, and to the attempt to solve the internal contradiction of the problem of measuring factors that are not measurable, which is regarded as a logical impossibility.

Current Trends

The problem of 'good-for-people' is connected with the functioning of society. At the moment we live in a time of crisis, i.e. an era of invalidation of old thoughts and the bringing forth of new ones. The old way of thinking arising from the depths of liberalistic thought, according to which man has to strive continually towards new objectives, belongs to the past but still has some influence upon social organizations and institutions. Emphasis is still placed on the omnipotence of economic growth as a guarantor of the basic potentialities of societal measures. The evolutionary thinking of economic growth, which has been transmitted from the industrialized to the developing countries,[7] is deeply rooted in societal decision-making. At the same time it has formed the theoretical background on which social indicators have been constructed.

A new industrial revolution characterized by automation and the restructuring of the working process has begun in the industrialized countries. In the background a tendency to economize (cf. Engelhardt 1981), which is associated with general scarcity and which has an influence upon economic activity and thus on the whole life of the people is recognizable. Rising prices on the world markets cause predominance to be given to the scarcity of raw materials and energy. The cost of labour has risen in the industrialized countries as social security and social services have been extended. Machines are used at an ever-increasing rate for a variety of purposes, and work is being restructured.

It has been suggested that the tendency to economize while in the whirls of automation will force the economy and all human life to divide into two sectors, the hard and the soft: i.e. into a dualistic economy. The top employees of the hard sector run production; the remainder of the population lean on their home environment. With the help of automation, routine jobs can be so decentralized that they can be done at home. Experiments have already been carried out in the USA to see how people employed in tertiary industries can work at home using computer terminals.[8] These are mainly intended for married women who function as subcontractors, for instance, for banks or insurance companies. It has been calculated that firms save enormous amounts in the form of social costs because, through these arrangements, they are freed from employing people on routine and subordinate jobs. So far, even within service industries, people carrying-out routine tasks have been hired as employees, but it is now becoming possible to buy the work of these people as a final product. The employees become comparable to private entrepreneurs but without their benefits. The control exercized by the trade unions will be weakened in this way.

Such developments mean that the whole realm of life (life spheres) of these people will change. The notion of work will also change. Lives of people can no longer be weighted with the present criteria; the importance of social indicators will decrease. The emphasized significance of employees in the hard sector is also connected with this: people functioning in planning, control and maintenance tasks are still important. The gap between the soft and the hard groups in regard to their societal significance will increase. The problem of the existence of elites will multiply and the gap between social classes will widen. And these are problems that cannot be captured conceptually by social indicators.

Employees in the hard sector hold important positions in society, and work and the working environment will continue to play an essential role in their lives. Their life style will be mobile and will have more possibilities than that of people who are obliged to work in the home environment. The number of unemployed is also expected to grow as a result of technological change. It is obvious, therefore, that work-centered life is going to lose way among the values of people who, under the force of circumstances, become the prisoners of their housing environment. Different matters become important to the 'good-for-people' when days are spent in the home environment rather than working outside it, even though the time spent at home might include paid working hours.

The largest of the Western industrial countries have taken their first steps in this process and the smaller nations are following suit. Not only economic but also social factors follow the path of economic conditioning. The matters under consideration are processes associated with socialization, through which, for example through education and training, members of society are guided to adopt those forms of behaviour that correspond with predominant cultural norms and which allow limited freedom for truly independent action.[9] Some time ago Fromm stated that people want to do what they are expected to do. Marx, for one, used the notion of 'character mask' in reference to the same phenomenon.

If 'good-for-people' is measured with social indicators, it must be asked whether this 'good', regarded as worthy of aspiring to, is only a product of the kind of socialization process discussed above. When projecting problems into the future, it is justifiable to ask what the society that we consider as worth aspiring to should be like. This is especially relevant now that the economizing tendency seems to be leading towards the formation of a dualistic society, even in countries where the actualization of democratic ideals has so far been regarded as important.

The various social and societal processes act continuously to cause changes to the essential limits of human life. Also, the contents of social indicators might be transformed, as far as the meaning of indicators is concerned, into something completely different to the original meaning if the situation is analyzed in these altered circumstances. Take education as an example. In traditional social indicator research, attempts would be made to measure the opportunities given to the population to participate in learning and in acquiring knowledge by using different kinds of indicators, such as pupil/teacher ratio, and the percentage of young people participating in primary, secondary and tertiary education. The situation in industrial countries might already be that while education is universal and maintained through the use of societal resources, schools actually become storage places for some pupils. It is assumed that school is a better place than the street for those who cause disturbances. In reality, therefore, the contents of social indicators such as learning and increasing knowledge should be transformed to refer (also) to the social function of schools, i.e. their meaning in referring to knowledge (educational services) has changed to refer to social welfare functions (social services). This being the case, the use of social indicators might yield biased results when their meaning in relation to the community under study is considered.

Research on the quality of life, whose aim is 'to measure the combined effect that both the facts of life and people's wellbeing' (Szalai 1980: 14), is not necessarily more successful in revealing the truth. If, for instance, pupils are asked why they attend school, when they have been manipulated through the process of socialization to consider the school as a place for learning and increasing knowledge, they are likely to respond: 'for the sake of learning', although they would not appreciate that at all. The meaning of school as a storage place can be perceived only through a hermeneutic study of the collective mind. Correspondingly, in the planning of services for the disabled it often seems that the understanding of their life (life as a whole) is inadequate.

The matter under consideration refers to the problem of correspondence between the logic of societal measures as this appears, for example, in policies of education or social security, and the logic of people's life. The logic of social policies no longer reaches the logic of people's life whereas, during periods of construction of society such as the decades following World War II, these types of logic were congruent. Research using the social indicators approach suits periods of social evolution, but does not correspond with the challenge of altered social reality; neither can the new challenge be responded to with quality of life research.

It is interesting that as the time of construction of society gradually gives way, the tendency towards popular participation and action which springs up amongst the people arises to counterbalance the tendency of economic conditioning (economizing). In all Western industrial nations the 1970s marked the era of ever-increasing demands for participation. People want to have direct access in order that they may participate in the decision-making process concerning questions close to their own interests, and thus bypass the bureaucracy and the official decision-making machinery. In particular, this demand for the right to participate concerns people's immediate environment, such as the living and working environment.

This refers to the new kind of concept of human being (*Menschbild*) which is coming into focus in Western social thought. The concept of human being which is incorporated in the social indicators approach is based on the image of a citizen who, through receiving goods and services, satisfies his needs. The participatory approach is founded on the active concept of a human being, i.e. a person who participates in the processes of society and is dynamic. This active concept of a human being, however, has only been adopted in working life to a very limited extent, without taking into consideration those few participatory organizations of working life which have been developed in Western countries. Participation in fundamental decisions concerning production does not exist in these countries. The active man actualizes himself mainly outside his working sphere.

In the early 1970s this active concept of human being was transmitted into Scandinavian research on welfare through the so-called research into the resources of people. While the satisfaction of needs through the flow of goods and services had been the focus of research on the level of living, the notion 'command over resources' now became crucial. Society provides its members with resources; by utilizing these, people can participate in social action and societal decision-making. It is essential to know what possibilities are available to the citizens on their own behalf. In general, they are in unequal positions with regard to these resources. Thus, it is important that, in planning society, primary attention is given to increasing the economic, political and social resources that are available to its members on an egalitarian basis.

It was later discovered that, in practice, research using the resources' approach was similar to that on the level of living, because resources are actually made up of goods and services. On the other hand, the notion of political resources was new. It gradually became obvious that to increase resources as such does not make social conditions more egalitarian since people utilize their resources to differing degrees.

In Swedish society, for instance, the aim was to guarantee the highest possible standard of housing for all people. After a while, however, it was noticed that increasing this material resource did not activate people, nor did it make them more equitable. Additional factors, such as the use of migrant workers made necessary by the expanding economy, had arisen. The problem of integrating these foreigners into Swedish society made application of the resources' approach even more complicated. People did not behave in the way expected of them, i.e. the logic of people's life differed from the logic of social policies.

Against this background it is understandable that, in the research on welfare, attention has been turned to analysis of the dimensions of this logic. New winds are blowing in this field of research, especially in Scandinavia. The main emphasis is now on research into the mode of life and the way of life.[10] The aim is to discover the meaning of the different background factors of living in relation to the formation and manifestations of a certain way of life. In Finland in particular, where since World War II the process of urbanization has been the most turbulent of all European countries, it has been found important to pay attention to the way of life as a collective and societal concept, i.e. as a process of totality. The tendency to economize causes people to move from one place to another. What kind of community is formed from these personal histories? How does a community continuously change its form? And how does this transition in turn influence the lives of individual members of the community and their families? These are the questions currently being examined.

A recent Finnish research report on the way of life (Kortteinen 1981) has observed, for instance, that, within a very short period of time, a suburban community continuously changes its character and internal relations. This kind of development becomes especially clear when a community is analyzed from its very beginnings. In observing old settlements, on the other hand, it is noticeable that, even decades after their origin, continuous motion is taking place which is in dialectic relationship with what is happening in the lives of individual people. The community with its members forms part of a whole which is in a state of motion (Koskiaho 1981).

Within the community lifestyles vary, dependent on the type of people under consideration. When measuring circumstances in a suburban community with social indicators, for instance, it is possible that quite even values will be obtained. The material standard of living is approximately the same in the case of all residents. However, the style of life of permanent urban dwellers differs considerably from that of other people living in the same suburb who have newly moved from the countryside to the town. The systems of social interaction, mutual appreciation, etc. of these two groups of residents will vary. Therefore, measurement of the level of living does not reach that substance which differentiates and divides people into different social classes in this area.

Research into the quality of life may also not reveal this because only people's own ideas and assessments are asked. The respondent might not be able to analyze the situation deeply and, unlike the researcher, cannot examine the totality theoretically. People who have moved from 'not so good material conditions' to a community with higher material standards, possibly regard being content as 'obligatory' during the first few years of their residence in the new place because they have been successful in achieving a share of higher standard. The meaningfulness of living in the new circumstances only later becomes an object of consideration.

Research on changing the way of life can be incorporated with the participatory approach and with the tendency of popular participation and action. For instance, UNRISD (Pearse & Stiefel 1980) as part of its research policy of recent years, has adopted the participatory approach in its research activities on the rural communities of developing countries and on improvement of their living conditions. This line of research has developed close to the tradition of action research: people functioning as objects of research are activated to take command of their own affairs. This gives rise to its own problems which cannot be dealt with here. Similar action research is carried out in various kinds of projects in Western industrial countries.[11]

In this case, 'good-for-people' is understood as participation in action rather than as results from which people can benefit and are able to share in, regardless of how this outcome is arrived at. Here, action itself is in focus, whereas research using the social indicators approach emphasizes the results achieved and used for increasing the level of welfare.

In the current stage of social change, tendencies towards people's participation and towards societal economizing have to contend with one another. To project the active concept of human being into research into 'good-for-people' means that the old procedures and notions are no longer applicable; research into 'good-for-people' must be accommodated with predominant social reality. Thus, research using the social indicators approach is no longer essential but has become one of the minor means of analysis of 'good-for-people'.

If the economizing tendency means that technological change, with automation and the use of computers, is in its totality projected into every aspect of production and other spheres of societal activity, then new approaches must be developed for research into 'good-for-people'. The 'way of life' approach suits the present critical time because it explains the current situation. But it is not a means of planning society in the sense that society would in future be oriented towards actualization of 'good for people'. Rather, research on the way of life analyzes the situation of the present and of the past.

The basic difficulty of social research is, in fact, its limited ability to mark the road to the future. Prognoses are based on the existing understanding of the world which might prove outdated while factors acting in the situation are changing. Non-measurable information, which forms a great deal of the information concerning 'good-for-people' cannot be utilized, for example, in simulation models.

Notes

1. The national statistical units of various countries have extensively developed social indicators of national systems. The UN statistical unit has also developed lists and measurements for global social indicators.

2. The values of the official culture derive from such developed theory which is based on the principle of valuation associated with industrialization and emphasis on economic growth. In political theory the same is regarded as the theory of modernization. Social indicators measure the world according to this notion of development. The remaining factors are not considered important and are not taken into account (Koskiaho & Kovero 1981).

For example, a Swedish research group was given the task of analyzing development differences in Portugal, giving special attention to regional aspects (Erasmie 1966). The differences were analyzed in respect of the level of industrialization, productivity and general educational structure. The group developed social indicators for comparing regional socio-economic conditions, ending-up with the term 'welfare'. In addition, they tried to analyze the situation in the light of indicators, i.e. predictors of development.

The indicators were selected according to this approach. It might then be asked: which important factors for the welfare of these people have been forgotten? Some regions are very underdeveloped in the sense of economic growth. Why do we investigate the life of people in that sense when this point of view is not characteristic of the community?

3. Examples of research into welfare in the socialist countries are Manz 1975, 1979, and Koskiaho, Staufenbiel, Tanninen & Brandt 1979.

Diagram 1 (Manz 1979) illustrates this system of terms. Level of living forms the material basis for the satisfaction of total needs such as biological and cultural needs. Way of life is a parallel term to mode of production. It consists of the collective way of life of people, including the way of thinking and moral rules, as well as the activities of the people. Style of life describes the manner by which an individual or a family behaves.

Diagram 1.

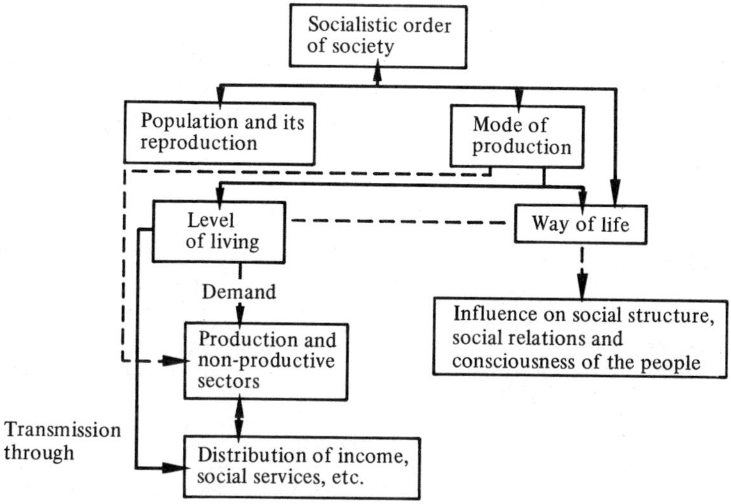

4. Essential reports of the UNRISD series on the level of living include Drewnowski 1966, 1970; Drewnowski & Scott 1966; Drewnowski et al. 1970; McGranahan et al. 1970; Scott et al. 1973; *Compilation of Development Indicators* 1969.

5. My own doctoral thesis was completed in connection with UNRISD activities (Koskiaho 1969a). A shorter version of this has been published in English (Koskiaho 1969b).

Other Finnish academic theses with a close connection to UNRISD research include Vepsä 1973; Noponen 1971; Roos 1973; Salavuo 1969.

6. The works of Polish researchers have been published in Polish in the series of the Statistical Office of Poland: Wiadomosci Statystyczne. In 1969-71, for example, the following researchers analyzed the concept of level of living and its measurement: Stanislaw Bartczak, Andrzej Luszniewicz and Wladyslaw Welfe.

7. For example, the attitude of Western industrial countries concerning development in the developing countries is still based on the idea that progress in these countries must follow past development patterns of the industrialized countries (Koskiaho & Kovero 1981).

8. A research project that critically evaluates the social consequences of the new technological revolution is taking place in Sweden (Albons 1981).

9. Engelhardt has made a more profound analysis of socialization in conjunction with the economizing tendency (Engelhardt 1981).

10. Examples of such studies include a Swedish research report (Björnberg et al. 1980, a Danish one (Christiansen 1980), and a Finnish one (Kortteinen 1981).

Some characteristics of this type of research are very old; see, for example, the British tradition of conditions of life studies in Petty (n.d.), the German one in Lengerke (1849) and the American one in Rowntree (1900).

11. Many such projects were carried out in Western industrial countries during the 1970s. Some have had a regional approach (e.g. on villages in Northern

Norway); research has been done on housing areas (e.g. on slum areas in the Federal Republic of Germany and in Great Britain, on the reconstruction of old housing areas in Denmark, and on new housing areas in conjunction with community work in Finland), and on the democratization of working places (e.g. in Norway).

Action research, which has a close connection with the participatory approach, has also been evaluated and criticized, for example by Moser 1975 and Moser ed. 1978.

The main problem of participation research is to combine demands for the actualization of research in the scientific manner, and to exercise participation in a practical manner. Practically-inclined people are seldom good researchers, and *vice versa.*

References

Albons, B. (1981): 'Den nya smygkontoriseringen – i vardagsrummen', *Arbertsmiljö*, 3.

Björnberg, U., et al. (1980): *Livsformer i en region. En jämförande analys av familje- och samhällsliv i 1970-talets Sverige* (Kungälv).

Christiansen, P.O. (1980): *Fire landsbyer. En etnologiskt rapport om nutidige livsformer* (København, Landsbykommissionen).

Drewnowski, J. (1966): *Social and Economic Factors in Development. Introductory Considerations on their Meaning, Measurement and Interdependence* (Geneva, UNRISD, February; Report No. 3).

— (1970): *Studies in the Measurement of Levels of Living and Welfare* (Geneva, UNRISD, Report No. 70.3).

— (1974): *On Measuring and Planning the Quality of Life* (The Hague, Mouton, for the Institute of Social Studies).

Drewnowski, J., et al. (1970): *Studies in the Methodology of Social Planning* (Geneva, UNRISD, Report No. 70.5).

Drewnowski, J. & W. Scott (1966): *The Level of Living Index* (Geneva, UNRISD, Report No. 4).

Engelhardt, W.W. (1981): 'Die Frage der Auswirkungen von Ökonomisierungs- und Ökonomismustendenzen auf die Sozialisation und zu den Voraussetzungen der Gegensteuerung mittels Sozialpolitik, Sozialpädagogik und Kooperation', *Sozialer Fortschritt*, 1-2.

Erasmie, T. (1966): *Basic Needs and Education in Portugal* (Linköping University, Department of Education, Report Lill-PEK-R-66).

Johansson, S. (1973): 'The Level of Living Survey: A Presentation', *Acta Sociologica*, 16, 3.

Kortteinen, M. (1981): *Asumalähiö ja elämäntapojen muutos. Sosiologian pro gradu-tutkielma. Helsingin yliopisto* (Helsinki).

Koskiaho, B. (1969a): *Elintason osatekijöiden kasautumisesta ja elintasoon vaikuttavista tekijöistä Länsi-Euroopassa* (Tampere, Acta Universitatis Tamperensis. Ser. A. Vol. 30).

— (1969b): *Level of Living and Industrialization* (Jyväskylä Studies in Education, Psychology and Social Research, 20).

— (1981): *Pispala, kappale suomalaisen yhteiskunnan sosiaalihistoriaa* (with English summary: Pispala, A Specimen of Social History in Finland; Sociaalihuollon näköaloja).

Koskiaho, B. & S. Kovero (1981): *The Problem of the Least Developed Countries* (University of Tampere, Department of Social Policy, Research Report 57 b).

Koskiaho, B., F. Staufenbiel, T. Tanninen & K. Brandt (eds) (1979): *Lebensweise und Lebensniveau – Wohnen und Wohnumwelt* (Tampere).

Laitinen, H. (1981): *Kvalitatiivisesta ja kvantitatiivisesta sosiaalitutkimuksesta* (with English summary: On Qualitative and Quantitative Social Research; Sosiaalihoullon näköaloja. Acta Universitatis Tamperensis. Ser. A vol. 127).

Lengkerke, A.V. (1849): *Die ländliche Arbeiterfrage* (Berlin).

Manz, G. (1979): *Zur Auffassung von der Lebensweise und Lebensniveau in der sozialistischen Volkswirtschaftsplanung der DDR.*

Manz, G., et al. (1975): *Das materielle und kulturelle Lebensniveau des Volkes und seine volkswirtschaftliche Planung* (Berlin).

McGranahan, D.V., et al. (1970): *Contents and Measurement of Socio-Economic Development: An Empirical Enquiry* (Geneva, UNRISD, Report No. 70.01).

Moser, H. (1975): *Aktionsforschung als kritische Theorie der Sozialwissenschaften* (München).

– (ed.) (1978): *Internationale Aspekte der Aktionsforschung* (München).

Noponen, J. (1971): 'Hyvinvointi objektiivisena ja subjektiivisena tekijänä. Helsingin yliopisto, sosiaalipolitiikan laitos', *Tutkimuksia* No. 3 (Helsinki).

Patton, M.Q. (1978): *Utilization-Focused Evaluation* (Beverly Hills).

Pearse, A. & M. Steifel (1980): *Debaters' Comments on 'Inquiry into Participation': A Research Approach* (Geneva, UNRISD Participation Programme, Occasional Paper No. 80.5).

Petty, W. (n.d.): *The Political Anatomy of Ireland.*

Randolph, R. (1979): *Pragmatische Theorie der Indikatoren. Innovative Unternehmensführung* (Göttingen, Vol. 5).

Roos, J.P. (1973): 'Welfare Theory and Social Policy', *Commentationes Scientiarum Socialium*, 4 (Helsinki).

Rowntree, B. Seebohm (1900): *Poverty. A Study in Town Life* (New York).

Salavuo, K. (1969): *Taloudellisen tason asteikko elintason mittana* (Turku).

Scott, W., et al. (1973): *The Measurement of Real Progress at the Local Level. Examples from the Literature and a Pilot Study* (Geneva, UNRISD, Report No. 73.3).

Szalai, A. & F.M. Andrews (eds): *The Quality of Life. Comparative Studies* (Beverly Hills).

UNRISD (1969): *Compilation of Development Indicators (for 1960)* (Geneva, UNRISD/69/C.31).

Vepsä, K. (1973): *Elintason muutos Suomessa v. 1906-1965* (Helsinki).

PART THREE

SELECTED AND ANNOTATED BIBLIOGRAPHY ON LEVEL OF LIVING INDICATORS

Matty Klatter

I State of the Art and Review Literature

Abrams, M.: *A Review of Work on Subjective Social Indicators 1971 to 1975* (London, SSRC Survey Unit, 1976).

Occasional papers in survey research.

America in the Seventies: Some Social Indicators, ed. by C. Taeuber. *Anals of the American Academy of Political and Social Sciences* (1978), 435.

Special issue on social indicators, discussing the significance of data, trends and patterns given in the 1976 *Social Indicators Report*, issued by the US Office of Management and Budget.

Baster, N. (ed.): *Measuring Development. Journal of Development Studies*, 8 (1972), 3, pp. 1-182 (Also published as a book by Frank Cass, London, 1972).

Special issue on development indicators, using a variety of indicators for the analysis of socio-economic development. Contr. by D. Seers, J. Drewnowski, D. McGranahan, I. Adelman & C. Taft Morris, J. Galtung, etc.

Duncan, O.D.: 'Social Forecasting: The State of the Art', in *Public Interest*, 17 (1969), pp. 88-118.

Dusen, R.A. Van (ed.): *Social Indicators, 1973: A Review Symposium* (Washington DC, Social Science Research Council, Center for Coordination of Research on Social Indicators, 1974).

Horn, R.V.: 'Social Indicators: Meaning, Methods and Applications', in *International Journal of Social Economics*, 7 (1980), 8.

Reviews the state of the art of social indicator literature and discusses some of the major issues.

Johnston, R.: 'Review of New Compendia of Social Statistics and Social Indicators in Five Western Countries', *Social Science Information*, 15 (1976), 2-3, pp. 349-370.

Review of compendia of social statistics and indicators, issued by statistical offices in Canada, France, UK, Norway, USA. The compendia are compared in terms of developments in the compilation and reporting of social statistics and of their coverage of subject matter.

Klages, H.: 'Assessment of an Attempt at a System of Social Indicators', *Policy Sciences* (173), 4, pp. 249-261.

Review article assessing some of the first attempts to develop comprehensive systems of social indicators.

Luster, E.J. & K.C. Land (eds): *Social Accounting Systems: Essays on the State of the Art* (London, Academic Press, 1982).

Oborn, P.T.: *Review of the Literature on Social Indicators* (Denver, USA, Social Welfare Research Institute, University of Denver, 1972).

Broad overview of the field of social indicators.

Rao, M.V.S., K. Porwit & N. Baster: *Indicators of Human and Social Development; Report on the State of the Art* (Tokyo, The United Nations University, 1978).

Examines the purposes and contexts of development indicators in various conditions prevailing in different types of countries as well as related to the activities of international bodies.

Seminar on Concepts of Poverty in Asian Countries, Parts I and II. *Philippine Economic Journal*, 43-44 (1980-81), 4 and 2.

Special issues on a seminar on poverty concepts and poverty indicators, including articles on concepts of poverty in various stages of economic development, estimation of poverty lines, measurement of poverty in several Asian countries and an appendix on statistics for studies on poverty in Asian countries.

Sheldon, E.B. & K.C. Land: 'Social Reporting for the 1970s; A Review and Programmatic Statement', in *Policy Sciences*, 3 (1972), 2, pp. 137-151.

Reviews the criteria, uses and proposed development of social indicators.

Social Goals and Indicators for American Society, Vol. I, ed. by B.M. Gross; *Annals of the American Academy of Political and Social Science* (1967), 371.

Special issue on social indicators, examining the objectives of social indicators, data availability and data needs.

Socio-Economic Indicators: Theories and Applications. International Social Science Journal, 27 (1975), 1.

Special issue on social indicators, including contributions by K.C. Land & Z. Gostkowski (on theories), M.V.S. Rao (application to planning), R.G. Cant (application to Asia), and K.T. de Graft-Johnson (application to West Africa).

Szalai, A. & F.M. Andrews (eds): *The Quality of Life: Comparative Studies* (London, Sage, 1980. Sage Studies in International Sociology No. 20).

Collection of papers about comparative studies on the quality of life, illustrating the current state of the art in this field. The papers reflect the discussion at a symposium on comparative studies of life quality which formed part of the Ninth World Congress of Sociology, held in Uppsala, Sweden, in August 1978.

United Nations Research Institute for Social Development: *Measurement of Real Progress at the Local Level: A Review of the Literature and a Pilot Study*; ed. by W. Scott, H. Argalias & D.V. McGranahan (Geneva, UNRISD, 1973).

Verwayen, H.: 'The Specification and Measurement of the Quality of Life in OECD Countries', in A. Szalai & F.M. Andrews (eds): *The Quality of Life: Comparative Studies* (London, Sage, 1980).

Review of the OECD Social Indicator Development Programme.

II Bibliographies

Conroy, M.: *Social Indicators: Methodology; A Selective Bibliography* (Dublin, The National Institute for Physical Planning and Construction Research, 1981).

Gilmartin, K.J., R.J. Rossi, L.S. Lutomski et al.: *Social Indicators, An Annotated*

Bibliography of Current Literature (New York, Garland Publishers, 1979).

Bibliography of social indicator literature, containing about 600 abstracts related to a variety of social indicators research issues.

Simonis, H. & V.E. Simonis: *Quality of Life: Methods and Measurement* (Kiel, Bibliothek des Instituts für Weltwirtschaft, 1976; Kieler Schrifttumkunden zu Wirtschaft und Gesellschaft, Nr. 21).

Bilingual (German/English) bibliography on social indicators.

Taylor, J.B.: *Annotated Bibliography and Selected References on Social Indicators* (Washington DC, Agency for International Development, 1971).

Bibliography compiled for use of the Task Force on Social Indicators of AID.

Wilcox, L.D., R.M. Brooks, G.M. Beal et al.: *Social Indicators and Societal Monitoring, An Annotated Bibliography* (Amsterdam, Elsevier, 1972).

Extensive literature study and overview of social indicators literature, containing over 1000 listings.

III Conceptual and Methodological Issues

Adelman, I. & C.T. Morris: *Society, Politics and Economic Development* (Baltimore, Johns Hopkins Press, 1967).

Allardi, E.A.: 'Welfare Model for Selecting Indicators of National Development', in *Policy Sciences*, 4 (1973), 1.

Gives a frame of reference for selecting social indicators on the basis of values inherent in the concept of social welfare. A scheme is presented for selecting indicators of comparative relevance by cross-tabulating the basic value categories with a second set of categories called elements of society.

Andrews, F.M.: 'Social Indicators of Perceived Life Quality', in *Social Indicators Research*, 1 (1974), 3, pp. 279-299.

It is sometimes suggested that perceptual indicators suffer from methodological weaknesses associated with their validity, interpretability, completeness and utility. Each of these possible weaknesses is discussed, the conclusion being that not one of them is sufficient to invalidate the development and use of perceptual indicators.

Andrews, F.M. & S.B. Withey: *Social Indicators of Well-Being* (New York, Plenum Press, 1976).

Atkinson, A.B.: 'On the Measurement of Inequality', in *Journal of Economic Theory*, 2 (1970), pp. 171-185.

Banerji, D.: 'Measurement of Poverty and Undernutrition', in *Economic and Political Weekly*, 16 (1981), 39, pp. 1579-1582.

Comment on some of the critical issues involved in the debate on poverty and hunger.

Bauer, R.A. (ed.): *Social Indicators* (Cambridge, Mass., MIT Press, 1966).

Bayless, M. & S. Bayless: 'Quality of Life Indicators: Some Theoretical and Methodological Concerns', in *The American Journal of Economics and Sociology*, 41 (1982), 4, pp. 421-437.

Examines several recent attempts at direct measurement of the quality of life directly.

Beckermann, W.: *Human Resources and Economic Development; Some Problems of Measurement* (London, University College, 1972).

Bertholt, G. & B. Evers: *Measuring Socio-Economic Development* (Tilburg, Catholic University, 1965).

Bunge, M.: 'What is a Quality of Life Indicator?' in *Social Indicators Research*, 2 (1975), 1, pp. 65-79.

A social indicator is characterized as an observable variable assumed to point to some other variable. A quality of life indicator is one that allows degrees of well-being to be estimated. Some of the problems posed by this definition are discussed.

Buttel, F.H., E.A. Wilkening & O.B. Martenson: 'Ideology and Social Indicators of the Quality of Life', in *Social Indicators Research*, 4 (1977), 3, pp. 353-369.

Examines the possibility that social-psychological, evaluative measures of social well-being/quality of life perceptions may embody unintended ideological elements.

Carchedi, G.: 'Cultural Biases and Levels of Living Indices', in *De Economist*, 120 (1972), 6, pp. 550-562.

Examines various levels of living indices, evaluates them as tools of social engineering and shows that, when applied to LDCs, such indices are culturally biased.

Carley, M.J.: *Social Measurement and Social Indicators; Issues of Policy and Theory* (London, Allen and Unwin, 1981).

Chandrasekar, K.: 'Productivity and Social Indicators', in *Annals of the American Academy of Political and Social Science*, 453 (1981), January, pp. 153-168.

Discusses the relationship among changes in productivity, economic output and significant aspects of societal welfare which are measured by social indicators.

Christian, D.E.: 'International Social Indicators; The OECD Experience' in *Social Indicators Research*, 1 (1974), 2, pp. 169-186.

Describes and appraises the operational-level set of international social indicators developed by the OECD, and suggests a governmental strategy for developing more comprehensive social indicators in the longer term context.

Dandekar, V.M.: 'On Measurement of Poverty', in *Economic and Political Weekly*, 16 (1981), 30, pp. 1241-1250.

Discussion of the criticism by V.K.R.V. Rao and P.V. Sukhatme of the author's measurement of poverty, arguing that this criticism is based on a confusion between 'poverty' and 'under-nutrition'. A comment by P.V. Sukhatme is published in *Economic and Political Weekly*, 16 (1981), 32, pp. 1318-1324.

Delors, J.: *Les indicateurs sociaux* (Paris, SEDEIS, 1971).

Drewnowski, J.: 'The Practical Significance of Social Information', in *Annals of the American Academy of Political and Social Science* (1971), 393, pp. 82-91.

Examines the kind of information on social matters that is most urgently required and argues that economic indicators are inadequate. Discusses four kinds of social indicators and level of living indicators.

— : 'Social Indicators and Welfare Measurement: Remarks on Methodology', in: N. Baster (ed.): *Measuring Development; Journal of Development Studies*, 8 (1972), 3, pp. 79-90.

Elaborates a methodology of measurement welfare by means of indicators and indices, based on observable and measurable facts.

— : 'Frustrated Development', in *Development and Change*, 5 (1973-74), 2, pp. 101-105.

Distinguishes five classes of causes of frustrated development and explains this phenomenon in terms of appropriate economic and social variables.

— : *On Measuring and Planning the Quality of Life* (The Hague, Mouton for the Institute of Social Studies, 1974).

Outcome of Drewnowski's work for UNRISD during the years 1964-69, concerning the methodology and particularly the measurement of social elements of development with their relations to economic variables, and the problem of giving social orientation to development planning. Proposes the 'level of living index' and the 'state of welfare index'.

— : *The Definition and Measurement of Poverty* (Address delivered on the occasion of the Dies Natalis of the Institute of Social Studies, The Hague, 1976).

— : 'Poverty: Its Meaning and Measurement', in *Development and Change*, 8 (1977), 2, pp. 183-208.

Argues that indicators should be limited to observable and measurable phenomena and that subjective indicators do not provide clear guidance for action.

— : 'The Affluence Line', in *Social Indicators Research*, 5 (1978), pp. 263-278.

In the discussion of distribution problems an affluence line that determines the level above which consumption need not and should not rise is required in addition to the poverty line. The concept of the affluence line is introduced in this article.

— : 'Basic Needs and Social Indicators: A Suggestion for an Integrated Approach', in *Labour and Society*, 4 (1979), 3, pp. 261-275.

In writings on basic needs little reference is made to work on social indicators. A plea is made for an integration between the basic needs approach and the work on social indicators: social indicators provide quantitative information about the state of satisfaction of basic needs and can reveal insufficiencies in basic need satisfaction and where their causes can be found.

— : 'Social Indicators, Quality of Life and Economic Theory', in *Philosophica*, 25 (1980), 1, pp. 15-32.

A suggestion for establishing a theoretical basis for social indicators and quality of life research.

Duncan, O.D.: *Toward Social Reporting: Next Steps* (New York, Russell Sage Foundation, 1969. Social Science Frontiers Series Paper No. 2).

Economics of Social Measurement Processes; Some Questions of Public Policy Indicator Design. International Journal of Social Economics (special issue), 9 (1982), 1.

I. Introduction
II. Reflections on key measurement issues in the history of economics: 1890–1950.
III. Toward a general theory of policy indicators.

Ellis, G.F.R.: *The Quality of Life Concept: An Overall Framework for Assessment Schemes* (Cape Town, South African Labour and Development Research Unit, University of Cape Town, 1980).

Environmental Protection Agency: *The Quality of Life Concept; A Potential New Tool for Decision-Makers* (Washington DC, Office of Research and Monitoring Environmental Studies Division, 1973).

Collection of papers presented at the Quality of Life Concept Symposium, held in Warrenton, Virginia in 1972.

Fox, K.A.: *Social Indicators and Social Theory* (New York, Wiley, 1974).

Galnoor, I.: 'Social Information for What?', in *Annals of the American Academy of Political and Social Sciences* (1971), 393.

Discusses the usefulness of the cluster of ideas on social information for advanced industrialized countries as well as for development efforts in LDCs. The plea for new kinds of information is examined in terms of its specific context in these countries.

Galtung, T.: 'World Indicators Program', in *Bulletin of Peace Proposals*, 4 (1973), pp. 354-358.

Discusses the world indicators programme developed by a transnational study group founded during the 1973 World Congress of the International Political Science Association in Montreal. Such a programme should have a number of special characteristics, which are discussed in this article.

— : *Goals, Processes and Indicators of Development; A Project Description* (Tokyo, The United Nations University, 1978).

Progress report on a project on goals, processes and indicators of development of the UN University's Human and Social Development Programme.

Galtung, J., A. Guha, A. Wirak et al.: 'Measuring World Development I and II', in *Alternatives*, 1 (1975), 1 and 4, pp. 131-158 and 523-555.

Discusses how the old and rather technocratic idea of expressing the state of affairs in a society in numbers by means of social indicators, can be given a more radical content.

Galtung, T. & T. Hoivik: *On the Definition and Theory of Development with a View to the Application of Rank Order Indicators in the Elaboration of a Composite Index of Human Resources* (Oslo, International Peace Research Institute, 1968).

Paper prepared for the UNESCO Expert Meeting on the Methodology of Human Resources Indicators, Warsaw, 11-16 December 1967.

Gerson, E.: 'On "Quality of Life"', in *American Sociological Review*, 41 (1976), 5, pp. 793-806.

Two approaches to the conceptualization of quality of life are distinguished: the 'individualist' emphasizing the position of individuals, and the 'transcendentalist' stressing the overall order of society. Individuals and society are not seen as separated but as logically connected categories, generating each other in a process of 'negotiation'.

Ghai, D.P. & T. Alfthan: 'On the Principles of Quantifying and Satisfying Basic Needs', in D. Ghai et al.: *The Basic Needs Approach to Development: Some Issues Regarding Concepts and Methodology* (Geneva, ILO, 1977).

Gillingham, R. & W.S. Reece: 'Analytical Problems in the Measurement of the Quality of Life', in *Social Indicators Research*, 7 (1980), pp. 91-101.

Presents a theoretical framework for quality of life measurement based on individual utility maximization.

Gross, B.M.: *The State of the Nation: Social Systems Accounting* (London, Tavistock Publications, 1966).

Harbison, F.H., J. Maruhnic & J.R. Resnick: *Quantitative Analysis of Modernization and Development* (Princeton, Industrial Relations Section, Princeton University, 1970).

Study based upon the work carried out within the UNESCO project on human resources indicators.

Harewood, J. & R. Henry: 'Problems of Defining and Measuring Poverty in the Caribbean', in *Caribbean Issues*, 4 (1978), 3, pp. 5-23.

Examines some of the problems involved in operationalizing the concept of poverty, arguing that most of these problems are derived from the relative nature and subjective evaluation of poverty. In this context the technical problems involved in constructing indicators of poverty are explored.

Henderson, D.W.: *Social Indicators: A Rationale and Research Framework* (Ottawa, Economic Council of Canada, 1974).

Hicks, N. & P. Streeten: 'Indicators of Development: The Search for a Basic Needs Yardstick', in *World Development*, 7 (1979), 6, pp. 567-580.

Reviews social indicators, social accounts and composite indices of development approaches as better measures of development than the growth of GNP. Concludes that the use of social and human indicators is the most promising supplement to GNP, particularly if work on social indicators is done in areas central to the basic needs approach.

Horn, R.V.: *Indicators for Basic Needs Strategy* (Auckland, ANZAAS Conference, 1979).

International Labour Organization: *Employment, Growth and Basic Needs* (Geneva, ILO, 1976).

— : *On the Measurement of Basic Needs*, by S. Radwan (Geneva, ILO, 1977).

— : *Economic and Social Factors in Development* (Geneva, ILO, 1979).

Johnston, D.F.: 'Discussion: Problems in Social Indicator Development', in *Social Indicators Research*, 6 (1979), 2, pp. 207-213.

Reflects on the critical comments of five reviewers of US government publications in the field of social indicators.

Johnston, D.F. & M.J. Carley: 'Social Measurement and Social Indicators', in *Annals of the American Academy of Political and Social Science* (1981), 453, pp. 237-253.

Discusses the interdependence and the conceptual distance of social indicators and social measurement and distinguishes five types of indicators. Three broad problem areas in respect to developing social indicators are dealt with: technical, socio-political, and communication.

Kakwani, N.: 'Welfare Measures; An International Comparison', in *Journal of Development Economics*, 8 (1981), 1, pp. 21-45.

On the basis of previous work by Sen and the author, alternative welfare measures are proposed which take into account both the level and distribution of income. It is shown that there are substantial differences among countries with respect to the level of welfare, even among subgroups such as mature capitalist economies.

King, B.: *What is a SAM? A Layman's Guide to Social Accounting Matrices* (Washington DC, World Bank, 1981; World Bank Staff Working Paper No. 463).

Koskiaho, B.: *Level of Living and Industrialization; A Study on the Cumulation of Level of Living Components and on the Societal Factors Affecting Level of Living in Western Europe* (Iyvaskyla, Finland, Iyvaskylan Yliopisto, 1969).

Examines the basic dimensions of the level of living and the structural factors and functions of society associated with industrialization.

Land, K.C.: 'On the Definition of Social Indicators', in *American Sociologist*, 6 (1971), pp. 322-325.

— : *Theories, Models and Indicators of Social Change* (Urbana, Illinois, Department of Sociology, University of Illinois at Urbana-Champaign, 1974).

Land, K.C. & S. Spilerman (eds): *Social Indicator Models* (New York, Russell Sage Foundation, 1975).

Identifies analytical indicators of the social process.

Larson, M.A. & T. Wilford: 'The Physical Quality of Life Index: A Useful Social Indicator?', in *World Development*, 7 (1979), 6, pp. 581-584.

Assesses the usefulness of the physical quality of life index developed by the Overseas Development Council, which combines infant mortality, life expectancy and literacy into a single index for each of 150 countries.

Lee, T. & R.W. Marans: 'Objective and Subjective Indicators: Effects of Scale Discordance on Interrelationships', in *Social Indicators Research*, 8 (1980), 1, pp. 47-64.

Studies utilizing both subjective and objective measures indicate that, although relationships between them exist, these are often not strong. The article suggests several explanations for such imperfect relationships.

Liu, B.: 'Quality of Life; Concept, Measure and Results', in *American Journal of Economics and Sociology*, 34 (1975), 1, pp. 1-14.

Develops an analytical framework to guide empirical work on defining and measuring the quality of life and establishes a set of quality of life indicators. These in turn reflect the social well-being and can be evaluated over time in such a manner that timely and efficient actions towards the improvement of future quality of life can be taken.

Mitchell, A., T.J. Logothetti & R.E. Kantor: *An Approach to Measuring Quality of Life* (California, Stanford Research Institute, 1971).

Mokrzycki, E.: 'The Negative Indicators of Social Development; The Critical Versus Utopian Perspectives in the Theory of Development', in *The Polish Sociological Bulletin* (1980), 1, pp. 19-22.

Criticizes the welfare indicators proposed by UNRISD and argues that measuring devices require factual knowledge even though they help to produce it. Compares two categories of indicators: positive indicators, providing information relating to a model of good society, and negative indicators, providing information related to a critical social diagnosis.

Morris, M.D.: *Measuring the Condition of the World's Poor; The Physical Quality of Life Index* (New York, Pergamon Press, 1979).

Moser, C.: 'Social Indicators – Systems, Methods and Problems', in *The Review of Income and Wealth*, 19 (1973), 2, pp. 133-141.

Social indicators are frequently normative and are often concerned with outputs rather than inputs. A social indicator should represent or summarize a broader concept than itself and should belong to a structure or system of social indicators.

Mukherjee, R.: *On the Construction of Social Indicators* (Calcutta, Indian Statistical Institute, 1974).

Nieuwenhuijze, C.A.O. van: *Recent Developments in Development Studies; Some Reflections on the Message of Futuribles, Social Accounting and Social Indicators* (The Hague, Institute of Social Studies, Occasional Paper No. 22, 1972).

Organization for Economic Cooperation and Development: *List of Social Concerns Common to Most OECD Countries* (Paris, OECD Social Indicator Development Programme, 1973).

— : *Subjective Elements of Well-Being*, by B. Strumpel (Paris, OECD Social Indicator Programme No. 2, 1974).

Presents a conceptual model for social indicators, discussing the usefulness of the concept of subjective well-being.

— : *Measuring Social Well-Being: A Progress Report on the Development of Social Indicators* (Paris, OECD, 1976).

— : *Towards the Measurement of Work Satisfaction*, by A.A. Pornigal (Paris, OECD Social Indicator Programme, Special Studies No. 1, 1976).

— : *Basic Disaggregations of Main Social Indicators* (Paris, OECD Social Indicator Programme, Special Studies No. 4, 1977).

— : *Measures of Leisure, Equality and Welfare*, by W. Beckerman (Paris, OECD, 1978).

Rao, B.: 'Measurement of Deprivation and Poverty Based on the Proportion Spent on Food: An Exploratory Exercise', in *World Development*, 9 (1981), 4, pp. 337-353.

A review of measurements based on monetary and nutritional norms. Data on the proportion spent on food by per capita expenditure can be used to measure the incidence of poverty. Data for rural India are used to illustrate the measurement of deprivation and poverty.

Rossi, R.J. & K.J. Gilmartin: *The Handbook of Social Indicators: Sources, Characteristics and Analysis* (New York, Garland STPM Press, 1980).

Russett, B.M., H.R. Alker, K.W. Deutsch et al.: *World Handbook of Political and Social Indicators* (New Haven, Conn., Yale University Press, 1965).

Scott, W.: 'Poverty Monitoring in Developing Countries', in *Development and Change*, 10 (1979), 3, pp. 445-459.

Suggests the use of systematic monitoring at the local level as a means of providing supplementary data, controls, and explanations. The village or small town may be a suitable level at which to analyze the interrelationships of factors associated with poverty, supplementing other kinds of analyses at the national level. Integration of data series into comprehensive systems is needed.

Seers, D.: *Active Life Profiles for Different Social Groups: A Contribution to Demographic Accounting, A Frame for Social Indicators and a Tool of Social and Economic Analysis* (Brighton, Institute of Development Studies at the University of Sussex, 1982).

Sen, A.: 'Poverty, Inequality and Unemployment: Some Conceptual Issues in Measurement', in *Economic and Political Weekly*, 8 (1973), 31-33, pp. 1457-1464.

Reviews some analytical results on the welfare aspects of inequality measurement, presents an axiomatic framework for inequality measurement, and proposes an alternative measure of poverty.

— : 'Poverty: An Ordinal Approach to Measurement', in *Econometrica*, 44 (1976), 2, pp. 219-231.

Examines the problem of constructing an index of poverty using available information on the poor. A method for aggregate measurement of poverty expressed by a single indicator is proposed. An axiomatic approach is used to derive the measure.

— : 'Real National Income', in *Review of Economic Studies*, 43 (1976), 133, pp. 19-39.

Presents a general approach to real income comparisons which makes distribution an integral part of them. This permits the treatment of real national income comparison as generating a partial ordering of a complete welfare indicator rather than a complete ordering of a partial welfare indicator.

Sheldon, E.B.: 'Notes on Social Indicators, Promises and Potential', in *Policy Sciences*, 1 (1970), 1, pp. 97-111.

Sheldon, E.B. & W.E. Moore (eds): *Indicators of Social Change, Concepts and Measurements* (New York, Russell Sage Foundation, 1968).

Singer, H.W.: *The Quest for an Employment Strategy in Developing Countries and its Relationship to the Work on Human Resources Indicators* (Brighton, Institute of Development Studies at the University of Sussex, 1972).

Strumpel, B. (ed.): *Economic Means for Human Needs: Social Indicators for Well-Being and Discontent* (Ann Arbor, Michigan, Survey Research Center, Institute for Social Research, University of Michigan, 1976).

A review by J. Drewnowski in *Social Indicators Research*, 4 (1977), 2, pp. 241-245, questions the usefulness of the concept of subjective well-being.

Tahir, P.: 'The Service Element in National Accounts; A Preliminary Basis for an Alternative Formulation', *Pakistan Development Review*, 17 (1978), 3, pp. 302-315.

Pleads for the combination of 'serviceless' GDP and social indicators in order to delineate real growth from spurious growth.

United Nations: *Report on the International Definition and Measurement of Standards and Levels of Living* (New York, UN, 1954).

— : *International Definition and Measurement of Standards and Levels of Living, An Interim Guide* (New York, UN, 1961).

— : *Compendium of Social Statistics* (New York, UN, 1963).

— : *Aspects of Social and Economic Growth: A Pilot Statistical Study*, prepared by N. Baster and M. Subramanian (Geneva, UN, 1965).

— : *Social and Economic Factors in Development, Introductory Considerations on Their Meaning, Measurement and Interdependence*, prepared by J. Drewnowski (Geneva, UN, 1966).

— : *Feasibility of Welfare-Oriented Measures to Supplement the National Accounts and Balances; A Technical Report* (New York, UN, 1977).

— : *Social Indicators: Preliminary Guidelines and Illustrative Guidelines* (New York, UN, 1978).

United Nations Economic and Social Council: *Social and Demographic Statistics: Draft Guidelines on Social Indicators, Report of the Secretary General* (New York, UN, 1976).

United Nations Educational, Scientific and Cultural Organization: *Mathematical Methods in the UNESCO Project on Human Resources Indicators: An Evaluation and Alternative Analytical Methods*, by L. Lebart (Paris, UNESCO, 1972).

— : *Synchronic and Diachronic Approaches in the UNESCO Project on Human Resources Indicators*, by S. Fanchette (Paris, UNESCO, 1972).

Discusses the Wroclaw Taxonomy and Bivariate Diachronic Analysis.

— : *Towards a System of Human Resources Indicators for Less Developed Countries*; Papers prepared for a UNESCO Research Project, ed. by Z. Gostkowski (Paris, UNESCO, 1972).

— : *The Methodology of Development Indicators*, by M. Bunge (Paris, UNESCO, 1974).

Report of a UNESCO meeting on indicators of social and economic change, 20-22 May 1974.

— : *Social Indicators: Problems of Definition and of Selection* (Paris, UNESCO, Reports and Papers in the Social Sciences No. 3a, 1974).

Proposes methods for the selection of 'key' or 'core' indicators of socio-economic development. Three contributions:
- 'Social Indicators: Problems of Methodology and Selection', by S. Fanchette
- 'A Method for the Selection of a "Compact" Set of Variables', by Z. Hellwig
- 'A Method of Establishing a List of Development Indicators', by B. Jvanović.

— : *Communication Indicators: Communication Indicators and Indicators of Socio-Economic Development.* Summary of a Study made by R.C. O'Brien, E. Cooper, B. Perkes et al. (Paris, UNESCO, Mass Communication Documentation Centre, Communication and Society No. 3, 1979).

— : *Women and Development: Indicators of Their Changing Role* (Paris, UNESCO, Socio-Economic Studies No. 3, 1981).

United Nations Research Institute for Social Development: *Social and Economic Factors in Development; Introducing Considerations on Their Meaning, Measurement and Interdependence*, by J. Drewnowski (Geneva, UNRISD, 1966).

— : *The Level of Living Index; Old Version*, by J. Drewnowski & W. Scott (Geneva, UNRISD, 1966).

— : *The Level of Living Index; New Version*, by J. Drewnowski (Geneva, UNRISD, 1968).

— : *A Suggestion for an Empirical Production Function Representing the Productivity Effect of Social Factors*, by J. Drewnowski & M. Subramanian (Geneva, UNRISD, 1968).

— ; *Measuring Social Variables in Real Terms; A Survey of Issues and Possible Solutions*, by J. Drewnowski (Geneva, UNRISD, 1968).

— : *The Level of Welfare Index*, by J. Drewnowski (Geneva, UNRISD, 1968).

— : *Social Aims in Development Plans; A Report on a Tentative Investigation into the Social Significance of Development Plans*, by J. Drewnowski & M. Subramanian (Geneva, UNRISD, 1969).

— : *Studies in the Measurement of Levels of Living and Welfare*, by J. Drewnowski (Geneva, UNRISD, 1970).

I. Measuring Social Variables in Real Terms
II. The Level of Living Index – New Version
III. The Level of Welfare Index.

— : *Contents and Measurement of Socio-Economic Development*. A staff study by D.V. McGranahan, C. Richard-Proust, N.V. Sovani and M. Subramanian (New York, Praeger, 1972).

— : *Research Data of Indicators for 1970* (Vols I and II) and *1960-1970 Comparisons* (Vol. III) (Geneva, UNRISD, 1976).

— : *International Comparability of Statistics of Income Distribution*, by D.V. McGranahan (Geneva, UNRISD, 1979).

— : *Concepts and Measurement of Poverty*, by W. Scott (Geneva, UNRISD, 1981).

Presents empirical data showing the arbitrary nature of poverty lines and the imprecise and relative nature of the concept. Suggestions are made as to how data on poverty could be improved.

Zapf, W.: 'Social Indicators: Prospects for Social Accounting Systems', *Social Science Information*, 11 (1972), 3-4, pp. 243-277.

Describes the efforts of a group of social scientists engaged on the development of social reports, social indicators and social accounting systems.

— : 'Systems of Social Indicators; Current Approaches and Problems', *International Social Science Journal*, 27 (1975), 3, pp. 479-498.

Discusses the meaning, use and dimensions of 'systems of social indicators'.

IV Applications to Planning and Policy and Country Studies

Andorka, R.: 'Long-Term Social Development of Hungary, Measured by Social Indicators', *Social Indicators Research*, 8 (1980), 1, pp. 1-13.

Uses social structure indicators to study the development of Hungarian society from the capitalist period to the present. The impact of socialist transformations leading to economic reforms is investigated.

Apthorpe, R.: *Development Indicators* (Manila, National Development Research Centre, University of the Philippines. Cooperative Rural Regional Development Project, Working Paper No. 4, 1973).

— : 'Social Reporting in Papua New Guinea', in R.J. May (ed.): *Research Needs and Priorities in Papua New Guinea* (Port Moresby. Institute of Applied Social and Economic Research, 1976).

Booth, T.A.: 'Economics and the Poverty of Social Planning', *Public Administration*, 60 (1982), 2, pp. 197-214.

Examines the principal reasons for the poor state of social planning in Britain and argues that the main obstacle is the subordination of social goals to economic objectives, caused by the failure to define social objectives and by the neglect of social indicators in contrast to the sophistication of economic statistics.

Boulding, E.: 'World Welfare Measurement as Social Action', *Alternatives*, 2 (1976), 1, pp. 71-87.

Develops indicators for system processes: participation, production, distribution and 'nurturance' (emphatic responses that enhance human growth).

Brand, J.: 'The Politics of Social Indicators', *British Journal of Sociology*, 26 (1975), 1, pp. 78-90.

Discusses two aspects of social indicators: their relation to policy goals, and their use by a political organization for goals that may have nothing to do with the domain of the indicators.

Bull, R.: 'Social Accounts, Social Indicators and Development Planning', *Development and Change*, 9 (1978), 4, pp. 613-630.

Discusses which data are necessary as inputs to the development planning process and examines the balance that has to be achieved in the production of economic and social statistics when statistical resources are scarce. Demonstrates when statistical resources are scarce. Demonstrates how a social accounting matrix can be constructed.

CEPAL: *Indicadores del desarrollo economico y social en America Latina* (Santiago, CEPAL, 1976).

Chander, R.: *Social-Economic Indicators and National Policy; Paper Prepared for the Conference on Statistical Policy in Less Developed Countries* (Brighton, Institute of Development Studies at the University of Sussex, 1975).

Cohen, S.I.: *Production, Manpower and Social Planning; with Applications to Korea* (Rotterdam, Rotterdam University Press, 1975).

— : 'Simulations of Socio-Economic Development Policies', in *ITCC Review*, 5 (1976), 1, pp. 1-10.

A brief account of a completed study of the integration of socio-economic aspects in development planning models. A description is given of ways in which the conventional multi-sector model is extended to take account of social development and social planning. Results of an empirical application of the extended system to South Korea are presented.

Correa, H.: *Population, Health, Nutrition and Development; Theory and Planning* (Lexington, Mass., Lexington Books, 1975).

Correa, H. & K.A. Khan: *A Simulation Model for Planning Population Growth, Health, Nutrition, Education and Economic Development* (Pittsburgh, University of Pittsburgh, 1974).

Drewnowski, J.: *Two Concepts of Social Planning* (The Hague, Institute of Social Studies; Draft Discussion Paper, 1969).

Ewusi, K.: 'Disparities in Levels of Regional Development in Ghana', in *Social Indicators Research*, 3 (1976), 1, pp. 75-100.

Reviews some of the techniques for analyzing socio-economic indicators, selects the Wroclaw Taxonomic Technique for more detailed analysis, and applies the model to Ghana.

Ferriss, A.L.: 'National Approaches to Developing Social Indicators', *Social Indicators Research*, 2 (1975), 1, pp. 81-92.

The bases for selection of social indicators in ten national publications are primarily measures of welfare and measures reflecting public policy and social concern. The orientation of volumes from the USA, France, Canada, Norway, Philippines, Malaysia and Great Britain are discussed.

Franco, R.: 'Latin American Typology; An Essay on Measuring Social Discontinuities', *Social Indicators Research*, 3 (1976), 3-4, pp. 275-372.

Review of the literature on some social indicators that are usually employed in planning. Some alternative options are discussed and a classification is given of economic and social aspects of development of Latin American countries.

Galnoor, I.: 'Social Indicators for Social Planning; The Case of Israel', *Social Indicators Research*, 1 (1974), 1, pp. 27-57.

Argues that efforts should be directed towards developing social indicators for social planning. Israel's experience is presented as an example of the background to specific types of state intervention.

Gostowski, Z. (ed.): *Toward a System of Human Resources Indicators for Less Developed Countries* (Warsaw, The Polish Academy of Sciences, Institute of Philosophy and Sociology, 1974).

Study based on the work carried out within the UNESCO project on human resources indicators.

Government of France: *Indicateurs sociaux et économiques; rapport du groupe de travail* (Paris, Commissariat General au Plan, La documentation française, 1976).

Government of Great Britain: *Social Trends, No. 6* (London, Central Statistical Office; HMSO, 1976).

Government of the Netherlands: *Social and Cultural Report* (The Hague, Staatsdrukkerij, 1974).

Government of the United States of America: *Toward a Social Report* (Washington DC, Department of Health, Education and Welfare; U.S. Government Printing Office, 1969).

— : *Social Indicators 1973* (Washington DC, Office of Management and Budget, Department of Commerce, 1973).

— : *Social Indicators 1976* (Washington DC, Office of Management and Budget, Department of Commerce, 1976).

Hoffmann, H.: *Social Indicators and Their Role in Development Policy in Latin America* (Hamburg, Institut für Ibero-Amerikakunde, 1978).

Examines in which contexts the subject of social indicators came to the fore in recent literature on development, and whether a hierarchy of development indicators can be established.

Hongkoo, L., K. Kyong-Dong, & C.S. Doh: 'Perceptions of Quality of Life in an

Industrializing Country: The Case of the Republic of Korea', in *Social Indicators Research*, 10 (1982), 3, pp. 297-317.

Analyzes data collected from a national sample survey in Korea. The results do not accord with those from research undertaken in industrialized countries.

Horn, R.V.: 'Social Indicators for Development Planning and Analysis', in *International Labour Review* (1975), pp. 483-506.

Examines the main features and 'sequence' of statistics and indicators used in development planning, and considers the practical application of social indicators to planning, with their advantages and limitations.

Innes de Neufville, J.: *Social Indicators and Public Policy; Interactive Processes of Design and Application* (Amsterdam, Elsevier, 1975).

Johansson, S.: 'The Level of Living Survey: A Presentation', in *Acta Sociologica*, 20 (1973), 3, pp. 211-219.

Text of an address to a Review Symposium on the 1968 level of living survey in Sweden.

Khan, M.H. & M. Iqbal: 'Socio-Economic Indicators in Rural Pakistan: Some Evidence', in *Pakistan Development Review*, 21 (1982), 3, pp. 217-230.

Lisk, F.A.N.: 'Indicators for Basic Needs-Oriented Development Planning; Some Issues and Illustrative Examples', in *Labour and Society*, 4 (1979), 3, pp. 241-260.

Examines some of the main issues involved in the formulation of social indicators and their application to a basic needs planning framework.

— : 'Popular Participation in Basic Needs-Oriented Development Planning', in *Labour and Society*, 6 (1981), 1, pp. 3-14.

Presents an operational framework that is appropriate to planning for basic needs satisfaction, placing the concept of popular participation in the framework of a basic needs strategy within the formal planning system.

Lütkenhorst, W.: 'Operationalizing Basic Needs: A Few Fundamental Reflections', in *Intereconomics* (1982), 5, pp. 244-250.

Examines whether indicators exist which could provide for a sufficiently exact operationalization of at least basic physical needs, and whether these would enable improved measurement of the degree to which target levels are reached.

Mangahas, M. (ed.): *Measuring Philippine Development: Report of the Social Indicators Project* (Tagaytay City, The Development Academy of the Philippines, 1976).

Extensive social report on the Philippines, monitoring the social system by a list of about forty-five indicators, some sixteen of which are experimental.

Mukherjee, R.: 'On the Use of Social Indicators for Planning', in *Social Indicators Research*, 9 (1981), 2, pp. 184-195.

A properly constructed set of indicators may suggest not only the planning measures that should be employed, but may also lead to a better formulation of the targets, goals and even objectives of planning.

Obudho, R.A.: 'Social Indicators for Housing and Urban Development in Africa; Towards a New Development Model', in *Social Indicators Research*, 3 (1976), 3-4, pp. 431-449.

Reviews the literature on social indicators and shows how they can be applied to measuring social progress in urban and housing development in the international, national, regional and local environments.

Pyatt, G., A. Roe et al.: *Social Accounting for Development Planning with Special Reference to Sri Lanka* (Cambridge, Cambridge University Press, 1977).

Pyatt, G. & E. Thorbecke: *Planning Techniques for a Better Future* (Geneva, ILO, 1976).

Sen, A.: 'Public Action and the Quality of Life in Developing Countries', *Oxford Bulletin of Economics and Statistics*, 43 (1981), 4, pp. 287-319.

An examination of economies that have performed remarkably well in terms of quality of life indicators. This progress is related to the nature of these economies and to the public policies followed. Lessons from this experience can be drawn, not through the blind imitation of policy instruments, but through understanding their functional roles.

Shonfield, A. & S. Shaw (eds): *Social Indicators and Social Policy* (London, Heinemann, 1972).

Social Indicators for the European Community 1960-1975 (Luxembourg, Statistical Office of the European Communities, 1977).

United Nations: *Social Reports; Their Contributions to Integrated Development Planning* (New York, UN, 1976).

Report of a Seminar at Saint Pierre, Aosta Valley, Italy, 20-30 April 1976, discussing social reports including a review of reports in twelve countries.

— : *Social Reporting and Social Indicators in Developing Countries* (New York, UN, 1977).

United Nations Educational, Scientific and Cultural Organization: *The Use of Social Indicators in Developing Planning*, by S.H.K. Yeh (Paris, UNESCO, 1976).

— : *The Use of Socio-Economic Indicators in Development Planning*, ed. by N. Baster (Paris, UNESCO, 1976).

— : *Socio-Economic and Communication Indicators in Development Planning; A Case Study of Iran*, by M. Tehranian (Paris, Mass Communication Centre, UNESCO, 1979).

— : *Socio-Economic Indicators for Planning: Methodological Aspects and Selected Examples* (Paris, UNESCO, 1981).

United Nations Research Institute for Social Development: *A Planning Model for Social Development*, by J. Drewnowski (Geneva, UNRISD, 1969).

— : *Studies in the Methodology of Social Planning*, by J. Drewnowski et al. (Geneva, UNRISD, 1970).

— : *Measurement and Analysis of Progress at the Local Level*, by W. Scott et al. (Geneva, UNRISD, 1978).
Vol. 1. An Overview
Vol. 2. Country Case Studies in Ghana, India and Poland.

The overview report recommends a scheme for local level measurement and analysis.

— : *Measurement and Analysis of Progress at the Local Level*, ed. by W. Scott (Geneva, UNRISD, 1979).
Vol. 3. Country case studies in Argentina, Iran, Mexico, Nigeria and Papua New Guinea.

— : *A Development Monitoring Service at the Local Level; Socio-Economic Observation Areas in Kerala*, by N.T. Matthew & W. Scott (Geneva, UNRISD, 1980).

Walabyeki-Kibirige, G.: *Social Indicators in Development Planning* (Vienna, Vienna Institute for Development, 1978).

Yeh, S.H.K.: *Some Observations on the Use of Social Indicators in Development Planning, with Special Reference to Levels of Living* (Hawaii, University of Hawaii, Department of Urban and Regional Planning, 1974).

NOTES ON CONTRIBUTORS

Raymond Apthorpe is a Professor of Social Anthropology and Sociology of Development at the Institute of Social Studies, The Hague, The Netherlands.

Nancy Baster is a Researcher and Consultant in Social Development and Social Planning.

Hector Correa is Assistant Professor at the Graduate School of Public and International Affairs at the University of Pittsburgh, USA.

G.F.R. Ellis is a Professor in Applied Mathematics at the University of Cape Town, South Africa.

Jan van Heemst is a Senior Lecturer in Economics at the Institute of Social Studies, The Hague.

Jos Hilhorst is a Professor of Economics and Regional Planning at the Institute of Social Studies, The Hague.

Matty Klatter is a Documentalist at the Institute of Social Studies, The Hague.

Briitta Koskiaho is an Associate Professor of Social Policy at the University of Tampere, Finland.

Chris van Nieuwenhuijze is a Professor of Sociology at the Institute of Social Studies, The Hague.

N.V. Sovani is Professor at the Gokhale Institute of Politics and Economics at Pune, India.

Marshall Wolfe is a Consultant in Social Policy and Social Development, and was formerly with the UN Economic Commission for Latin America, Santiago, Chile.

